RAGE, RECONCILIATION AND SECURITY

Rage, Reconciliation and Security

Managing India's Diversities

B.G. VERGHESE

PENGUIN
VIKING

DPG

VIKING
Published by the Penguin Group
Penguin Books India Pvt. Ltd, 11 Community Centre, Panchsheel Park, New Delhi 110 017, India
Penguin Group (USA) Inc., 375 Hudson Street, New York, New York 10014, USA
Penguin Group (Canada), 90 Eglinton Avenue East, Suite 700, Toronto, Ontario, M4P 2Y3, Canada (a division of Pearson Penguin Canada Inc.)
Penguin Books Ltd, 80 Strand, London WC2R 0RL, England
Penguin Ireland, 25 St Stephen's Green, Dublin 2, Ireland (a division of Penguin Books Ltd)
Penguin Group (Australia), 250 Camberwell Road, Camberwell, Victoria 3124, Australia (a division of Pearson Australia Group Pty Ltd)
Penguin Group (NZ), 67 Apollo Drive, Rosedale, North Shore 0632, New Zealand (a division of Pearson New Zealand Ltd)
Penguin Group (South Africa) (Pty) Ltd, 24 Sturdee Avenue, Rosebank, Johannesburg 2196, South Africa

Penguin Books Ltd, Registered Offices: 80 Strand, London WC2R 0RL, England

First published by Penguin Books India 2008

10 9 8 7 6 5 4 3 2 1

ISBN 978-0-67008-172-1

Typeset in Sabon MT by Eleven Arts, New Delhi

Printed at Chaman Offset Printes, New Delhi

Copyright Acknowledgements

Every effort has been made to contact copyright holders. The publishers shall be happy to make good in future editions any errors or omissions brought to their attention. The author would like to thank the following for permission to use copyright material in this book:

For excerpt from *The Agrarian Prospect in India* by Daniel Thorner (1965); second edition 1973, Allied Publishing Limited, New Delhi; for poetry extract by Namdeo Dhasal (1975) in *An Anthology of Dalit Literature*, (eds.) Eleanor Zelliot and Mulk Raj Anand, second edition 1992, Lokayata: Mulk Raj Anand Centre, New Delhi.

Contents

Foreword

Security, which had for very long been perceived primarily as a requirement of the state, is now widely accepted as equally the citizens' need. This growing emphasis on human security and non-traditional threats to security has captured the imagination of people globally. It has also led to a growing corpus of studies and reports at the United Nations and in all major think tanks of the world.

In the new discourse on security, the Delhi Policy Group had brought forward the concept of Comprehensive Security involving economic, societal, environmental and political dimensions of security. The idea of Comprehensive Security had also been spread in South Asian states. The Delhi Policy Group instituted a Chair on Non-Traditional Security in 2005. This had been made possible by a grant from the Ford Foundation. The first product of the Chair on Non-Traditional Security was the well-received book, 'Understanding Security: A New Perspective'.[1] The book had examined security from a sociological perspective.

The current Chair on Non-Traditional Security is George Verghese, noted author, columnist, advisor to governments on media, and winner of the Magsaysay Award. He has worked extensively on issues of ethnic conflicts and insurgencies in India. Verghese examines conflicts and unrest by going to the fundamental challenge of a country like India. He views security from a new perspective, by examining insecurities that cause unrest and conflicts. This book examines the societal, economic and cultural landscape and identifies the diversities inherent in the Indian mosaic, and their linkages with internal conflicts

[1]T.K. Oommen, *Understanding Security: A New Perspective*, Delhi: Macmillan India Ltd, 2006.

that have raged for decades. Verghese's emphasis on societal spaces, livelihoods and community as essential building blocks, for a national fraternity arising from the insecurities of diversity, is a path-breaking study in the arena of Non-Traditional Security. Verghese's analysis is equally applicable to other South Asian states.

This persuasive and illuminating book covers the issues of security from the unique vantage point of diversities. The Delhi Policy Group is confident of its being received as a valuable addition to studies in Non-Traditional Security.

V.R. Raghavan
Lt General (Retd)
Advisor

Delhi Policy Group
Core 5A, India Habitat Centre, Lodhi Road, New Delhi 110003
delhipolicygroup@gmail.com; Telephone. 26149571;
www.delhipolicygroup.com

Preface

The Delhi Policy Group has been undertaking a series of studies on non-conventional or human security from which has emerged a wider concept of comprehensive security, which it is now engaged in exploring further. Traditionally, the idea of security has largely revolved around national security from external aggression or threats to the state or internal security from internal subversion and the collapse of public order through force, subversion or mis-governance. Diplomacy, appropriate social policies, policing and a call to arms have been the obvious instruments for defending the state against these dangers.

Growing awareness of the relevance of human rights, both group and individual, and a quality of life that makes the citizen or Demos believe that the state is worth defending, lies at the heart of human security. Human rights are inherent in life and not a gift of governments or international conventions, though those in authority often tend to think otherwise. Democratic states recognize fundamental rights but place reasonable restrictions on their exercise in the interests of other individual or collective rights. Gandhi went even further in stating that rights flow from duties well performed.

The condition of human security and challenges to it are determined by place, time and changing circumstances. Security is not a static concept and is influenced by internal developments, whether individual, local, community or national, as much as by changes in the external environment.

India, for example, is an ancient civilization but a relatively young nation state or state nation as some would define it, moving from traditional moorings towards modernity. The very processes of nation building and development entail multiple changes in power, social and economic relationships, cultural norms, patterns of governance, control over and management of resources, attitudes and behaviour, aspirations and goals. Technology has powerfully impacted society and has created new problems in its wake. We live today in a global village and an instant world in which national, political and social boundaries are no longer always inviolate. Changing demographic profiles, migration, climate change and pandemics pose ever-new problems that threaten security at one level or another.

Gross poverty and disparities are unacceptable. They are violative of rights and threaten security. Growth is necessary, but at what cost and at whose cost? Bhutan has wisely decided that gross national happiness is more important than mere gross national product. Happiness implies contentment and security. Is Bhutan more or less secure than the United States, the world's most powerful nation?

The canvas is extremely wide, and constantly changing. It would therefore be best to focus only on a part of the paradigm. This volume accordingly endeavours to look primarily at a few problems confronting India at the turn of the twenty-first century. India is shining for some and in some places, but not for all or everywhere. Insurgency and Naxalism have emerged as stubborn problems or security threats that are essentially rooted in other parameters that include self-perception, differentiation, divergent world views, human rights, dignity, socio-economic factors and so on. Issues of language and culture, dalits and caste, tribals and minorities and conflicts over land, forests, urbanization, industrialization and globalization have come to the fore. Climate change underlines the need for sustainable development and interrogates lifestyles. New uncertainties arise as old paradigms are challenged.

India is a huge country of enormous diversity and potential power. But it cannot steamroller everybody and everything by some pre-determined definition of the greater common good or the 'mainstream'. Such readymade definitions or majoritarian diktats threaten others' identity, security, self-interest, esteem, traditional values, cultural pride and democratic beliefs. Even in the 'heartland', the matter of reservations and community identity has rocked the country. Underlying these issues have been tensions between many layers of 'we' and 'they'.

Insurgency has been limited to the Northeast and Jammu and Kashmir. It has been based on either asserting independence from the Indian state or seeking greater autonomy within the country.

There is tension between the centre and the periphery. Naxalism is very different. It aims to capture state power for the 'people' through class annihilation and the destruction of the existing bourgeois–imperialist edifice. It has won some affection among the exploited, neglected and oppressed underclass, the wretched of India, who have lived beyond the pale for generations. There is today a Naxalite or Maoist 'problem'; but Left-wing Extremism as it has come to be termed, cannot be crushed. These elements have to be won back. Many layers of insecurity need to be negotiated with patience and understanding to achieve a common or comprehensive security. What has to be secured is not just borders or material gain, but minds and hearts.

The Preamble to the Constitution vests sovereignty in 'We, the People'. But the 'People' comprise many kinds and layers in different stages of economic and social growth reflecting enormous diversity. This in itself causes 'we' or 'us' to be posited against 'the other' in general and a multiplicity of 'theys' and 'thems'.

These numbers and interactions are not static or frozen in time but dynamic and accelerating. This is because the hitherto dormant, voiceless, under-mass is upwardly mobile and steadily getting empowered, challenging stable social equations and power relationships in the process.

However, change can be disconcerting, even threatening. So there is need for dialogue to establish a new social contract on development and change. Insecurity is often engendered among individuals by current and future uncertainties. Societies risk pandemics, natural disasters and, now, global warming. Individuals fear unemployment, illness and old age and suffer trauma from having to cope with development that may entail displacement or technological change affecting their status, residence and way of life.

The status quo suits some. It is burdensome for others. Tribals may wish to be left alone or at best enabled to develop at their own pace. However, modernization and development have excluded them by arbitrarily declaring their habitats to be reserved forests or natural parks, converting traditional rights into privileges dependent on laws and rules and the grace of petty functionaries. No wonder the Raj was dogged by tribal revolts. However, these freedom fighters continue to be exploited and their forest habitats have shrunk and been transformed by population pressures, development and modernization.

While free-spirited tribals have been losing their lands and rights, dalits are mostly landless and chafe at a status quo that has been hurtful to their dignity and well being. They seek equality and equity and an end to caste oppression. So, paradoxically, while those who would prefer to be left alone face involuntary inclusion in the form of intrusion, those seeking inclusion remain socially and economically excluded.

All available indices position dalits and tribals at the bottom of the heap. They are among the poorest and most deprived, largely assetless (in a modern monetary sense) and unable to compete for lack of education. Bondage, debt, hunger, unemployment and migration have been their lot. Little wonder then that they have been easy recruits to Left-wing Extremism. Unable to change their condition—as the law has quite often been blatantly employed to maintain the established order—they are enticed by the option of revolutionary change. Marx's battle cry, 'Workers of the World Unite! You have nothing to lose but your chains', has not lost its ring. Many only discover too late that violent change is a trap. Wrong means tend to defeat right ends.

As India's multitudinous but hitherto dormant diversities come to life, identities are asserted and jostle for a place in the sun. Issues of majority and minority, centre and periphery, great and little traditions, rural and urban values, tradition and modernity and all of Naipaul's million mutinies have to be negotiated and managed. This management of diversity within multiple transitions is a delicate and complex process aggravated by inexorable population growth.

Tribal India is astir. Certain rights to living in the forest and enjoying its usufruct are in the process of being restored. Even while the basic needs of the tribal people are yet to be properly met, the quiet woods are being increasingly opened up to mineral-based industries—coal mining, steel, aluminium, cement, non-ferrous metals—and the infrastructure development and urbanization that must necessarily accompany them. Is this to be a clash of civilizations? Some fear this is inevitable. Need it be so?

It is often said that India lives in its villages and is primarily an agricultural society. Yet, within another twenty-five years a majority of Indians will be city dwellers and agriculture will contribute less to GDP than industry and services. The country's population has tripled since Independence and will probably only stabilize at around 2050 at something approaching 1600 million.

With a falling land-man ratio, the countryside can no longer hold rising numbers gainfully everywhere. A growing stream of rural to urban migration has spawned inadvertent cities responding more to in-migration than any specific demand for labour. There is also the phenomenon of rural to rural migration with labourers moving from depressed to more prosperous regions and seasonal migration from the poverty belt of eastern Indian to areas of opportunity elsewhere. Migration has sometimes bred hostility among the host population even as it has encouraged vote bank politics.

It is in this context that there has been an outcry against diversion of farmland for industry and infrastructure and resultant displacement. Land acquisition for mega projects and Special Economic Zones in West Bengal, Orissa, Chhattisgarh and Jharkhand has been fiercely contested. Three issues have been raised. First, are the costs and benefits being shared fairly? Why is good, irrigated agricultural land being acquired and is this being done with informed consent? Who will feed India? Thirdly, is a onetime payment of compensation adequate? Jobs are ephemeral. Land is forever.

On the one hand it is argued that higher growth at 9–10 per cent will, like the rising tide, lift all boats. But, a tsunami can also play havoc. Safety nets can provide comfort during critical periods between transition and transformation. Small projects have their own place. However, mega investments, including dams, can trigger larger area development in hitherto sequestered and inaccessible areas that have suffered neglect and exploitation as their mineral and forest wealth has been extracted for the benefit of others elsewhere. This is where Gandhi's concept of trusteeship should more broadly define corporate social responsibility as a means of harnessing corporate wealth and experience to the tasks of promoting welfare and good governance within a democratic, but not paternalistic, framework.

Many issues are involved. Among them has to be a new approach to land, farming and country life. Land is a primeval factor of production, which, with labour, has created capital and given impetus to entrepreneurship. But land, like everything else, needs to be put to the most productive use. If agricultural productivity assures requisite farm production and permits diversion even of arable land where necessary for industry and urbanization, should this be resisted? If some forest diversion produces an equivalent or conceivably larger benefit, should that too be denied? No person, especially simple tribals and peasants, should be coerced; but should they not have the right to exercise a free and informed choice?

These are all sensitive questions and impinge directly or more subtly on matters of identity, status, well being, ways of life and notions of security and contentment. Urbanization and industry are certainly not problem-free and have given rise to all manner of ills and tensions. Some may find virtue in poverty, citing Gandhian ideals of simple living and the Biblical injunction, 'Blessed are the meek, for they shall inherit the earth'. Perhaps they might weigh this against the concept of creating wealth as a trust for the common good. In modern parlance this would be to build a truly welfare state ensuring government by and of but equally for the people. It is in such a regime that diversities will be better cushioned against insecurities because of change.

It is said that a stranger is but a friend whom one had not met before. Many layers and segments of Indians are meeting for the first time. We have to see 'the other' as just another, like any one of ourselves. *Vasudhaiva kutumbakam,* meaning, the world is my family, is an axiom and exhortation of ancient Indian wisdom. It implies that there is no 'other' beyond one's extended self as embodied in the family. Globalization too may then be perceived as not something foreign but a part of the extended family.

What India confronts as it journeys on is both a challenge and an opportunity. There is no single, simple answer to the many perplexing questions and conflicts that must be negotiated. As we approach another crossroads it is prudent to consider whether roads less travelled can bring reconciliation as a step towards happiness. In so doing, I have examined a variety of insecurities that trouble people's minds and how these keep changing for various players. Ultimately, security lies in common security whether internally, within nations and among peoples, or internationally. At the end of the day, a sense of common citizenship must prevail against narrower community or group identities, which must be subsumed and can be well preserved within the larger whole.

Acknowledgements

This volume is the outcome of my tenure as the Delhi Policy Group's Chair on Non-Traditional Security through 2006–08. I deem it an honour to have been invited to hold the Chair.

I would like to acknowledge the unfailing support, encouragement and consideration that I received from the Advisory Group for the Chair. I would also like to thank Lt. Gen. V.R. Raghavan (Retd), Pradeep Rao, Amritha, Nidhi and others in the DPG office.

Those who assisted me one way or another are legion. I spoke with many, maybe indirectly at times, to discuss and clarify ideas. I am most grateful to the Librarian at the Centre for Policy Research, Kamaljit Kumar and the assistant librarian, Gopal. They have been a permanent help over many years. As much thanks to Sushma Zutshi and her very able and ever-obliging staff at the India International Centre. They too could always find a book, document, paper or reference and procured material on inter-library loans for the asking.

Then there were those I formally interviewed, most often off the record the more freely to garner their views and insights. Those of them who read this work will possibly recognize a detail here, a reference there, a quotation or reflection. They were unsparing of their time and generally candid in their expression. I gained much from these conversations with academics, politicians, bureaucrats, police officials, corporate personnel, social workers, media persons and activists. They shared the distilled wisdom of their work and both personal and institutional experiences in their offices and homes at odd and, sometimes, late and often over long hours and gladly rearranged their busy schedules at short notice to accommodate a stranger, patiently educate him and satisfy his curiosity.

I list no names. A short list would leave out too many; a long list could be tedious for those not there to share the learning and friendships made. The DPG and other occasions enabled me to travel, meet many interesting and useful sources and attend seminars and discussions where I benefited from a variety of contacts and stimulating interactions and papers. Geography influences perspectives.

These visits took me to Guwahati, Shillong and Dibrugarh in the Northeast; to Jammu and Srinagar in J&K; Raipur, Jagdalpur, Dantewada, Konta, Kanker and Bijapur in Chhattisgarh; Siliguri and Kolkata, Katihar and Patna, Ranchi, Bhubaneshwar, Hyderabad, Mumbai, Bhopal, Chennai and Bangalore.

Long absences and hours at the computer sorely tried the patience of my wife, Jamila who, at the end of the day was most understanding, as she has been for over fifty-five years.

And finally my thanks to Penguin Books. Ravi Singh, the editor-in-chief, took no time to signal acceptance of the manuscript and handed me over to the safe editorial care of Kamini Mahadevan, now in Chennai, an old friend with whom it has been my pleasure to be associated earlier.

B.G. Verghese

{1}

Mapping the Landscape

People everywhere desire to lead a secure and serene life of their own volition, free from want and harm. Is happiness then an index of human security? Happiness has to mean something more than hedonism or the mere pursuit of pleasure to indulgence and excess. Perhaps the goal we seek is more truly the assurance of contentment, satisfaction and peace with oneself and the world around through the instrumentality of self-determination.

Contentment, however, though adequately assuring individual well being, may not quite comprehend the myriad anxieties of large social groups, let alone nations, especially when their members are stratified and differentiated. Moreover, even individuals and, certainly, states do not necessarily rate happiness as their prime concern. For them, freedom, economic growth (riches), power and status often count for more. Some might of course prefer to *be more*, deriving satisfaction from service and good deeds, rather than *have more* in order to pander to their acquisitive instincts. Bhutan, remarkably, would prefer to measure progress not by the size of its gross domestic product, GDP, but by the yardstick of gross national happiness (GNH). The elements it would include in a basket of indices for this purpose are adherence to its particular persuasion of Buddhism, preservation of its traditional way of life, sustainable development, avoidance of undue disparities between persons or regions, and desisting from progressing faster than the kingdom's ability to absorb change. Thus tourism has been limited to manageable proportions by price rationing, making Bhutan a highly up-market destination, while the inception of television was consciously delayed for some years.

However, pressures to conform rigidly to stringent norms can sometimes induce distortions. There is neither any Shangri La nor a workaday time machine. Some choices are barred. The world is with us and real life is not obedient to the injunction contained in the title song of the post-World War II musical of the 1940s, *Stop the world, I want to get off*.

The late environmentalist, Anil Agarwal, proffered another view captured in the term Gross Nature Product. He believed that at least in terms of sustainable development, this was a better index of national advancement than GDP, which might well be enhanced by destructive measures to force (short-term) growth. Yet power often scorns virtue. Recall the Big Three meeting at Yalta towards the close of World War II. Stalin made a proposal. Churchill interjected that the Pope might not take kindly to it. To which Stalin famously retorted, 'And how many divisions has the Pope'? That settled the argument for the moment. But can force resolve the moral dilemmas of our time?

Most societies are plural, at least to some degree, though narrow nationalism, the market and ideology tend to exercise a homogenizing influence. The United States was for long regarded as a melting pot that Americanized its vast migrant heterogeneity. Europe was more homogeneous, with language and culture as the hallmark of nationality among competing nation states. It is only more recently that the phenomenon of multiculturalism has surfaced with non-European migrants streaming in as post-colonial legatees, refugees and asylum seekers and, increasingly, to find or fill jobs. This has brought a variety of social tensions in its train, not all of which have been mitigated in the passage to a second or even third generation.

India, however, boasts an unparalleled diversity of language, race, religion, caste, culture and regional flavours. The genius of Hinduism has been accommodation, with the result that there has been no overriding homogenizing principle at work as in so many situations elsewhere. Thus, it has been an early and welcoming home or refuge to all the great world religions. The Buddha, Mahavira and Guru Nanak were indigenous reformers alongside many others that sought to restore certain pristine values to 'Hinduism', an appellation of recent coinage. Their spiritual message transcended boundaries. But for many Hindus, the new faiths established were enveloped within the Hindu fold.

The Apostle St Thomas brought Christianity to the shores of Kerala in 52 AD while Islam came to Malabar with Arab traders in the lifetime of the Prophet, well before Mohammad bin Kasim invaded Sind. The Jews sought refuge down the west coast in two or three waves many centuries ago and established settlements around Cochin and Bombay. The Zoroastrians fled persecution in Persia between the eighth and tenth centuries to find a home in Gujarat. All these faiths flourished on Indian soil, adding fragrance and colour to the rich diversity prevalent in the country.

In May 2007, India uniquely had a Muslim President, a Sikh Prime Minister, an Italian-born Christian Indian chairing the ruling national coalition, a Hindu Leader of the Opposition, a Scheduled Caste Chief Justice of India as well as a Chief Minister of its largest state, Uttar Pradesh, a Parsee at the head of its Air Force and more than one Tribal chief minister, apart from Buddhist, Jain and Bahai dignitaries holding positions of honour elsewhere. Nowhere else in the world has diversity been so celebrated.

The monumental *People of India* (POI) study by the Anthropological Survey of India (1992) under its then director-general, Kumar Suresh Singh, quotes Jawaharlal Nehru as describing India as 'a cultural unity amidst diversity, a bundle of contradictions held together by strong but invisible threads'. The survey enumerates 4,635 communities, consisting of 2,795 main communities, including 586 segments, located in 91 eco-cultural zones distributed throughout the country. Of the main communities, 2,006 were found to be restricted to one state or Union Territory from which the conclusion follows that nearly 78 per cent of these communities are not only linguistic and cultural but social categories. A further breakdown in accordance with recognized concepts lists 13,156 clans spread over several communities, irrespective of region or language. Many bear names of plants, animals or inanimate objects, indicating the survival of totemism with its close environmental links between man and nature. The POI survey further records 12,142 surnames (mostly derived from occupations), 8650 *gotra*s (Sanskritic clan derivatives), 1820 lineages and 2994 titles like Acharya, Choudhury, Naik and Patil.

Migration has added to local diversity. Vegetarianism, related to the spread of Jainism and Vaishnavism, was found to be limited to only about 20 per cent of the population and is probably more extensively practised in consequence of price rationing. But with migration, spread of communications and local availability, diets are becoming more national. Butter chicken in Cochin rivals the *dosa* in Ludhiana. Wheat and rice have crossed cultural boundaries over the past forty to fifty years, as have tea and coffee. The POI survey notes that 'milk-culture' has penetrated the Mongoloid and Proto-Australoid tribal population of the Northeast. Interestingly, like bilingualism and the use of borrow-words from neighbouring lexicons, many communities report following two faiths. The study reports 87communities who follow both Hinduism and Sikhism, 116 that follow Hinduism and Christianity, 35 Hinduism and Islam, 21 Hinduism and Jainism, and 29 both Hinduism and Buddhism. Several tribal communities are also found to profess their own faiths as well as one or other major religions: 94 Christianity, and 11 Buddhism.

The POI data on conversion reveals that people in 383 communities or their segments have entered the Hindu fold in recent times (possibly and in part through the process of what M.N. Srinivas termed Sanskritization). Members of 267 communities have embraced Christianity, 112 Islam and 63 Sikhism. Interestingly, among the 584 Muslim communities, 53 still recall their place in the Hindu four-fold *varna* system as do 86 from among the 339 Christian communities. These vestiges of casteism among Christians and Muslims suggest the strong pull of traditional social and occupational hierarchies in Indian society.

Within the bounds of Hindu society, the four-fold varna system by birth was a post-Vedic or post-Buddhist intrusion that gradually hardened into caste (Nadkarni, 2003). It instituted itself as an organizing principle that gave rise to a certain social division of labour akin to occupational guilds found in medieval Europe. This gradually hardened into a hereditary encrustation, with ritual characteristics that stratified society into many layered highs and lows by birth and beyond class on the basis of an elaborate concept of purity and pollution. It precluded social and occupational mobility and differed from class, being hierarchical and ordained by birth. To the four-fold varna was added a fifth caste of untouchables, engaged in what were considered unclean and menial tasks. Despite efforts at social reform, the system for many remained discriminatory, oppressive, divisive and without redress.

The continental dimensions of India, a geographical expression encompassing the territories bounded by the Himalaya–Karakoram–

Hindu Kush shield and the Indian Ocean, spawned several major languages and numerous dialects, each with a script and rich literature of its own. This should be no surprise. But Sanskrit emerged as a lingua franca or mother language which, with some exceptions, ensured a common alphabet and classical tradition that was cultivated and preserved by the Brahmanical order and its royal patrons. Sanskrit was to India what Latin was to Europe.

There were of course regional kingdoms and petty principalities that waxed and waned, conquered neighbouring territories and peoples, including those beyond the confines of 'India', and were in turn subjugated by these others. Great pan-Indian empires rose and fell at various times, separated by centuries—the Asokan, Gupta and Mughal Empires among others. Then followed the British Raj, culminating in Partition and Independence in 1947. Understandably, therefore, the Indian narrative is made up of many histories of nations and sub-nationalities, myriad cultures, ethnicities and racial intermingling. The varied topography, ranging from coastal to alpine, plateau, swamp and desert, the monsoon and soil types defined numerous agro-climatic zones, each with its own seasonal cycle and rhythm of life, distinctive styles of rural and urban habitation, food and dress, architecture, fairs and festivals, customs and large and little traditions. A great many tribal communities steadily pushed back into the 'interior' could live reclusive lives in the hills and receding forests until the world rudely intruded into their domain. Migrant streams entered India from its northwest and northeast portals that were great crossroads of history.

The North-West Frontier was romanticized by the British as it marked a point where powerful empires met and set the stage for the Great Game with Russia. These territories are now in Pakistan. The Northeast Frontier was even more sequestered and diverse. It was a gateway for migrant waves of tribal peoples who entered clockwise from Nepal and Tibet as well as from central China, Laos, Thailand and Burma into Bangladesh and India. There were conquerors too, like the Ahoms from their redoubt in the Shan Hills. Racially, the Northeast is Mongoloid and it is here that South-east Asia begins or ends.

India's diversity spans both space and time. Each dimension has posed problems of integration in the process of nation building. Localism, sub-nationalism and regionalism by whatever name challenge the larger nationalism. Equally, India exists in multiple layers in keeping with many levels of development. This is evident not merely as rural and urban categories but in terms of adaptation to different levels of social organization, ideas and technology. Thus the bullock cart, bicycle and trendiest automobile jostle along the same road. Likewise, nuclear power and cow dung cakes provide energy to people living cheek by jowl even as jhuggis hug modern high-rise apartments. The contrasts are enormous. Contradictions and disparities breed tension.

It is commonplace to talk of India's unity in diversity. In truth, the appearance of unity in the early years of Independence was masked by the fact that the major part of the country's extraordinary diversity was submerged and passive. Vast numbers lacked political and social consciousness or economic freedom and were mute observers rather than active participants in governance. With increasing development and the concomitant spread of literacy and communications, cohort after cohort of those at the bottom of the pyramid have gained empowerment. A culture of silence has yielded to protest. Some thirty years ago, Govind Nihalani made a film, *Aakrosh*, in which the hero, a bonded labourer, did not utter a word throughout the film which was otherwise punctuated by groans and gasps as he was brutally belaboured and abused by his master's henchmen. Such a film would be unthinkable today and, even if scripted, would be unlikely to find a producer. The upsurge from below and associated churning has stirred the pot; but the process of moving all of India's deprived and traditional millions from 'Bharat' to 'India', the extant social duality of rich and poor, the liberated and the disempowered, will take more than a few decades to exhaust itself.

Western democracy as we know it was the culmination of a long and turbulent process of social and economic change that took a century or more to find fulfilment. In contrast, India's founding fathers reversed the natural order of things and stood history on its head. They consciously chose democracy as the instrument for effecting a social and economic revolution that would enable the country to make the transition from a highly stratified, traditional, poverty-stricken society to a modern, modestly well-off and more egalitarian nation.

Accommodation of diversity through access and participation necessitated not only democracy but also secularism and a multi-tiered federalism. This encompassed territorial units, often with distinct histories of their own, bringing together peoples with shared identities. These states in turn comprised decentralized units of local governance for purposes of administrative devolution as much as to provide representation or self-determination for various communities and particularities through autonomous or regional councils and other devices.

Gandhi advocated the principle of subsidiarity, with each tier of government from the grass-roots upwards vested with the responsibility of doing whatever lies within its competence and then entrusting upwards that which is admittedly beyond its capacity. This bottom-up approach was not followed. Instead, there was devolution of power from the top downwards, though sovereignty is nominally vested in 'We, the People'. This too is changing with empowerment, the annihilation of space and time by technology, deregulation, the unleashing of market forces (though not laissez faire), globalization and the makings of an increasingly borderless world.

It is not widely realized that of the hundred largest economic entities in the world, more than half are corporations. Even within India, Reliance, Tata, the ONGC, State Bank of India and other corporate giants today dispose of larger incomes than most states, some of which hold smaller populations than those inhabiting the large metropolitan centres. In thirty years from now, urban India will outstrip village India in numbers. In many ways, as Amartya Sen argued, development is and should be seen as freedom. The relative weightage of the traditional factors of production, Land, Labour, Capital and Enterprise has undergone change and, perhaps most important of all, to them has been added a fifth factor—Knowledge.

The ferment of integration, change and burgeoning numbers has inevitably generated tensions aggravated by the clash of diversities, with upwardly mobile communities asserting their identity and attendant rights. Although absolute poverty constitutes a grim assault on human rights and freedom, relative deprivation as between individuals and regions can be particularly galling. Envy more easily turns to antagonism when communal, caste, linguistic or other clearly defined social groups see others enjoying comforts, privileges and advancement, whether real or sometimes imagined, that they seem to lack. Such differences are easily exploited to build a constituency so that 'we' can be mobilized to confront 'them'.

Given its population explosion, India is finding that its last frontier has been all but reached. Demographic pressures on land, water and other natural resources and opportunities, without commensurate development gains that might have ensured a sufficiently larger cake to share, have fanned discontent. At the root of poor governance is the fact that privileged elites and corrupt elements do well for themselves by manipulating the system. Those that are excluded, especially tribals, dalits and minority groups, have long suffered but are now protesting the cumulative neglect and oppression of the past and are determined to fight for their rights and safeguard what is left of their diminishing and degraded commons. Marginalized but aspiring communities are staging their 'million mutinies'. The periphery challenges the centre.

In the struggle to maintain law and order, the rule of law has often been subverted to maintain the established order with all its inequities and structural violence. We label these uncomfortable manifestations as 'Insurgency' and 'Left-wing Extremism'. This is perhaps not entirely untrue but it may equally well be less than the whole truth, which has many layers and is multifaceted.

Closer examination may reveal that some problems, though not all, stem from our failure to understand the dynamics of the 'clash of diversities' in a process of development and change. From this follows our further inability to manage and reconcile the human insecurities and anxieties inherent in the multiple transitions of different social formations with their varied points of departure and divergent trajectories. The task then is to shepherd singular group identities towards a common and equal citizenship, not by obliterating the former but by accommodating them at ever-higher levels of satisfaction. Clinging to the past, even while quite properly preserving what is best in our heritage, will not win the future.

The process of modernization and change produces both differentiation and intermingling. Whatever the divisions at the top, driven by political considerations feeding on social competition and real or contrived apprehensions and grievances, interactions among communities at the grass-roots are everyday necessities and a fact of life. The POI study analyses 777 traits or unique cultural values and finds many of them are shared. A very high correlation of traits was found between Scheduled Castes and Tribes, between Scheduled Tribes and Hindus, Hindus and Sikhs, Hindus and Jains and, notably, Hindus and Muslims. Folk traditions bind communities, perhaps in response to ancestral memory.

As far back as in 1891, H.H. Risley, another of *Tribes and Castes of Bengal*, found a sense of 'Indianness', howsoever elusive it seemed. Nehru felt it emotionally but 'discovered' India in his prison cell as an ancient nation collectively reached out to freedom. The making of the Constitution and the integration of the princely states were manifestations of 'Indianness' and an idea of India that many doubted, not a few at home, many more abroad.

In a memorable closing address to the Constituent Assembly after the Constitution was adopted, Dr B.R. Ambedkar, its principal pilot, uttered a caution. Referring how India had lost its freedom in the past, he asked, 'Will Indians place the country above their creed or will they place creed above country?' He argued that democracy was not unfamiliar to Indians as the ancient Buddhist sanghas functioned in accordance with parliamentary procedure.

But if we wished to maintain democracy, not merely in form but in substance, 'the first thing in my judgement we must do is to hold fast to constitutional methods of achieving our social and economic objectives'. Civil disobedience, non-cooperation and satyagraha could be justified when constitutional avenues were barred, but no more now that Independence was won. 'These methods are nothing but the Grammar of Anarchy and the sooner they are abandoned, the better for us'.

Bhakti, the path of devotion or hero worship, he said, possibly played a larger part in Indian life than elsewhere. 'Bhakti in religion may be a road to the salvation of the soul. But in politics, Bhakti is a sure road to degradation and eventual dictatorship.'

His final caution was perhaps the most relevant. He urged that India should not be content merely with political democracy but must cultivate a robust social democracy as well.

> On the 26th of January, 1950, we are going to enter a life of contradictions. In politics we will have equality and in social and economic life we will have inequality. In politics we will be recognising the principle of one man, one vote and one vote one value. In our social and economic life, we shall, by reason of our social and economic structure, continue to deny the principle of one man, one value. How long shall we continue to live this life of contradictions? . . . We must remove this contradiction at the earliest possible moment or else those who suffer from inequality will blow up the structure of political democracy, which this Assembly has so laboriously built up.

Coupled with this exhortation, Ambedkar stressed the centrality of fraternity or 'common brotherhood'. He denounced caste divisions as 'anti-national . . . (as) they bring about separation in social life. They are anti-national . . . and generate jealousy and antipathy between caste and caste. But we must overcome all these difficulties if we wish to become a nation in reality. For fraternity can be a fact only when there is a nation. Without fraternity, equality and liberty will be no deeper than a coat of paint.' Powerful words, still as true as the day they were spoken.

The contradictions remain—not only of social ideology but of emerging and assertive diversities. Yet much has changed for the better and continues to change.

This, however, is often resisted as change is unfamiliar and threatens the long-established status quo.

India's diversity is not a weakness but an asset. It imparts colour, vibrancy and hybrid vigour to the nation. At the same time the tensions it could or, in fact, does generate must be anticipated and managed as the country makes the transition from community and group identities towards a common citizenship as enshrined in the Constitution.

Meanwhile, the unfamiliar, unfolding future constantly challenges the familiar past and present and fogs the mind. Years ago, in 1967, Regis Debray warned of this in *Revolution in the Revolution*? We are never completely contemporaneous with our present, he wrote.

> History advances in disguise; it appears on stage wearing the mask of the preceding scene, and we tend to lose the meaning of the play. Every time the curtain rises, continuity has to be re-established. The blame, of course, is not history's but lies in our vision, encumbered with memory and images learned in the past. We see the past superimposed on the present, even when the present is a revolution.

India too is witnessing multiple revolutions within the Revolution.

{2}

Not Peripheral but Equal

The Northeast was always far away. But for and from whom? The seat of the empire often seemed distant and subaltern rulers and satraps sought comfort in the mantra 'Delhi *dur ast*', Delhi is far away. Being proximate or far away is not necessarily measured by distance but by affection or a seeming lack of it. Secession too need not always entail physical separation. It can find expression through emotional rejection and alienation.

India's progress from a civilizational idea and episodic empire to a modern state has understandably traversed the same road. Whatever the earlier history of the region, Assam and the eastern marches of India were not subdued by the Mughals. The Ahoms, a Shan people from Burma, overran Assam in the fourteenth century, making it their home and ruling it until the nineteenth century. Lower Assam fell to the British in 1826 and Upper Assam followed twelve years later. The Muttocks, a fiercely independent people inhabiting the head of the Brahmaputra Valley, remained restive and rebellious for some time thereafter.

The rich natural endowments of the region were soon apparent and tea gardens, coal mines, oilfields, saw mills and plywood factories sprouted, bringing Bengali administrators and professionals and Middle India tribals, Nepalese and even some Chinese workers in their wake. These migrants manned the new enterprises, reclaimed new farmlands and developed the communication infrastructure to consolidate the administration, promote commerce and win revenue for the exchequer. Assam was until Independence one of India's more globalized states.

However, in order to protect the valley against tribal marauders from the surrounding hills, the British drew an Inner Line in 1873, signifying an administrative boundary. Beyond that lay the nominal political frontier along the Himalayan rampart. The tribal people inhabiting the intermediate territory were largely left to their own devices. These designated Frontier Tracts were partially or wholly 'excluded' from the civil administration and placed directly under the governor and outside the purview of the Assam government when popular ministries took office under the 1935 Act. They remained under the tutelage of British political officers and were virtually untouched by the nationalist movement.

Strenuous efforts were made to avoid Partition in the course of the frenetic negotiations leading up to the transfer of power. The Cabinet Mission proposed a certain grouping of provinces, excluding princely India, as a basis for working out centre–state relationships within the federation. The Muslim majority regions in the northwest and east of the country were placed in Groups B and C, separated by a residual Part A. Assam was grouped with Bengal under this scheme. The Congress was prepared to go along with this arrangement but its Assamese leadership was vehemently opposed, fearing that this would entail immediate domination by Bengal and even ultimate detachment from India as the Muslim League reserved the right of provinces to opt out and secede to form Pakistan, if the federal experiment failed.

Earlier in 1941, some British officials and subsequently the Cabinet Mission's adviser, Reginald Coupland, mooted a proposal to carve out the Assam–Burmese tribal belt as a Crown Colony. Both the Nagas and Mizos spurned this idea and decided to throw in their lot with India, at least for an initial period of ten years. Nehru had earlier been influenced by Soviet thinking and while in Ahmednagar jail in 1944 had contemplated conceding constituent units of the Indian federation the right to secede if they so chose, but only ten years after Independence, in an atmosphere of detachment free of external influence. He resiled from that position and subsequently wrote as Congress President to T. Sakhrie, Secretary of the Naga National Council (NNC), stating that the Naga territory in eastern Assam was clearly much too small to stand by itself, politically or economically, sandwiched as it was between two huge countries, India and China. Part of it also consisted of 'rather backward people who require considerable help . . . . Therefore this Naga territory must form part of India'. But, he added,

'It is our policy that tribal areas should have as much freedom and autonomy so that they can live their own lives according to their own customs and desires'. (Ramunny, 1988) He was later to spell out these ideas in his Foreword to the Northeast Tribal Adviser, Verrier Elwin's *A Philosophy for NEFA*.

However, the NNC leadership entered into a Nine-Point Agreement with the Assam Governor, Akbar Hydari in June 1947. This set off a controversy. Point 9 read: 'The Governor of Assam, as Agent of the Government of the (sic) India, will have a special responsibility for a period of ten years to ensure the due observance of this agreement; at the end of this period the NNC will be asked whether they require this agreement to be extended for a further period or a new agreement regarding the future of the Naga people be arrived at.' (Verghese, 1996) Controversy ensued, with the NNC claiming that this phrasing implied an option to seek independence. The language employed clearly does not say so and Hydari interpreted it as signifying no more than a right to renegotiate the terms of union within India. The NNC leader, A.Z. Phizo (who had served as a corporal in the INA in Burma to win a common independence), rejected this view, arguing that the Nagas were neither Indian nor ever part of India. The British had conquered India and the Naga homelands and had as a matter of convenience ruled them centrally, though dividing the Naga territories administratively between India and Burma. Hence, once the British withdrew, both India and the Nagas would be free to go their own way. This marked the beginning of the Naga breach with India.

Interestingly, *The Naga Chronicle* (Nuh, 2002) prints what it calls a 'Modified' version of the Nine-Point Agreement amending the last portion to read '. . . at the end of this period, "the Nagas will be free to decide their own future"'. The modification was unilateral.

Be that as it may, if the long 'excluded' Northeast tribal communities feared too quick or too warm an Indian embrace, Indian leaders too were equally wary about them. In 1950, Sardar Patel wrote to Nehru of 'our northeastern approaches'. In his view, 'From the point of view of communications they are weak spots . . . . The contact of these areas with us is by no means close and intimate. The people inhabiting these portions have no established loyalty or devotion to India. Even the Darjeeling and Kalimpong areas are not free from pro-Mongoloid prejudices.' (Durgadas, 1973) Years later, Morarji Desai refused to consider inclusion of Nepali in the Eighth Schedule of the Constitution. It is a foreign language, he said!

It was left to the Bordoloi Committee of the Constituent Assembly to give shape to the Nehruvian promise of tribal autonomy in the Northeast. The wholly excluded areas of Assam were placed in the Sixth Schedule with provision for the constitution of autonomous district and regional councils. But the Nagas would have none of it. The first shots were fired in 1955. India's oldest insurgency had commenced.

The Japanese invasion of India during World War II was halted at Kohima and Imphal. That marked the turn of the tide. The Northeast had become a war zone, a base for the Allied armies for the Burma campaign and flying the 'Hump' to China. The INA under Subhas Bose also registered a fleeting presence there. The Burma Road and Stilwell Road were constructed. All this churning ended the earlier quietude of the region. Indian Independence was followed by Britain's withdrawal from Burma, torn by war and now by ethnic unrest and Kuomintang inroads in search of a base area against the military triumph of Communist China. The People's Liberation Army entered Tibet in 1951. Peasant communism was on the march. The 1948 Cominform Congress in Calcutta proclaimed a radical revolutionary (Zhdanov) line for Asian communism. The region was awash with arms. The Cold War was joined with opposing ideologies in contention.

In the sub-continent, Partition had left a bitter legacy of blood and refugees. Kashmir erupted, and trouble in Junagadh and Hyderabad lent urgency to the nagging problem of national integration and of redefining and securing national boundaries against any challenge. Against this background, earlier thoughts of a decentralized polity inspired by Gandhi yielded to a stronger Union that was fashioned in the Constituent Assembly and further underpinned by Nehru's inclination to embrace socialist planning.

Friction in the Northeast

It was in this mood and environment that 'India' encountered the 'Northeast', now a geo-political construct carved out by Partition, beyond the slender Siliguri neck. Immediately, and almost inevitably, two tendencies clashed. The metropolitan integrationist pull confronted the shield of differentiation constructed by the somewhat surprised and bewildered assortment of tribal and settled communities of the Northeast, who needed time and understanding to come to terms with a radically new situation in a strangely different world that had closed in on them.

Even Assam pleaded for dual citizenship to protect an Assamese identity that appeared under siege as a result of the refugee influx from East Pakistan. Gopinath Bordoloi's plaintive pleas to Nehru in this regard were brusquely brushed aside in correspondence with the Assam Chief Minister. (*Selected Works of Jawaharlal Nehru*, 7 August 1949) Certain non-resident Indians enjoy this privilege today as do state subjects of Jammu and Kashmir (J&K) and of Sikkim. Pressures to integrate were mistaken as steps towards annexation or forced assimilation. This was as far from the truth as differentiation, a holding out for time to consider and consult, was interpreted as separatist or secessionist.

The Naga issue

Not all Northeastern insurgencies are secessionist or monolithic. The Naga Nationalist Council launched an independence movement but sections of its following broke away and settled for a 16-Point Agreement in 1960 that led to statehood for Nagaland three years later. Notwithstanding the Shillong Accord of 1975, the Phizo faction persevered in its demand but soon splintered. The more radical National Socialist Council of Nagalim (NSCN) came to the fore in 1980 but broke into warring Khaplang (K) and Isak Swu-Muivah (IM) factions in 1988. All these different formations have distinct tribal affiliations, which has been the cause of much fratricidal strife and grief.

The Government of India negotiated a ceasefire with the NSCN (IM) in 1997 and this was later extended to the NSCN (K) group as well. The ensuing dialogue with Th. Muivah and Isak Swu, was initiated at the level of the Prime Minister and has since been patiently conducted in Bangkok, Amsterdam and Delhi by the Government's interlocutor, K. Padmanabhiah and, at the political level, by Oscar

Fernandes. A joint communiqué issued in July 2003 noted that the Union Government 'recognises the unique history and situation of the Nagas'. At one level this does no more than give formal recognition to a Naga identity that was always implicit, but the NSCN (IM) saw it as a step forward in pressing its case. Its two outstanding demands have been sovereign independence and unification of all Naga areas in Nagaland, Manipur, Assam and Arunachal (and, beyond that, in Burma) to constitute Nagalim. In more recent rounds of discussion, there has perhaps been a subtle shift of emphasis from independence to internal self-determination. With regard to integration, the Government's position is that no change in state boundaries is possible without the willing consent of the others concerned. Manipur has strongly protested against any dismemberment and Assam and Arunachal too have decried any challenge to their territorial integrity.

Even if the territorial claim is arguably validated on ethnographic considerations, can the same be said historically? Dimapur, Nagaland's prime urban and commercial centre, was for centuries the capital of the Dimasa (Kachari) kingdom until it was abandoned in 1540 in favour of Maibang, in what is now the Autonomous District of North Cachar, with the expansion of Ahom power. (Barpujari, 1994) The Jadikhe Naisho Hoshom, the apex Dimasa body, is emphatic on this point. (Dutta and Bhuyan, 2007) Dimapur along with an area of 150 square miles around it was subsequently transferred to the Naga Hills District in order to provide it a railhead. The Dimaraji Revival Demand Committee petitioned Narasimha Rao for the return of this tract when he was prime minister. But history, alas, is not easily unscrambled.

The idea of independence is perhaps beginning to yield to the realization that interdependence with significant local autonomy could be a more viable and practical proposition. Hence both sides appear moving towards exchanging views on whether Nagaland could have a constitution defining certain limits of extended jurisdiction by renegotiating centre–state relations. Differences might yet remain on how to link these two constitutions, whether on the model of the J&K constitution, which has an organic link with the Constitution of India, or otherwise. If the India–Pakistan peace process throws up an informal confederal-type resolution for J&K, this might suggest another model, with suitable adaptations. Vesting these entities with symbols of distinctive identity and entrusting them with certain elements of delegated authority could be packaged into a settlement, provided that this gives emotional satisfaction without derogating from national sovereignty. Some fear a domino effect, but there is good reason to look on both the Naga and J&K issues as sui generis.

Article 371A of the Constitution already sets out a special dispensation for Nagaland, as do the succeeding Articles for Assam, Manipur, Sikkim, Mizoram and Arunachal and Article 370 for J&K. This family of Articles provides a key that can unlock other doors.

It may be possible to respond to the Nagalim sentiment by treating the Naga collective as a people. Their aspirations to peoplehood can then be enabled to find fulfilment in a non-territorial restructuring of inter-state relationships without undermining the territorial integrity of any of the partners. Naga culture, language and way of life generally can be uniformly guaranteed across state boundaries with designated Naga-inhabited areas being brought under the Sixth Schedule for purposes of local governance and development administration. The existing Naga Ho Ho could appropriately watch over collective community interests in keeping with traditional practice. Given growing economic ties, friendship and cooperation between India and Myanmar and the development of growth bilaterals between adjacent Naga territories on either side, such a peoplehood arrangement could conceivably take on a trans-boundary character over time.

The stumbling block to such an unfolding is not so much the perceived obduracy of the Government of India as the sorry state of mistrust and internecine tribal strife between the Nagas themselves. A Naga reconciliation mission mounted some years ago by a widely representative body of Nagas and the NSCN (IM) led to admissions of mutual excesses and past wrongs. Unfortunately, that mood of reconciliation was not sustained. The Nagaland Baptist Church Council (NBCC) has rued the sorry state of intra-Naga relationships, strongly condemning factional conflicts and killings, rampant extortion by lawless elements, the telling of past history and events in different versions, an unyielding personal and tribal agenda of resentment, provocations, revenge and counter-revenge, with factionalism taking centre stage. 'Hurts not transformed are always transferred', it warns, and concludes with the imperative of 'restoration of trust and relationship' within the Naga fold. (NBCC, 2006)

The estimated sixty-six Naga tribes and sub-tribes lack a common language that can unify them, though Christianity has to some extent come to provide a common though not a universal religious denominator. The NSCN and others have taken 'Nagaland for Christ' as their motto. The Church clearly plays an important role in Naga society, as among the Mizos, but tribal differences remain. Of the leading dramatis personae, Muivah is a Thangkul Naga from Manipur whereas Khaplang is a Hemi Naga from Burma. This should not matter. But it does—critically. The NSCN (K) has served a quit notice on Thangkuls in Nagaland. The two NNC factions, named after their leaders Adino and Khadao, are dominated by Angamis who have remained quiet but may not have been entirely marginalized.

Some commentators have observed that a sharpening of ethnic identity has overshadowed civic identity. (Srikanth and Thomas January 2006). This is not merely a Naga or Northeastern syndrome. This is a trap from which India as a whole has to extricate itself.

Troubled Manipur

Other than fending off vivisection from any move to concede Nagalim, Manipur's grievances against the Indian state have other roots. The majority Meiteis, the traditional ruling clan, are islanded in the Imphal Valley, surrounded by the far more expansive hill region with its twenty-nine scheduled and some more unspecified tribes. The Naga tribes are dominant and occupy the surrounding hills, with Kuki and other tribes concentrated in the south. The Meiteis are seventeenth-century Vaishnavite converts who still retain traits of their original tribal Sanamahi faith. But they claim to having always lived in harmony with the predominantly Christian tribals and the small Pangal (Muslim) community. Manipur has an unbroken history going back to 33 AD, recorded in its royal chronicles, and came under the Raj in the late nineteenth century when the British planted their flag over the Kangla Fort, the citadel, sacred domain, court, library, theatre and prime symbol of Meitei culture and pride.

It is against this background that subsequent events must be viewed. Manipur acceded to India on 11 August 1947 but went on to adopt its own constitution and hold elections under universal suffrage. A popular ministry was installed under the Maharaja's brother, Priyabrata Singh, in September 1948. Its Marxist inclinations under the radical influence of Hijam Irabot Singh caused disquiet in Delhi. This led to pressures for Manipur's merger with the Union which the Maharaja signed a year later in Shillong without being able to consult his council of ministers or seek ratification by the state assembly. Manipuris felt further slighted at being demoted to a Part C State (a category since abolished) and then being designated a Union Territory, even as others with lesser credentials were given full statehood. Thereafter, Nehru formally ceded to U Nu the Kubaw Valley, a fertile tract that had changed hands between Manipur and Burma more than once in the past. This merely reconfirmed the de facto 'restoration' by the British of the tract to the court of Ava in 1834 in lieu of a monthly 'stipend' to the Manipur ruler.

It was only in 1972 that Manipur became a full-fledged state and it took until 1992 for the Manipuri language, with its long literary tradition, to be placed in the Eighth Schedule, a classification of little real meaning but of some emotional significance. There were other hurts too. Under its revenue regulations, Meiteis, classified as an Other Backward Class, are barred from purchasing land in the hills whereas tribals and outsiders may do so in the Imphal Valley. Then again, Manipur tribals enjoying reservation soon gained more positions in the all-India and Central services, thus making them administrative overlords in the state in a galling role reversal, despite the Meiteis' better educational status. The in-migration of outsiders and foreigners also aggravated unemployment among local youth.

All this rankled and fostered Meitei revivalism in a bid to restore a faded glory, leading to a more radical assertion of secessionism and insurgency. A pan-Mongolian movement gave birth to the United National Liberation Front (UNLF), dedicated to self-determination and socialism. Links were forged with the Naga and Mizo underground and contact established first with Pakistan and Bangladesh and then with China through Bisheshwar, who broke with the UNLF to form the Peoples Liberation Army in 1978 with a view to liberating the entire 'eastern front'. Several other revolutionary groups followed with acronyms like PREPAK, KCP, KYKL, PULF, and a couple of Islamic fronts, 'K' in these acronyms standing for Kangleipak, an ancient name for Manipur. To hold Imphal, the Assam Rifles operated until recently out of the hallowed Kangla Fort, unthinkingly, but unwisely, adding insult to injury. Alliances with the United Liberation Front of Assam, the Kuki National Army and NSCN (K) saw the creation of an Indo-Burma Revolutionary Front.

These bewildering permutations and combinations have been part of a continuing pattern of coalition building and fragmentation throughout the Northeast in response to different pulls and pressures and initiatives from new leaders. Manipur in turn witnessed Meitei–Pangal riots, NSCN (IM) domination of four of its five Naga-inhabited districts, and bloody Naga–Kuki clashes following Kuki resistance to NSCN (IM) control of the border town of Moreh, a pivotal hub for a thriving smuggling trade that the NSCN (K) group has also been eyeing. Drug-trafficking through Myanmar has led to the spread of HIV-AIDS through shared use of hypodermic syringes. As in Nagaland, extortion and easy money has led to criminalization and adventurism. Development has suffered and unemployed youth are ready recruits to agitational and revolutionary politics.

Police action has inevitably resulted in repression, human rights violations and further alienation. The Armed Forces Special Powers Act provides a legitimizing shield for security forces operating in remote and difficult combat zones. But its prolonged use has made it a special focus of popular ire. A committee that reviewed its working recommended its scrapping and partial incorporation in a modified form with safeguards in other extant legislation. A women's group, Apunba Lup, has spearheaded the agitation, with the Meira-Paibas (women torch-bearers) in the lead and Irom Sharmila Chanu having to be nose-fed for over six years to keep her from fasting unto death in protest. But the intended reform is yet to be legislated.

Clearance for the multi-purpose Tipaimukh dam on the Barak (Meghna) in Manipur, near its trijunction with Mizoram and Assam, has latterly become a prime target of opposition on grounds of environmental loss and possible seasonal submergence of a waterfall sacred to the Zeliangrong Nagas. However, the Hmars and others see the project as a potential boon. Unfortunately, a lack of transparency and inadequate public information has allowed rumour and conjecture to get the better of facts regarding the area of possible submersion, the nature and value of crop or plantation loss and the number of persons likely to be displaced. The project could be transforming if imaginatively handled, and would open up a backward and disadvantaged region and bring employment and wider opportunities to this part of Manipur as well as adjacent areas in Mizoram, Cachar and Bangladesh, which must also be brought into the loop as potential beneficiaries.

The general election in Manipur held in February 2007 registered an 83 per cent turn out despite the anti-AFSPA and anti-Tipaimukh agitation and only six out of eleven NSCN (IM)-supported United Naga Council candidates (favouring Nagalim) were elected. Furthermore, the incumbent Congress regime was returned to power. All this appears to suggest that notwithstanding subversion of governance as a result of insurgency, extortion and agitational politics over the years, popular opinion is signalling a yearning for stability, peace and development.

Mizoram's different track

Events in Mizoram followed a very different track. Early opinion favoured remaining in India and prospering with it. However, a sense of remoteness, neglect and distress caused by tardy famine relief transformed frustration into anger when the periodic *mautam* or bamboo flowering led to an enormous proliferation of rats that ate up standing crops in 1965. The Assamese Language Bill of 1960 had also aroused fears of cultural erosion. Presbyterian Church leaders counselled patience in vain. The Mizo National Front (MNF) struck on 28 February 1966, taking control of Lungleh, parts of Aizawl and other administrative centres. Laldenga, the MNF chief, went on to declare independence and establish a sovereign government on foreign soil.

The Government of India was taken unawares but took immediate countermeasures. The rebels were soon on the run. To deny them food and intelligence, the rural population from 466 villages was regrouped, in four phases, in so-called protected and progressive villages along a strip of ten kilometres marking the principal road axes. The measure was harsh and 82 per cent of the population was thus involuntarily relocated. The MNF moved into the Chittagong Hill Tracts and sought assistance from Pakistan and China but to no avail. The tide had turned. Educated Mizos and MNF cadres knew that they must come to terms. The liberation of Bangladesh came as a further blow and secret negotiations were initiated with the Government, which finally fructified in a Memorandum of Settlement in June 1986. The sitting Congress chief minister vacated his seat and Laldenga formed a government that the electorate confirmed some months later. Mizoram was separated from Assam and granted statehood and has since remained a peaceful outpost of the Northeast.

The basic terms of the Mizoram settlement were incorporated in Article 371G of the Constitution. Development of border trade with Myanmar and Bangladesh was envisaged to end its geo-political isolation. This, alas, has made slow progress although border trade posts have been designated. A more recent understanding with Myanmar, previously Burma, for construction of the Kaladan Corridor, a road-cum-inland navigation link from southern Mizoram to Sitwe and the upgradation of that port holds promise.

Ethnic tensions between the dominant Mizo community and the Brus (Reangs) and Hmars in the east and north have been resolved with the guarantee of special development programmes for these minority groups. However the Government expressed its inability to concede unification of all Mizo-inhabited areas except with the consent of all the parties concerned. Problems remain with immigrant Chins from Myanmar and Chakmas from Bangladesh. It is noteworthy that 'de-grouping' after the peace accord has not restored the earlier pattern of rural habitation. Grouping had led to a 'loosening of village solidarity' and a tendency towards urbanization (a concomitant of 'modernization'). By the mid-1990s Mizoram was India's most urbanized state (over 46 per cent), with Aizawl graduating to a Class I town with a population of 155,500 people.

Tripura's travails

Tripura's story is very dissimilar. There, a continuing influx of, first, licit and then illicit Bengali settlers and refugees across its western border reduced the tribal population of this ancient and once powerful tribal state to a minority, confined to the larger but less-hospitable and less-developed eastern hill tracts. As in the fable, at the end of the day the camel had occupied the tent and even the specially established tribal reserves came under relentless pressure. This demographic transformation aroused anguish and anger leading to ethnic violence and insurrection. It is true that land-leases to Bengali farmers had in earlier times brought revenue to the state whose ruler found it convenient to adopt Bengali as the language of administration and education in the principality.

Two parallel streams emerged from growing discontents. Responding to the formation of the Eastern India Tribal Union (EITU) in 1954, tribal militancy grew in opposition to rising Assamese assertion if not chauvinism, and there was growth of leftist influence under the tribal leader, Dasarath Deb, that catapulted the communists to power. Pleas to stem the increasing alienation of tribal lands finally secured the creation of a tribal autonomous council region that in turn aroused Bengali opposition and gave birth to the militant Amra Bangali movement in the 1970s. The situation was ripe for conflict. The Tripura Upajati Juba Samity (TUJS) called for the expulsion of all 'foreigners' who had entered the state after its merger with the Indian Union on 15 October 1949. A petty incident triggered rumours of a tribal boy having been knifed and lit the spark that led to an ethnic conflagration. Hundreds were massacred and 300,000 persons were compelled to seek refuge in camps.

Meanwhile, Bijoy Hrangkhwal, a TUJS activist had established the Tripura National Volunteers (TNV), an armed cadre trained by the MNF, and set up an underground government in exile in the Chittagong Hill Tracts in 1982. Realization soon dawned that independence was a far cry and, following the MNF lead, the TNV laid down arms and negotiated a peace settlement in 1988. The Tripura Tribal Areas Autonomous District Council, covering 68 per cent of the state, had by now been brought under the Sixth Schedule and was further reorganized to enhance its tribal pre-eminence.

Not all the TNV cadres were pleased at this turn of events. Two breakaway groups successfully formed the All-Tripura Tribal Force (ATTF) and the National Liberation Front of Tripura (NLFT). The ATTF abjured violence in 1993 and negotiated certain cultural safeguards for the preservation of heritage sites and development of Kok-Borok and other tribal languages. Two factions of the NLFT, committed to reviving indigenous Borok pride, also gave up arms later even as still other splinter groups took up arms. Violence has not totally abated but most erstwhile militant elements have turned to development, which is the critical challenge of not only Tripura but of the entire Northeast. Opening up to Bangladesh could powerfully impact both.

Peace and development go hand in hand. The Gomti hydroelectric dam (with an installed capacity of 15 MW) has been fully amortized. The area of forty-six square kilometres it submerged displaced a large number of tribals while the electricity generated largely benefited an urban Bengali population, engendering new resentments. Power output has significantly declined over the years with silting of the reservoir and a consequent reduction in plant efficiency. Fortunately, Tripura increasingly depends on thermal power generated from locally discovered gas. If, therefore, the Gomti dam is decommissioned and its reservoir drained and restored to cultivation, 46,000 displaced and landless families could be resettled on a hectare apiece. This would not only give a fillip to the farm economy but could bring about a significant measure of ethnic reconciliation and send a powerful message across the Northeast.

Assam splinters

The Khasi, Jaintia and Garo Hills have had a relatively smoother passage, possibly because of Shillong's greater cosmopolitanism as united Assam's former capital and on account of the personality of its farsighted Hill leaders. J.J.M. Nicols Roy and Williamson Sangma steered the Khasis and Garos towards merger with India with the promise of district autonomy under the Sixth Schedule. The Hill districts thus formally became part of Assam in December 1949 against the background of the economic and cultural hardship caused by disruption of market and communication links with and through East Pakistan. This remains to be fully overcome.

Moves to declare Assamese the official language of the state were countered by the demand for a separate hill state by the Eastern India

Tribal[Hills] Union. The States Reorganisation Commission declined to break up the composite state of Assam and matters came to a head with the introduction of the Assam Language Bill in 1960. By now the united hill state demand had fragmented into demands for separate states Nagaland, Mizoram and what was to become Meghalaya, which graduated to full statehood in 1972 after an intermediary tenure as a sub-state of Assam.

The adjacent and more Hinduized Dimasas, Kacharis and other tribes in the United Mikir and North Cachar Hills were, however, persuaded to remain within Assam with the assurance of district autonomy. This was also sought in order that Assam might retain contiguity with its predominantly Bengali-speaking Cachar district in the Barak Valley. However, growing disquiet over creeping 'Assamisation' following the Assam agitation in the 1980s, led the United Mikir and North Cachar Hills to demand the constitution of autonomous councils for Karbi Anglong (Mikir Hills) and the North Cachar Hills, with wider powers than hitherto devolved on such bodies. Interestingly, the CPI (Marxist-Leninist) Party took office in Karbi Anglong, marking the first occasion that a Naxalite breakaway revolutionary Maoist group anywhere chose to come to power through the parliamentary route.

In Meghalaya itself, party splits and defections led to opportunistic politics at the State level while overlapping jurisdictions between the State administration, district councils and Khasi Syiem durbars led to bickering and rivalry. The anti-foreigner/outsider agitation in Assam sparked similar sentiments elsewhere in the region and Shillong witnessed rioting between tribals and non-tribals in 1992, though not for the first time, fanned by market rivalry, rising unemployment among educated youth and controversies over job reservations. The fallout was twofold. There was a rise of Khasi (HALC) and Garo (ALMA) militancy and the demand for a separate Garo state was voiced. The arrival in Siliguri and Darjeeling of Nepalese, who had fled Shillong, encouraged Subhas Ghising to launch his Gorkhaland movement. There was also a Seng Khasi movement for Khasi cultural revival, part of a widespread trend among modernizing communities searching for roots.

From NEFA to Arunachal

Nowhere is the Northeast's diversity more evident than in Arunachal, whose steady evolution from a state of atomized isolation of a multitude of secluded tribes to a naturally-inculcated sense of oneness, as Arunachalese, has been a quite remarkable saga of nation building. Nehru's policy of encouraging the tribes to progress at their own pace and in accordance with their own genius was codified by his tribal adviser, Verrier Elwin, in *A Philosophy for NEFA* (the North East Frontier Agency as it was then known). Tribal institutions were not rudely discarded. Village elders were employed as *gao bura*s, who provided a link with the incipient administrative structure that took the form of a simple single-line administration under a political officer for each of several so-called frontier divisions. A cadre of specially selected Indian Frontier Administrative Service officers, oriented towards field administration, manned the government. These officers would trek through forest and mountains, sing and dance with the people and were not headquarter- or file-bound.

These beginnings gave birth to panchayats, a panchayat assembly and finally the apparatus of a full-fledged state. Nefamese (a pidgin Assamese) provided a lingua franca. Hindi was popularized and English developed more slowly but ultimately extensively. There has been no militancy in Arunachal but there has been agitation against the settlement of Chakma refugees (displaced from the Kaptai dam in Bangladesh) as well as of Hajongs and even Tibetans in parts of the state. The numbers involved are modest but large enough for a state made up of essentially small communities. Like all migrants, these people are hard-working and thrifty and have forged ahead to the envy of the others.

The state is particularly well endowed with hydroelectric potential and bio-diversity. With regard to the first, Arunachal is chary of displacement by large dams and has so far preferred run-of-the-river or modest storage projects, which it would like to develop with private capital unfettered by any Central or Northeast Water Resource Authority (NEWRA) as proposed. The region's bio-diversity needs fuller mapping and guidelines to prevent its unscientific harvesting and unregulated export by predatory elements. The obverse of this is local development of a whole range of horticultural, herbal and floricultural products, which entails managerial, technical and marketing inputs and economies of scale best achieved through partnerships with corporate bodies on appropriate terms of mutual cost–benefit sharing.

Land in the hill regions of the Northeast is very largely held by individuals or tribal communities and cannot be alienated to non-tribal entities. Concepts of 'tribal interest' (corresponding to 'public purpose' under the Land Acquisition Act) and land leases are being explored as options for providing land for developmental purposes. However, there are ever more reports, as from Nagaland too, of the privatization of community lands by new tribal elites and their alienation by some to outsiders and foreigners (Bangladeshis and Nepalese) through concealed tenancies, benami holdings and marriages of convenience. This is creating a new feudal order or rentier class within what have traditionally been egalitarian tribal communities and is a tendency that merits watching and possible regulation to avoid any future backlash.

In Meghalaya too, shallow coal deposits on land owned by the community have been wastefully mined from outcrops with child workers burrowing laterally into the thin seams from small vertical shafts. They win as much coal as possible before the 'mine' is abandoned so as not to risk a roof collapse. This 'rat-hole' mining, illegal after coal nationalization, remains a thriving industry though it is unsafe, a health hazard, liable to spontaneous combustion and responsible for environmental blight. Coal is smuggled down the escarpment to Bangladesh and the rest is disposed of in Assam. Heavy trucks have pitted the roads and a mafia has grown around the trade. This 'industry' needs regulation and a scientific work plan if permitted to continue. The point essentially is to prevent environmental abuse and alienation of community-held tribal lands.

Assam's woes

If the hill tribes have their problems, Assam has had its own share of worries. It had successfully staved off Mughal invasion but fell prey to the Raj. The Ahoms ruled from Sibsagar and then extended their sway over Lower Assam. British rule was first established in parts of what was to become Meghalaya and Lower Assam from Bengal and only then extended to Upper Assam, with the surrounding Hills being cordoned off behind an Inner Line. Conquest, administrative compulsions and finding the workforce to establish more tea gardens, manning forest and mineral-based industries and reclaiming new lands to augment revenues called for labour and services. Administrative and professional cadres were brought in from Bengal. Marwaris did the provisioning. Tea garden labour was recruited from tribal Middle India and Bengali immigrants were encouraged to settle on the land and Nepalese inducted into the security forces. Although 'lines' were drawn to mark the limits of such migrant settlements, the line system was breached. This marked the beginning of what was later to manifest itself in Assam's twin identity problems of language and 'the other', with the Bengali element metamorphosing from outsiders to foreigners after partition.

Trained 'writers' were brought to Assam from Calcutta and the local administration was conducted in Bengali, which was formally declared to be the official language of the province until 1873, with Assamese designated a mere Bengali dialect. Assamese sensitivities were outraged. Assamese students in Calcutta launched the Asamiya Unnati Sadhana Sabha in 1885 and the Assam Sahitya Sabha was founded in 1917. Similar sahitya sabhas were established thereafter by different ethnic groups and became engines of linguistic pride and competing cultural identities.

By the 1930s, the Bengali immigrant tide had registered a noticeable presence in certain border districts and a British State Census Commissioner was to describe this alarmingly as a 'silent invasion of Assam'. With the approach of Partition, the Muslim League began to lay claims to Assam, adding a communal dimension to what was until then primarily a linguistic contention. However, though Assam (minus the district of Sylhet) remained with India, Partition brought in waves of Bengali refugees as well as illicit immigrants from what was then East Pakistan. With their rehabilitation, various encroachments, the diversion of land for development programmes and construction of roads and other infrastructure, the empty spaces were soon filled and inroads made into the tribal belts and blocks established after Independence in order to protect the shrinking homelands of the plains tribals. The plains tribals, as opposed to the hill tribes, had long intermingled with others but now found they were increasingly fragmented within the general populace, which created a creeping sense of isolation and siege. And thus was born the plains tribals demand for linguistic and territorial recognition.

Assam's own geo-political isolation after Partition was overlaid with a feeling of Delhi's neglect and indifference to its problems and aspirations. On Independence Day, 1947, a local AIR station was attacked by some Assamese youth while *Jana gana mana* was being sung, as the anthem excluded reference to Assam. Thereafter, for almost five years, Assamese would sing the national anthem substituting Kamarup for Sindhu. (Mullick, 1972) The battle for an oil refinery in the State, after the discovery of new oil and gas fields in Upper Assam, yielded no more than a 'toy' refinery at Nunmati as the bulk of Assam's oil was pumped to Barauni and Haldia in Bihar and West Bengal respectively. The influx of foreigners continued and worse was to follow with Assam feeling abandoned following the evacuation of the North bank during the India–China conflict in 1962.

Smouldering resentment exaggerated hurt and made simple minds susceptible to myths and canards. One such fable was carelessly recorded as gospel in an otherwise absorbing and scholarly narrative by Yasmin Saikia (2005), reconstructing the growth of cultural identities in the course of the Tai–Ahom struggle. Budeshwar Gogoi, a high-school history teacher and founding chairman of the United Liberation Front of Assam (ULFA), told Saikia that while the Assamese heeded the call to defend the motherland, the Indian Army pulled out of Tezpur on 21 November 1962 after the Chinese breakthrough at Se La. The town was evacuated and Nehru's broadcast that evening shocked the people and heightened their sense of abandonment. Budeshwar Gogoi cites Nehru's broadcast that night as saying 'My heart goes out to the people of Assam'. Gogoi then interpolated the words, 'but I cannot do anything', which Nehru never uttered. A further embellishment followed: '. . . the government backed off and abandoned us . . . . On the other hand, the Chinese, who were supposed to be our enemy saved us'. How? According to Gogoi, the people fled leaving their paddy fields untended; but 'when we returned to our homes, we found that the Chinese soldiers had harvested the grain, tied them in bundles, and stored them in the barns. We could not believe it . . . We are farmers. Rice is our only wealth, and the Chinese gave it back to us'.

Gogoi's story is a total concoction. The Chinese did not enter Tezpur or the Assam plains, let alone harvest the crop. This writer was one of two Indians among a group of eleven newspapermen who did not leave Tezpur on 20–22 November and remained behind with bemused patients of the mental hospital who had been released when the North Bank was evacuated. The whole sorry business was undoubtedly a political disaster but that is another story. Lal Bahadur Shastri, then home minister, visited Tezpur a day later and Indira Gandhi a couple of days thereafter.

Nevertheless 1962 was a turning point. There commenced a slow cultivation of a distinctive Assamese identity that, especially in Upper Assam, harked back to earlier cultural roots. Ethnic infusions had made the Tai–Ahoms of Upper Assam consider themselves somewhat different from their cousins in Lower Assam though to most, differences in daily living were not easily discernible. The intellectual progenitors of ULFA (mostly drawn from marginalized communities and tribes in Upper Assam) recalled memories of Ahom rule and over a period of time sought to reconstruct an Ahomness around which their discontents began to feed.

The language and foreigners' issues sparked agitation through the 1960s and 1970s in a movement led by the All Assam Student's Union (AASU). While AASU saw danger in the continued influx of foreigners, ULFA dismissed this as populist sentiment and pointed to India as the main threat. Summoning the Indian Army in aid of civil power to contain ethnic and communal violence led in turn to charges of repression and human rights violations.

ULFA's philosophy veered from radical socialism to ethnic chauvinism, culminating in its leadership seeking refuge in Bangladesh and making common cause with its erstwhile sworn enemies in order now to combat alleged Indian hegemony! Udayon Misra (2001) cites ULFA literature as eulogizing 'East Bengal' immigrants as 'a major part of the national life of Assam' without whom 'our freedom struggle can never be successful'. ULFA's more recent pogroms have been directed against Hindi-speaking people in Upper Assam (mostly Marwaris and Bihari labourers) on whom quit notices were served.

Returning to Yasmin Saikia, the Tai–Ahom movement gained momentum 'after the Thai of Thailand adopted the Ahoms as one of their ancestors' at the first international Thai Studies Conference in New Delhi in 1981. 'A new representation of origins made it possible to imagine a history of Assam connected with Thailand that transcended the limits of nation-state and Indian national identity.' This also facilitated the forging of ties with Shan and Kachin rebel groups within a larger front of neighbouring local nationalisms.

At the same time, the continuing influx of Bangladeshi migrants was not deterred either by the fitful implementation of the Illegal Migrants (Determination by Tribunals) Act, 1983, or fencing the border. These only created new crises of identity for both Assamese Hindus and Muslims. Hindus continued to fear that they might be politically and culturally overwhelmed. Asamiya Muslims, who had begun to declare Assamese as their mother tongue in the census as part of a process of assimilation, now felt threatened along with the newer waves of Bangladeshi Muslim immigrants on grounds of faith and their earlier linguistic affiliation. The horrendous Nellie massacre of 1983 primarily targetted the new immigrant Muslims who had occupied Tiwa (Lalung) tribal lands, and like other communal incidents, did not altogether spare indigenous Muslims. Bodos, Bengali Hindus and ex-tea garden tribes settled in the area felt the heat.

Plains tribals' aspirations

The Nellie massacre was an ugly facet of plains tribal anger at being cribbed, cabined and confined by 'outsiders' within their traditional homelands. The States Reorganisation Commission had favoured consolidation rather than fragmentation of the Northeast. It rejected breakaway demands for a Hill State, Purbanchal (a Bengali consolidation around Cachar) and Kamatapur (a Rajbongshi unit straddling Assam and Bengal on both sides of the Siliguri neck). It instead recommended the merger of Tripura with Assam, which was not accepted either locally or in Delhi.

By 1967 the Plains Tribals Council of Assam had come into being and, encouraged by Nagaland's approaching statehood, proposed the consolidation of plains tribal areas in what was christened Udayachal within a federal Assam. The demand was rebuffed. The Assam movement saw the plains tribals stand alongside AASU in the hope that the struggle for Assamese identity would enhance respect of their own separate cultural identities. However, the record of the Asom Gana Parishad (AGP) government that took office after the Assam Accord proved disappointing.

The Bodos, the largest plains tribal group and the very oldest indigenous community in the region, were growing increasingly impatient. In 1987 they demanded autonomy within Assam, denouncing Prafulla Mahanta the AGP leader as 'an outsider from Kannuaj' and proclaiming that Assam should have a federal structure as its population consisted of people of 'Aryan, Mongolian and Dravidian origin'.

Hiteshwar Saikia, then chief minister and himself of Tai-Ahom stock, was not unsympathetic towards the cultural and economic predicament of the plains tribals. Other minority groups had by now joined hands against 'Assamese chauvinism' in a United Reservation Movement Council of Assam demanding autonomy for all tribal groups. Tortuous negotiations followed, interspersed with Bodo militancy, leading to a phased settlement. This went through the process of official encouragement to the Bodo language, acceptance of a Bodoland Autonomous Council (BAC) with jurisdiction over thirty-eight heads of administration in some 2,000 villages and twenty-five tea gardens, and finally an enlarged and further empowered Bodoland Territorial Council (BTC) within Assam. This appears to have quietened the insurgency, though one splinter group is still holding out for separation if not sovereignty.

The formation of BAC/BTC has not been without protest. While the Bodos feel that what they have got is but a pale shadow of their once extensive domain, they are very much of a minority within BTC and yet rule over far more numerous groups including Assamese, Rajbongshis, tea tribes and others. This is an anomalous situation and it remains to be seen whether and how long this arrangement will hold. Given accommodation and statesmanship, the experiment might work.

Hiteshwar Saikia was also instrumental in fashioning an ingenious formula to satisfy the corresponding demands of other far smaller and equally scattered North bank plains tribals such as the Rabhas, Mishings and Tiwas. He constituted non-territorial Apex Councils for each of these communities. Under this arrangement, non-contiguous villages with a majority of any one of these tribes have been grouped under an apex council with an elected executive, a development budget and educational and linguistic safeguards. Latterly, some other minority communities such as Sonowals and Deoris have been declared scheduled tribes and granted similar apex councils. This is an innovative arrangement that caters to the basic demands of such minority groups without detriment to the larger state entity or other communities. The principle of non-territoriality clearly holds out much promise in managing diversity.

Some may question whether it is prudent to re-tribalize communities or pander to the politics of fragmentation. They do have a point. And yet it must be said that such symbolic gestures towards ethnic and cultural sentiments do have a valuable buffering role in periods of multiple transition. Moods change. An Asom identity was once pressed. Two decades later, when the Assam Legislative Assembly adopted a resolution seeking the renaming of Assam as 'Asom' through a constitutional amendment, a large number of Assamese academics, littérateurs and professionals were up in arms. They argued that 'Assam' is not of British coinage but has been current since the thirteenth century. Moreover, retaining 'Assam' would be conducive to maintaining harmony among all sections of people in the State. (*Indian Express*, 17 January 2007)

Resurgence of Assamese pride is also being manifested in other ways. When ULFA mindlessly 'banned' the National Games to be held in Guwahati in February 2007, there were protests, most notably from Assamese sportspersons who have added lustre to the state by their performance in various games. ULFA later backed down and the National Games were held unhindered.

Sikkim and Gorkhaland

Sikkim, a former protectorate, was absorbed into India in 1975 in somewhat traumatic circumstances that could have been handled differently. It has an indigenous Bhutia–Lepcha population which, as in Tripura, has been overwhelmed by outsiders, in this case, Nepalese. The personalized rule of the Chogyal, as the prince was known, had evoked mounting demands for democratization by the Nepalese majority. Resistance to this would have crumbled in time but matters came to a head sooner with Indian pressure for change. A 'special opinion poll' or referendum dethroned the Chogyal and Sikkim in quick succession was first declared an 'Associate State' of what momentarily became a confederal India, and then merged with the Union in terms of Article 371 F of the Constitution. The Bhutia–Lepchas have been recognized as scheduled tribes and given weighted representation in the Legislative Assembly and some Nepalese communities have been designated OBCs.

Darjeeling was gifted by the Sikkim raja to the British in 1835 and was later enlarged with the addition of Kalimpong, which was annexed from Bhutan, to form a district within North Bengal. It soon acquired fame for its high-quality tea. Development necessitated import of labour, which mostly came from Nepal and changed the ethnic complexion of the principality. Unionization of the tea garden labour provided opportunity for the rise of communist influence and it was the Communist Party of India, in keeping with the Marxist belief in nationality rights that first made out a case for self-determination of the Darjeeling Gorkhas. The idea of local autonomy, though canvassed, never fructified and resultant uncertainties and frustrations led to the birth of the Gorkha National Liberation Front (GNLF) under Subhas Ghising in 1980.

The expulsion of Nepalese from Manipur and Meghalaya around 1985 and the arrival of these refugees in Siliguri and Darjeeling gave rise to a movement against 'outsiders' that resulted in clashes and several deaths and damage to property. The GNLF's demand for statehood was rejected and Ghising finally settled for a Darjeeling Gorkha Hills Council (DGHC) in 1988 'for the social, economic, educational and cultural advancement of the people residing in the Hill areas of Darjeeling District'. The DGHC Agreement defined Indian Nepalese as Gorkhas (not Gurkhas) and the Nepali language was included in the Eighth Schedule. Ghising continues to bargain for more, but earlier tensions have subsided. Talk of a Greater Sikkim, absorbing the DGHC area, has surfaced from time to time. But this is a controversial topic and many Sikkimese, zealous of their identity, would not favour the merger.

Kamatapur and North Bengal blues

The DGHC area and North Bengal together constitute a missing element in the official and popular conceptualization of the Northeast. This stems from failure to differentiate between mere geography and geo-political or geo-strategic imperatives. The Siliguri neck is a vital choke point for every kind of national connectivity—road, rail, pipeline, power transmission, microwave and telecommunication links, air corridor—and marks a broad ethno-cultural divide. Further, North Bengal harbours trends and forces that impinge on peace and tranquillity in the Northeast and therefore needs to be viewed holistically.

There appear to be some mini-nationalist ferments brewing in North Bengal, the original home of the Naxalite movement, with significant tribal participation. Of the 300 tea estates in Darjeeling, the Dooars and Terai, about thirty-four are reported sick and at least fourteen have been closed, with official efforts being made to reopen some of them. These gardens are said to have been purchased by get-rich-quick investors, worked to death and then abandoned as sick, leaving several hundred tribal estate workers in penury without back wages or statutory benefits. Yet, critics ask, if tea was facing a slump, why should 60,000 hectares of paddy and other subsistence cropland have been brought under tea in the neighbouring Islampur area since 1980 in a drive to commercialize agriculture? (Manas Dasgupta, 1998) The process of conversion displaced marginal farmers, including Muslim peasants who constitute a big part of the population here, breeding further discontent. Adding to this has been resentment over the pushing out of Nepalese from the Northeast to North Bengal as well as the expulsion of the Lhotshampa (Bhutanese of Nepalese extraction) from Southern Bhutan to Eastern Nepal where they are lodged in in refugee camps under the aegis of the United Nations High Commission for Refugees (UNHCR) in Jhapa.

In effect, it is said that both tribals and Muslims have lost land and employment over the years, a situation aggravated by the ingress of hard-working immigrant farmers from East Pakistan/Bangladesh. The lumpenization of land relations in the plains and 'Nepalization' of the hill region have occurred at a time when the Maoists have gained influence in Nepal and have reactivated themselves in West Bengal even as there has been a fresh stirring of Gorkha sentiment on the Indian side of the Indo-Nepal border.

Adding to this cocktail has been the revival of the Rajbongshsi aspiration for Purbanchal or, more likely, Kamatapur, both of which extend into the western part of Lower Assam. Suggestions favouring Sixth Schedule status for the DGHC area, rechristened the Gorkha Hill Council, Darjeeling (GHC) area, have been mooted; but this would require there to be a 60 per cent tribal population in such a designated territory. The present tribal composition of Darjeeling district (2001 census) is, however, only13 per cent. With the Bhutia-Lepchas and Hindu Tamangs and Limbus (Nepalese clans) being accorded tribal status within the DGHC area, the tribal population has risen to around 35 per cent. The GNLF is now trying to get Buddhist Tamangs and other upper-caste Hindu Nepalese to adopt indigenous tribal rituals and not observe Durga puja during Dusshera in a bid to muster tribal numbers. There have been murmurs of opposition, as altering the ethnic composition of the DGHC could strain the fabric of social relations.

The Rajbongshis have genuine grievances, some of which, as elsewhere, relate to loss of power and status with changing times. Historians believe that Koch tribals who inhabited the thirteenth century Kamatapur kingdom around Cooch Behar took on the name of Rajbongshi in the process of Sanskritization. Based on their Kamatapuri identity, centred on language, they sought autonomy or statehood, which was earlier rejected but has been renewed in view of pressures on their lands and livelihoods by immigrant settlers. A West Bengal committee did not uphold their claims and held Kamatapuri to be at best a dialect of Bengali. The plea for recognition as an Eighth Schedule language has not been entertained and the agitation has been firmly put down. A Kamatapur Liberation Organisation has come into being and the idea of Greater Cooch Behar has been floated. The

Kamatapur Praja Party is now trying to join hands with the All-Assam Koch Rajbongshi Students Union in a bid to forge a united front.

There is perhaps low probability of any of this coming to anything and many such movements are ephemeral. It might nevertheless be unwise totally to disregard the straws blowing in the wind.

Policy implications

Looking at the Northeast as a whole, it is clear that many problems and conflicts await resolution. However, despite continuing insurgency and alienation, things are on the mend. There is a better understanding all around about the factors and compulsions that have dictated given positions and events and, with that, a growing willingness to adjust and move on by thinking of the future instead of being locked in the past. There is enough political and cultural space in India to accommodate seemingly dissident elements by restructuring the Union as a cooperative commonwealth.

It would be mistaken to assume that economic prosperity can be a universal solvent but there is little doubt that young people in the Northeast are looking for new development and employment opportunities. Peace and development march together and it is here that the region is poised to make a leap forward both in terms of aspirations and achievements. Implementation of the envisioned Look East Policy could make a major contribution to this end if vigorously and imaginatively acted upon. With its very large external perimeter and age-old trans-border cultural and economic links, an opening up to its sundered neighbourhood could quite soon convert the Northeast from a forgotten and neglected cul-de-sac into a vibrant land bridge to some of the fastest-growing economies in the world in East and South-east Asia. In this process, the Northeast must be more than a mere bus stop or corridor and should itself become an economic hub for a variety of manufactures and services and a tourist destination. The potential is clearly there and its realization is part of the Northeast Vision 2020 that has been formulated and is in the process of adoption.

Though once in the vanguard of development, Assam was hard hit by partition, which disrupted connectivity and markets. The northeast today ranks lowest in the national scale in terms of per capita income and human development indices, with Assam at the bottom of the heap. Given a national economic growth rate of nine per cent up to 2020, the northeast must attain a growth rate in excess of 13 per cent over the next three plan periods while Assam must aspire to nearly 15 per cent growth to level up with the rest of the country by 2020 and eradicate poverty. The vision 2020 document spells out how this might be accomplished. The challenge is great but, with strong local purpose and participation and national will, by no means impossible. A recent World Bank study also reveals a correlation between rising militancy and unrest and unemplopyment, especially rural unemployment. The logic of that finding is compelling.

The Northeast is anxious to restore lost linkages. Mindsets in Delhi and in the corporate world will have to change and exaggerated fears of subversive elements and dumping laid to rest. This calls for fashioning a border policy as much as settling outstanding boundary disputes with China and Bangladesh. Boundaries are mere lines on a map that define the limits of territorial sovereignty. Borders are transition zones related to people, language, ecology, shared natural resources, culture, commerce and history. Interactions at the border can and do shape larger inter-country relationships. Hitherto, India, following the British lead, has let its eastern marches remain a region of undeveloped wilderness as a low-cost natural defence option.

Innovative approaches

Whatever the merits of such a policy in the past, it is clearly counterproductive in a globalizing world today and is now in the process of being corrected. Smaller growth bilaterals or triangles straddling any one or more of India's neighbours could be a potent means of promoting relevant infrastructure development and trade facilitation. This would set in motion a virtuous cycle of trade and exchange, leading in due course not only to enhanced border trade but burgeoning inter-country and transit trade as well. Such a development would automatically imbue hitherto peripheral regions with a new centrality as pivots in a productive international relationship. Thus, there is no need to limit trade across the recently reopened Nathu La Pass between Sikkim and Tibet's Chumbi Valley to old-fashioned border trade in traditional products like yak tails and daily perishables. True, Lhasa is now connected via Golmud in Qinghai province to Beijing. But Calcutta still remains Lhasa's nearest ocean outlet.

Sustainable development is now part of conventional wisdom. Yet blanket orders such as contained in the Supreme Court's ruling on tree felling under the Forest Conservation Act and barring storage reservoirs above the Lower Subansiri dam in Arunachal Pradesh need to be revisited. These could place large, unrequited burdens on the local population and should not stand in the way of possibly better solutions that could be negotiated.

In this context, Arunachal could be encouraged to trade flat lands in the plains for habitations and lands lost to submergence behind storage dams in the hills. The disputed forest strip running along the Assam–Arunachal boundary has become an untended and unproductive no-man's land for lawless elements. It could be appropriately declared a 'trusteeship zone' for the next thirty to fifty years, with the Central Government as a third partner. This could then be developed as a special economic zone with requisite infrastructure, transport linkages and incentives to attract investments to convert cheap Arunachal hydro-power into wealth through value addition and income and employment generation that could be shared between all the three partners.

Multipurpose storages in the Brahmaputra basin in Arunachal could generate large blocks of power, improve lean season navigation and moderate floods in Assam, which has been devastated and impoverished by severe and extensive annual inundation. Such risk reduction would facilitate double cropping and enhance farm productivity, employment and income generation and have a multiplier effect. Winter lift irrigation and cold storages would facilitate diversified cropping. The chain of positive impacts and outcomes would enable Assam once again to become a dynamo for growth and stability in the entire region.

In Tripura, the decommissioning of the Gomti hydel dam, which has been fully amortized and has outlived its utility, and the restoration of the vacated reservoir bed to tribal cultivation could open a new chapter in ethnic relations and help restore peace. Gas has since been discovered in the state and the 750 MW gas-fired thermal station currently under construction could more than fuel its power needs.

The Northeast does not lack budgetary or natural resources. Per capita Plan expenditures in the eight constituent states are possibly the highest in India. All the units are special category states, which receive funding on the basis of 90 per cent grant and 10 per cent loan and also benefit from a non-lapsable pool of Central funding from each line department. The problem is leakage through extortion by the underground, rent seeking and oftentimes a poor delivery system. Where the community is involved, as through village councils, expenditures are targetted and productive, as has been illustrated by Nagaland's communization programme. What this suggests is the need to revive and strengthen village councils and panchayats, which now offer more autonomy and power under the Seventy-third Amendment than available under the Sixth Schedule.

For the rest, the Northeast cannot be developed or treated as a 'security state' nor should any underground faction or group be under any illusion that it can impose a military solution on the Indian state, or vice versa. The only way forward is patient dialogue, local institution and capacity building, and participative development within a framework of imaginative cooperative federalism.

{3}

Confronting Historical Injustice in Tribal India

A tribe necessarily represents not so much an aborigine or original and indigenous group as a form of early social division or organization of a people claiming a common descent, culture or territory. In the Indian context, tribes are recognized and scheduled by the President on the recommendation of the state administrations after due study and inquiry. The criteria adopted are backward or primitive traits, remoteness and isolation, shyness of contact and a distinctive way of life.

The term evoked discussion when the United Nations debated the formulation of a draft declaration on the rights of tribal and indigenous people some years ago. The native aboriginal populations of the Americas and Australia for instance were certainly indigenous in relation to the Spanish, Portuguese and other settlers who established colonies there. The Western view was that 'tribal' and 'indigenous' were virtually interchangeable terms, and that 'indigenous' more appropriately captured a chronological precedence that they sought to pass off as universal, a proposition that India and some others disputed. All of mankind was tribal at the beginning of time; but then communities and societies evolved through various stages of civilization and social, economic and technological growth to arrive at their present condition.

Many of India's Northeast tribes originated in Central China or South-east Asia and migrated centuries ago to what is now India. The process has not entirely ended. Some tribes are still on the move, pushing onwards and outwards, seeking new pastures. According to the Anthropological Survey of India (ASI), almost two-thirds of India's tribals claim to have migrated to their recent habitats even up to recent times. When conflicts arise, as must sometimes happen, one of the most contentious issues never easily resolved is the question: when does history begin? There is a preceding history that also represents a valid truth and, for modernizers, an unborn future that should not be denied.

These caveats are a useful reminder that many social categories are not static but need to be viewed in dynamic terms. According to K. Suresh Singh (1994) a tribe is (also) an administrative and political concept in India. Only those tribes duly 'scheduled' are constitutionally recognized as tribes. In this listing, some tribes may be left out by omission and others because they may have graduated by process of Sanskritization or development. Some communities scheduled as tribes in one state may not be so recognized in another. Reservations and affirmative action have caused some groups to seek tribal status, or re-tribalization as in the case of Rajbongshis in North Bengal. In the same manner, other social groups have struggled and agitated to be declared backward in order to share the spoils available by inclusion in the list of Other Backward Classes. We are witness to such regression.

It is even more surprising to see inhabitants of whole territories declared 'tribal', irrespective of their status. Thus, all persons living in Kinnaur (Himachal), Jaunsar-Bawar (Uttarakhand) and Ladakh (barring one community) have been designated as tribes.

The total number of tribes identified by the Anthropological Survey of India (1994) was 471, or 635, if segments and territories are added. They account for about 8 per cent of the population or some eighty-five million and constitute the largest national tribal aggregate anywhere in the world according to the UN Working Group on tribal and indigenous people. The four largest tribes are the Gonds, Bhils, Santhals and Minas (Meenas) who inhabit the heart of Middle India, the first two with numbers now probably in excess of eight million each. In contrast, the Northeastern tribes are much smaller in size. Overall, there were ninety-six tribes with a population below 5000 in 1981, some of them being numbered just in tens or hundreds. Most tribes are concentrated in one or two states, thirty-nine (14 per cent) across three states and thirty (7 per cent) across four to six states, indicating their presence in well defined territories across overlapping administrative boundaries in many instances.

Four racial stocks are represented in tribal India: Negritos (in the Andamans, and the Sidis who were brought from Africa as slaves), Proto-Australoid (Gonds, Mundas and Oraons), Mongoloids (in the Northeast) and Caucasoid (the Nilgiri Todas, the Rabaris of Gujarat and the Gujjars). And finally, the languages spoken are Indo-Aryan, Dravidian, Tibeto-Burman, Austro-Asiatic and Andamanese. Altogether, tribal India exhibits the same great diversity as all of India. Many tribes have a rich oral tradition that they are now trying to record and script.

The tribes have largely remained outside the *varna* or fourfold caste system, though most have their own notions of hierarchy. Many have embraced Hinduism (378 tribes numbering 60 per cent of the total tribal population), Christianity (149 and 24 per cent)) Buddhism (44 and 7 per cent) and Islam (19 and 3 per cent). As many as 293 tribal communities follow their traditional faiths, including Donyi Polo in Arunachal. But interestingly, the ASI records many groups as following more than one faith, primarily their own religion and either Hinduism or Christianity. There has been a revival of tribal cults such as that of the sacred grove among the Munda, Ho and Santhal and the Gondi dharma reflecting what the ASI sees as a nascent process of identity formation and assertion among the tribal people.

Forms of private property have emerged and there has been growing dependence on the market and middlemen. A gradual process of modernization has seen a shift in occupations and from traditional to modern practices. Hunting-gathering, trapping, and shifting cultivation are giving way to settled farming, horticulture, animal husbandry and sericulture. More tribals are gradually finding employment in government, private enterprise, services and entrepreneurship, though still mostly at the lower end of the scale. Things have changed, but there is a very long way to go.

Four tribal epochs

This is one part of the tribal story. If things have not gone too well it is because the world has intruded rudely and often inconsiderately into the tribal domain, resulting in a historical injustice. Pradip Prabhu, National Convenor for the Campaign for Survival with Dignity (2003) lists four epochs of Indian tribal history. The pre-colonial phase covers early centuries during which tribal communities lost ground to conquerors and settled populations and gradually withdrew to their forest habitat as a survival strategy. Then followed two centuries of colonial rule where the British saw the forests as prized preserves with economic and revenue potential in what they regarded as *res nullius* or areas of wilderness that belonged to no man. The best of these forests could therefore be 'reserved' by and for the state, thereby converting all those lawfully residing within its boundaries into encroachers or intruders. The tribal people were pushed ever deeper into the forest or on to its margins, their historic rights being treated as mere privileges or concessions bestowed on them by a benign ruler but only so long as they conducted themselves with due deference to the new authority, which in practice meant its minions and lowest functionaries. Thus, at a stroke, homelands and livelihoods were alienated.

Resentment soon surfaced with further inroads and exactions. Tribal anger matched rising insecurity. There were a whole series of tribal revolts between 1778 and the coming of Independence through the length and breath of tribal India. (Raghavaiah, 1979) At a time when the 150th anniversary of what has come to be termed the First War of Independence is being celebrated it should never be forgotten that the doughtiest and most persistent flag-bearers of independence from foreign rule before and after 1857 were the tribal people of India.

The Mal Paharia uprising and that of the Pahariya Sirdars of the Santhal Parganas in the 1770s preceded the Great Santhal Insurrection of 1855–6, which was long and hard fought before it was brutally suppressed. Its origins lay in the mounting exactions of rapacious zamindars and their intermediaries and feudatory underlings created by the Permanent Settlement. The Santhal areas also got distributed among different administrative jurisdictions and the requirement of paying revenue in cash and not in kind as hitherto 'ushered in a process of sale, mortgage, transfer of proprietary rights, assets and crops all of which made the alienation of land a powerful factor in the peasants' life. This led to a dependence upon the moneylender and trader who could give money in advance to pay the revenue in cash'. (Desai, 1979)

This in turn spawned under-tenants, sharecroppers, landless labourers, usury, litigation, debt and bondage that caught the peasant, tribal and non-tribal in its deadly coils. The Santhals were bloodied but won back a united district of Santhal Parganas.

Other tribes rose in revolt in the increasingly unquiet woods. Among them, the Kolis of Maharashtra in 1784, and not for the last time; the Chota Nagpur tribes; the Kols (Munda, Ho and Oraon) and Khewars of Bihar in the 1830s; the Bhils in Gujarat and the Kondhs in Orissa; the great Birsa Munda uprising in 1895; the Bastar uprising in 1911; the Gond, Kollam, Koya and Warli revolts; and many more. There was a string of tribal revolts in the Northeast too. Some of the more recalcitrant and sometimes nomadic elements were declared criminal tribes. The thirteen tribal chiefs in the Dangs (Gujarat) never ceded their territory to the British who merely leased their forests against payment of royalty.

The coming of Independence, the argument runs, saw the commencement of a third epoch marked by 'internal colonisation of the forest-tribal by the timber lobby in connivance with the state'. (Prabhu, 2003) The forests continued to be commercial enclaves from which the tribals, their traditional stewards, were virtually excluded. The 1952 National Forest Policy continued the old colonial tradition of denying tribals access in the name of promoting scientific forestry. The princes sold their private forests to contractors fearing their takeover by the Indian state. Shifting cultivation or *podu* was banned in part of Adilabad distrct of Hyderabad state in 1950 and in Chandrapur in Maharashtra in 1978, causing great distress to the Kollam, Hill Marias and other affected local tribal communities. Still later, in 1986, Bhil tribals in Khargone district won an order from the High Court of Madhya Pradesh that they did not require passes to collect and carry away the droppings of their own cattle while grazing in the forest as such dung did not constitute 'forest produce'! Such petty harassment was not uncommon.

The National Commission on Agriculture (1976) noted that the contribution of the forestry sector to GDP was 'very small' and advocated further investments to change over from 'the present low-cost low-yield forestry'. To this end, it recommended 'a dynamic programme of production forestry, aiming at clear felling and creating large scale man-made forests with the help of institutional financing' and the establishment of state forest corporations for their management. Further, *nistar* or forest concessions and privileges should be reduced and shifting cultivation regulated and progressively ended by employing tribals to work the new policy as forest corporation employees.

The forests were worked for revenue after Independence, as before, under working plans and there was increased contractual felling for commercial purposes. Opposition to this and manifestations of the ecological impact of deforestation and awareness created by the 1972 World Environment Conference in Stockholm gave a fillip to the Chipko movement in Garhwal under the leadership of Chandi Prasad Bhat and Sunderlal Bahuguna. This had echoes elsewhere and encouraged a movement for sustainable development and conservation forestry in place of commercial forestry.

Land aquisition and displacement

Agricultural expansion, large dam construction, refugee resettlement, a variety of infrastructural developments, industrialization and exponential population growth had over the years entailed increasing land acquisition and inroads into the forests. So-called wastelands that were invaluable common property resources for many on the margin of subsistence were also appropriated. Pressure on the forests increased. The UP terai was cleared and a large refugee resettlement project was launched in Dandakaranya. The Hirakud, Damodar Valley, Nagarjunasagar, Tungabhadra, Chambal and other river valley projects submerged considerable forest areas and tribal habitats. The Chittaranjan locomotive factory, Sindri fertilizer plant, the Rourkela, Bhilai, Durgapur and Bokaro steel works, the Ranchi Heavy Engineering complex, a number of new coalfields and iron ore, bauxite and non-ferrous metal mines, thermal power stations, new railway lines and highways, the Koraput aircraft factory and related townships encroached on forests and displaced large numbers of people, many of them tribal. The terms of resettlement and rehabilitation were not very satisfactory, especially in the early years, and implementation often faltered. There were also instances of multiple displacements of those already once relocated and resettled. Cynicism and frustration mounted.

Forest dwellers and others living on the fringes of forests but dependent on them were among those primarily affected. Estimates of displacement under all categories vary, going up to 40 million since Independence. But according to an official expert group on tribal land alienation (Ministry of Rural Development, 2004), 8.5 million tribals were displaced between 1951 and 1989. Of these, 6.3 million were displaced by dams, 1.33 million by mines and 0.31 million by industries; but only a quarter of these or 2.1 million had been rehabilitated. More to the point, more than 40 per cent of overall development-induced displacement has been of tribals. It is argued, with some justification, that the number of tribals displaced is an undercount as many titles are held jointly by several coparceners and many more lack pattas or title deeds and are therefore excluded. Similarly, compensation at 'market value' is likely to be greatly undervalued if calculated, as required, by reference to the registered sale value of equivalent land recently disposed of in the near neighbourhood as sale prices are notoriously under-quoted in order to minimize payment of stamp duty.

Prabhu's fourth epoch of tribal history is set in 'the contemporary phase of contesting ideologies, one that seeks integration as a means of tribal development, while the other argues for their eviction in the name of conservation' (of rare plant and animal species). The 'Tiger versus People' argument is set out in the report of the Tiger Task Force (Government of India, 2005).

The State has used the Land Acquisition Act, 1894 (as amended in 1984) to take over ancestral tribal lands on the principle of 'eminent domain'. 'Public purposes', subjectively defined, have rudely superseded the tribals' right to homeland and livelihood. The Forest Conservation Act, 1980, extended the concept of public purpose to protect game parks, nature parks and biosphere reserves from all of which sentient beings were excluded. The tribal was declared an encroacher.

Scheduling of tribes

The scheduling of tribes started long back under British rule. Tribal unrest necessitated a new approach and new dispensations were made under Regulation I of 1796, outlining a Santhal policy, the Wilkinson Rules of 1839 and similar decrees. The Ganjam and Vizagapatam

Act created so-called Agency Areas in southern Orissa and adjacent parts of Madras Presidency in what is now Andhra Pradesh. A wider ranging Scheduled Districts Act was passed in 1874 prescribing norms and procedures for the administration of these areas. The Montague–Chelmsford Reforms of 1919 excluded these tribal areas from the jurisdiction of the provincial governments and divided them into wholly and partially excluded categories, the former limited to Assam. Special provisions were also prescribed for so-called Primitive Tribes. The 1935 Government of India Act further clarified these matters. Tribals living in wholly excluded areas were administratively left more or less to their own devices whereas those in Fifth Schedule areas were taken out of the purview of the provincial governments and entrusted to the Governor reporting directly to the Viceroy, without injury to their right to continue to regulate their lives in the traditional manner under customary law.

The country's new Constitution adopted in 1950 brought the wholly excluded areas of the Northeast into a new Sixth Schedule and retained the Fifth Schedule concept in the rest of the country, with some refinements. Local governance in Sixth Schedule areas was entrusted to district and autonomous councils with jurisdiction over districts or specific regions under the supervision of the Governor who is armed with special powers.

Areas of tribal concentration in the rest of the country were brought within the ambit of the Fifth Schedule. Such areas may be de-listed or their boundaries altered by the President. About 88 per cent of tribal India is located in the Central Tribal Belt of Middle and Peninsular India and about 9 per cent in the Northeast. The rest is scattered.

The Fifth Schedule areas are administered by the state governments, subject to certain crucial powers exercised by the governor in his sole discretion as the agent of the President. To this end, the governor is required to make an annual report to the President regarding the administration of the Scheduled Areas under his charge and the Union is empowered to issue directions with regard to their administration. A Tribes Advisory Council is mandated to advise the governor on all matters referred to it by him. Laws passed by Parliament or the State legislature shall not apply to all or part of any Scheduled Area or shall apply with such modifications as may be notified by the governor, who is required to act in all matters in consultation with the Tribes Advisory Council. The governor may 'make regulations for the peace and good governance' of a Scheduled Area, prohibit or restrict the transfer of land therein or regulate its allotment by or among members of the Scheduled Tribes. He may also regulate moneylending. All regulations, however, are subject to assent by the President.

However, it is important to recall the sprit underlying the discussions in the Constituent Assembly leading to adoption of the Fifth Schedule. A sub-committee that examined the matter reported that the policy of total or partial exclusion had not yielded tangible progress in the removal of the tribals' backward condition. Therefore, since such isolation could not be extended indefinitely, it was sought to ensure that their educational level and living standards was suitably raised so that they might in due course be assimilated with the rest of the population. (Shiva Rao, 1967) Thus the Fifth Schedule was seen as an interim or transient arrangement but nonetheless something in the nature of a solemn, though unspoken, social contract between the new Republic of India, speaking through the Union Government, and its historically deprived and disadvantaged tribal citizens. The Centre's responsibility in this regard was clearly paramount.

Jawaharlal Nehru, as prime minister, was sensitive to the tribal condition and appointed Verrier Elwin as Tribal Adviser for the North East Frontier Agency (NEFA) in view of his previous experience in Middle India. Elwin (1958) quotes the prime minister as observing: 'I am not at all sure which is the better way of living, the tribal or our own. In some respects I am quite certain that theirs is better. Therefore it is grossly presumptuous on our part to approach them with an air of superiority, to tell them how to behave or what to do or what not to do. There is no point of trying to make them a second-rate copy of ourselves.'

Panch Shila for tribal India

Elwin wrote on the evolution of governance in NEFA and sought a Foreword from the prime minister for both the first and second editions of *A Philosophy for NEFA* in 1957 and 1958, the second elaborating on the first after fuller reflection. It was in the 1958 Foreword that Nehru set out what came to be known as a Panch Shila for Tribal India. He said it was neither possible nor desirable in this day and age to leave the tribes alone by following a policy of drift. At the same time they should not be over-administered. He then went on to enunciate a middle path of five principles:

> 1. People should develop along the lines of their own genius and we should avoid imposing anything on them. We should try to encourage in every way their own traditional arts and culture.
> 2. Tribal rights in land and forests should be respected.
> 3. We should try to train and build up a team of their own people to do the work of administration and development. Some technical personnel from outside will no doubt be needed, especially in the beginning. But we should avoid introducing too many outsiders in tribal territory.
> 4. We should not over-administer these areas or overwhelm them with a multiplicity of schemes. We should rather work through, and not in rivalry to, their own social and cultural institutions.
> 5. We should judge results, not by statistics or the amount of money spent, but by the quality of human character that is evolved.

To this may be added another quotation cited by Elwin, this time from Bimala Prasad Chaliha, Chief Minister of Assam, whom he asked what 'magic' he had so successfully used in working the autonomous districts in his state. Chaliha's disarming reply was 'a little understanding, a genuine respect, a lot of affection'. Chaliha too had a way with him that won tribal respect. The careful and sensitive manner in which NEFA was nurtured to become Arunachal is noteworthy. A hugely disparate and largely unexplored tribal region with a bewildering tribal diversity was patiently knit together into a larger political entity in defined stages. This coming together in statehood and self-governance was a remarkable achievement. Unfortunately, things did not quite work that way elsewhere, especially in Middle India.

A number of studies and reports over the years identified certain problems and shortcomings leading to modifications in tribal policy. To ensure an integrated policy framework as well as area development, the tribal sub-plan (TSP) concept was introduced in 1974 at the commencement of the Fifth Plan. The TSP envisaged comprehensive development and specified a number of measures concerning land alienation, indebtedness, bondage, excise, forest policy and strengthening of the local administrative structure.

Tribals live in or near forests and are critically dependent on them. The Expert Group (2004) found that two-thirds of all tribals live within one and five kilometres of the forest. Land is held both communally and individually, but most households own marginal holdings of under a hectare and by and large practise subsistence farming. Whether in the form of shifting or settled cultivation, neither necessarily meets their year-round requirement of grain. Because of poor social development and being asset-poor, they suffer from both 'capability poverty' and 'income poverty'. Many are dependant on minor forest produce and use this modest cash income to see them through the lean months. Even so, many need to migrate seasonally in search of employment. The collection and sale of minor forest produce entails negotiation with and harassment from contractors and minions of the Forest Department who are wily and exacting.

The Expert Group was convinced that the tribals' future is bound up with forests. It accordingly argued that it was essential to recognize their customary forest rights and concessions, accept that minor forest produce is an integral part of their survival strategy and reaffirm their stewardship of forests as part of a symbiotic relationship.

While the Indian Constitution set out to protect the tribal interest, as the 1935 Act avowedly did, there was one vital difference. In the matter of application of laws to Fifth Schedule areas, the 1935 Act provided that in the absence of any positive declaration by the governor in this regard, state or Central laws would not apply. On the other hand, the position under the present Constitution is that all state and Central acts shall be deemed to apply unless the governor specifically debars them. Regrettably, governors have tended to be apathetic, thereby routinely causing many general laws to be applied to Fifth Schedule areas by default. With this en masse extension has come the imposition of a complex written legal system and due process in place of simple, well-understood oral traditions.

Indeed, many governors since 1950 have been guilty of evading the constitutional responsibility entrusted to them as guardians of tribal welfare under the Fifth Schedule. The Expert Group, headed by B.N. Yugandhar, presently a Member of the Planning Commission, is scathing in its comments:

> The position of a Governor of a Fifth Schedule State vis-à-vis the State Council of Ministers is clearly unique even in comparison with the position of the President vis-à-vis the Union Council of Ministers. In spite of the Expert Group's hard search, it has not been able to find any instance where Governors have pro-actively taken interest or action by virtue of their unique position in matters affecting the lives of the tribal people. Successive Governors of Bihar omitted to make any annual report to the President of India regarding the Scheduled Areas in that State as required under Clause 3 of the Fifth Schedule for a period of more than 15 years (1985–2000).
>
> There are many custodians of interest of the scheduled tribes namely: (I) The Tribes Advisory Council in States having Scheduled Tribes, (2) the National Commission for STs and SCs established under Article 338(i) of the Constitution, (3) The National Human Rights Commission, etc. There is neither focus nor dynamic coordination among all these venerable institutions. Their studies, reports and recommendations languish without any interest whatsoever. The neglect by Parliament of their work and recommendations is a matter of deep regret. The Expert Group seriously urges consultation among all these bodies and the launching of joint initiatives for concerted and compulsory action on their joint recommendations, which should become mandatory for Chief Ministers.

Lackadaisical approach

Evidence of this lackadaisical approach towards constitutional responsibility is to be found in the Twenty-eight Report to the President of the Commissioner for Scheduled Castes and Scheduled Tribes, Dr B.D. Sharma, for 1986–7. The Commissioner's post was vacant from November 1981 to February 1986 as the Government had set up a Commission for SC and ST by a resolution in 1978 but was only able to invest this body with constitutional status in September 1987. However, during this period of confusion, the Commissioner for SC and ST continued as an ex-officio member of the new Commission.

The Commissioner narrated a tale of woe:

> It is a matter of regret that not only years pass by but decades roll on with no significant action even with regard to those matters about which the Founding Fathers did not wish a single moment to be lost. The powers with the Executive, both at the Centre and in the States, have remained unused even after four long decades, not because an idyllic situation prevails in the tribal areas, which should better be left untouched but because the system has been rather unresponsive. Even some formal matters specifically provided for in the Constitution have not been attended to. The administration of the Scheduled Areas is not being reviewed systematically at any level. Steps have not been taken to spell even the basic parameters for peace and good government. Not a single rupee has been given for raising the level of administration of the Scheduled Areas even though the first proviso to Article 275(1) of the Constitution provides for automatic devolution of funds the moment the need is established.
>
> It is sad that the tribal people suffer and even face penal action for acts of omission and commission of the State . . . . The latent rights of the tribal people have remained non-justiciable and escaped the probe of the judicial system and its benign protection because the Executive failed to act in discharge its constitutional obligation of adapting the formal system to the people's need rather than allowing it to supersede their institutions and customs. This constitutes a virtual denial

> of constitutional safeguards to the bulk of the tribal people . . . . The rights of a community cannot be ignored simply because it is small; their voice cannot remain unheard simply because it is feeble, and public purpose is not necessarily what the strong and more populous plead for.

The Commissioner made a number of recommendations pertaining to legal protection and redress, prevention of land alienation (through debt, bondage, benami sale, marriages of convenience to tribal women, 'name-lenders', or by resort to creation of antedated records on fake stamp papers of an earlier era). He laid great stress on agrarian reform, credit and marketing, excise policy (since tribals have for long been barred from brewing their own liquor, which has made them prey to liquor contractors and alcoholism), forest issues, minimum wages and strengthening of the administration of scheduled areas. The National Development Council was urged to deliberate on the social consequences of growing economic inequality and 'unrestrained consumerism' with special reference to their implications for the social and economic situation of the Scheduled Castes and Scheduled Tribes.

Of special interest were a series of recommendations made in the Commissioner's Twenty-eighth Report urging a reasonable share to tribals in all commercial assets, enterprises and townships established on tribal lands. Forms of participation or partnership suggested included grant of equity, housing sites and training to equip tribals and those producing raw materials to benefit from emerging opportunities. As before, little ensued.

PESA safeguards aborted

Panchayati Raj was constitutionally embodied by the Seventy-third and Seventy-fourth constitutional amendments in 1992 as an instrumentality for local self-government. Noting that this could also address many of the problems confronting Scheduled Areas, the Panchayats (Extension to the Scheduled Areas) Act, or PESA, was enacted in 1996. This enjoined that that State laws on panchayats 'shall be in consonance with the customary law, social and religious practices and traditional management practices of community resources.' A village was defined as ordinarily consisting of 'a habitation or group of habitations or a hamlet or group of hamlets comprising a community and managing its affairs in accordance with traditions and customs'. Every village was mandated to have a gram sabha or village council 'consisting of persons whose names are included in the electoral rolls for the panchayat at the village level'. The gram sabha was deemed competent to safeguard and preserve the traditions of the people, their identity and culture, community resources and their customary manner of dispute resolution.

The duties of the gram sabha are clearly laid out. It must grant prior approval of all plans, programmes and projects for social and economic development before they can be implemented. It is responsible for the identification or selection of beneficiaries under poverty alleviation and other programmes. Most important, in the present context of land acquisition for corporate enterprise and special economic zones, 'the gram sabha or the panchayats at the appropriate level shall be consulted before making the acquisition of land (sic) in Scheduled Areas for development projects and before resettling or rehabilitating persons affected by such projects' though such schemes are coordinated at the state level. Further, the recommendations of the gram sabha or appropriate panchayat 'shall be made mandatory' prior to the grant or auction of a prospecting licence or mining lease for minor minerals in the Scheduled Areas. As institutions of self-governance, the Act endows gram sabhas with the ownership of minor forest produce and the power to prevent land alienation or to restore lands unlawfully alienated in Scheduled Areas. Finally, they may control moneylending and exercise control over local institutions and functionaries relating to the tribal sub-plan.

Tribal land may be alienated to individuals, to the State (through its power of eminent domain), or to corporate or other private institutions. However, the cardinal principle embodied virtually in all land acts and regulations, Central or state, is that tribal lands cannot be alienated to non-tribals in Scheduled Areas except in accordance with strict conditions and processes laid out in the Land Acquisition Act, the Fifth Schedule and PESA. Yet, regrettably, transfers continue to be effected through all manner of subterfuges such as choice of language at public hearings, falsification of gram sabha records and so forth. The Expert Group (2004) notes that court cases had been filed in respect of over 850,000 acres of allegedly alienated land but only half that acreage had been restored. Legal remedies exist but moving cases through courts and securing redress is by no means easy.

Samatha judgement

While there is unanimity that tribal lands cannot be transferred to non-tribals, a difference arose some years ago over whether government lands in Scheduled Areas could be transferred to non-tribals. Divergent views were expressed in this regard by two benches of the Andhra Pradesh High Court on a matter concerning the grant of mining leases on government lands in Scheduled Areas to private parties. The Supreme Court heard this matter in an appeal filed by one of the private mining lessees, Samatha, and delivered a majority judgment (1997) that still holds the field.

The Court ruled the State is a 'person' and that it was therefore not exempt from the regulatory framework established for the peace and good governance of Scheduled Areas. This being so, did a mining lease or acquisition of land for a 'public purpose' entail a transfer? The Court held that it did not. A lease merely separates temporary possession from ownership while in the latter case allowing land to be used for a public purpose, such as a hospital or bank, does not entail any transfer of interest in the government land in favour of a non-tribal.

A further contention examined was that since the rich mineral wealth found in Scheduled Areas is a national asset, should it be left unexploited? In the Court's view the competing rights of the tribals and the State 'required to be adjusted without defeating the rights of either' in the interest of national development. The Court noted that Article 298 empowers the governor 'as head of the executive, to sanction transfer of its lands (even in Scheduled Areas)'. But it added a most important proviso. In case of such transfer, the non-tribal lessee must then also assume the State's constitutional obligation to improve the social, economic and educational condition of the tribals. Therefore, the licensee or lessee should, as part of its project, 'incur expenditure' for reforestation and maintenance of the ecology of the Scheduled Area; maintain roads and communication facilities within the 'impact area' of the industry or enterprise, supply potable water, hospitals and medical cover to and sanitation for the tribals; establish primary and secondary schools and provide vocational training to the tribals to qualify them for employment in its plant or enterprise in accordance with their qualifications; and construct housing for tribals 'as enclosures' (sic). To this end, 'at least 20 per cent of the net profits should be set apart as a permanent fund' and reflected in the annual budget of the enterprise over and above the expenditure incurred for re-forestation and maintenance of ecology. For its part, the Centre should sanction exemption of this entire amount from income-tax.

The Samatha judgment in a sense elaborates on the principles enunciated by Dr B.D. Sharma, Commissioner for Scheduled Castes and Scheduled Tribes, in his 1986 report. It also finds partial application in the Court's ruling on the Lower Subansiri Project (2003) in Arunachal with regard to forest conservation. However, in the Bharat Aluminium Case (BALCO, December 2001) the Court declined to extend the Samatha ruling to Madhya Pradesh on the ground that the Andhra law was different. It held that it was the right of a government to have a public policy of its choice.

In the light of the ambiguity thus created, it is for the Centre and the states concertedly to establish clear norms for determining tribal rights in case of land acquisition in Fifth Schedule areas. The principles embodied in the Samatha judgment could usefully serve as a point of reference.

The Expert Group also made a series of recommendations and suggestions for action. Central to these was to call upon the Government to conduct and complete a survey and settlement operation to correct and update land records and establish clear titles to tribal land holdings in Fifth Schedule areas. This was to be accompanied by an 'enjoyment survey' to implement all land alienation regulations. These clear titles should then be recorded and computerized as is being done in Karnataka, Madhya Pradesh and Tamil Nadu. It urged extension of land alienation laws to tribals living outside Scheduled Areas, including the right to usufruct, and measures to prevent *benami* transactions as by power of attorney. In case of contradictory laws, provisos and interpretations, there must be a presumption in favour of upholding the inalienability of tribal land rights. In case of disputes, special peripatetic revenue courts should be required to rule within three months in proceedings conducted without the intervention of advocates. Tribal litigants may, however, be assisted by non-governmental or community-based organizations.

In view of the controversy surrounding land acquisition, the Expert Group disfavoured compulsory acquisition and felt that the only way to get the informed consent of gram sabhas under PESA would be to insist on transparency and a better compensation and rehabilitation package. It would be best to avoid indiscriminate acquisition by limiting it directly to the intended public purpose. A clutch of recommendations were also made with regard to regularization of alleged tribal encroachment in forests and recognition of their ownership of and right to collect minor forest products.

Close on the heels of this admirable report, another equally comprehensive report was tabled by the Standing Committee on inter-sectoral issues relating to tribal development under Dr B. Mungekar, Member, Planning Commission (October 2005). This recommended conversion of forest villages (often composed of non-tribals and set up by Forest Departments to work the forests) into revenue villages within a year and their development with a special allocation of funds. It deplored the exclusive trading rights in most valuable minor forest products by state forest corporations and the appointment by them of contractors who exploited the tribals. It wanted the Minor Forest Produce (MFP) trade to be reserved for Scheduled Tribes as provided under PESA and all forestry operations, including afforestation, to be handed to tribal self-help groups. It enjoined strict observance of PESA in all matters, especially with regard to the pivotal role of gram sabhas and called for amendment to the Indian Registration Act to prevent alienation of tribal lands by precluding sale deeds in the face of State regulations against transfer of tribal lands to non-tribals. It also advocated a concerted drive to restore to tribal possession lands alienated from them.

The Standing Committee outlined Eight Development Goals to deal with extremist-affected tribal and backward districts. These were the creation by the State of an 'impregnable protective shield' against tribal exploitation; the resolution of forest-related issues; intensive development of agriculture and allied sectors; livelihood security through an employment guarantee; universalization of elementary education and the strengthening of secondary and vocational education; ensuring universal primary health care and nutrition; reinforcing effective administration and planning; and ensuring Bharat Nirman (basic needs) in extremist-affected and backward districts with targets for minor irrigation, village electrification, road connectivity, provision of safe drinking water, housing for all, and universal telecom voice coverage within the next two to four years.

The importance of a clear tribal focus in all these programmes was emphasized. The capacity of tribal communities to absorb development would need to be enhanced and criteria and norms would need to be suitably modified to this end. Thus under the Pradhan Mantri Gram Sadak Yojana (the prime minister's village road programme) priority has been accorded first to connecting habitations with populations of 1000 and above and then 500 persons and above whereas tribal hamlets are invariably smaller; likewise most of the remaining non-electrified villages are in tribal areas and need separate and more liberal eligibility criteria. In order to ensure sufficient finances, the Standing Committee enjoined strict implementation of prescribed norms under the tribal sub-plan under which Central ministries/departments must reserve a minimum of 8 per cent of their funds and state governments a minimum percentage equivalent to the tribal population in the state under each annual Plan.

Tribal Commissions

Article 339 empowers the President at any time to appoint a commission 'to report on the administration of the Scheduled Areas and the welfare of the Scheduled Tribes' and to direct the states to execute certain schemes that it may recommend to this end. The first such Tribal Commission was appointed in 1960 under U.N. Dhebar, a former Congress president.

The Dhebar Commission summed up the tribal scene in these words:

> We stand on the threshold of a new era. The tribal people are prepared to make an entry into that area with other members of the (Indian) family. The only thing they expect is that the changes should not destroy the harmony of their life, and the context should not result in suppressing their distinctive personality.
>
> The problem of problems is not to disturb the harmony of tribal life and simultaneously work for its advance; not to impose anything on the tribals and simultaneously work for their integration as members and part of the Indian family.

More than forty years later a second National Tribal Commission was appointed in 2002 under Dileep Singh Bhuria, a former tribal MP and Chairman of the Commission for Scheduled Castes and Scheduled Tribes. Its report was submitted two years later in 2004. The Commission found that the situation had deteriorated on account of callousness and neglect and even the rules under PESA had not been notified. With growing encroachment and settlement by outsiders, almost 40 per cent of tribal sub-plan areas were found to be dominated by non-tribals. Worse, even the Bhuria report, like some of the more recent reports of the Commission for SC & ST, has not as yet been tabled in Parliament, thus precluding debate and action thereon. Many alibis can be cited for this masterly inactivity. However, it presumably reflects the establishment's reluctance to disturb, let alone confront, vested interests.

The Seventy-third Amendment on Panchayati Raj led to PESA being enacted as an instrumentality for tribal areas in rural India. The Bhuria Commission found no corresponding effort to extend the Seventy-fourth Amendment to tribal lands in municipal areas. This has left another gaping hole for urban and industrial encroachment on tribal lands.

The fitful process of regularizing and recording tribal land rights/pattas under the tribal sub-plan programme was interrupted with the passage of the Forest Conservation Act in 1980 and a Supreme Court order in 1995 to stop felling of timber in forests and to clear them of encroachers. Evictions followed and, with this, further uncertainty.

Tribal people share the universal right to a life with dignity, but their life support systems have been steadily eroded. At the same time, in certain other areas there are signs of a tribal transition from communitarianism to individualism and the privatization and commercialization of land with the grant of hidden leases to non-tribal elements.

National Tribal Policy

A National Tribal Policy was announced on 21 July 2006 with the objective of implementing these recommendations and bringing the tribal population on par with the rest of the nation in terms of human development, socio-economic conditions and basic infrastructure by 2020. A primary instrument for achieving this objective will be the linking of devolution of funds to improvements in a newly constructed and quantifiable tribal development index (TDI) and the preparation of a tribal-centric strategy for each sector, the introduction of a single line administration in tribal areas and devising an appropriate personnel policy.

Specific sectoral initiatives are proposed such as reviewing state land alienation laws, amending the Indian Registration Act to ensure proper land pricing, and establishing fast-track courts to deal with land alienation; granting recognition to age-old tribal occupation rights and ownership of MFP, conversion of some 3,000 forest villages into revenue villages; instituting more humane and compassionate policies in matters of displacement and compensation, including the payment of market value for land and adopting the concept of Net Present Value for evaluating other assets; mandating social impact assessments of all programmes; and participation by those displaced or affected in the stream of benefits from industrial and other projects.

Education being a key concern, every effort is to be made to ensure 100 per cent enrolment of tribal children in school by 2012. This will be achieved by locating schools within a kilometre of every tribal village and through the provision of hostels and sports facilities. Fellowships will also be granted for higher and technical studies. Enhanced access to health and sanitation facilities, including drinking water, and better food and nutrition security are proposed. Steps are to be taken to synthesize traditional Indian and tribal systems of medicine and to make this available together with modern medicine.

The National Tribal Policy envisages enhancing livelihood opportunities through training, skill and design development. Market linkages are to be strengthened and state tribal development cooperatives promoted. Tribal agriculture will be upgraded with 100 per cent support for minor irrigation and distress migration sought to be curbed through the National Rural Employment Guarantee scheme. An improved flow of institutional credit and consumption loans is expected to eliminate moneylending, and special packages are proposed for Primitive and what have been termed Particularly Vulnerable Tribal Groups. The importance of gender equity is being stressed in all these programmes.

The National Tribal Policy seeks to reorient tribal sub-plans by requiring all state governments and Central departments and public sector organizations to earmark funds in proportion to the relevant tribal population and consolidate them in a non-lapsable, non-divertible pool for organized, targetted spending to be coordinated by State Tribal Welfare Departments and relevant Central agencies. It is estimated that approximately Rs 15,000 crore and Rs 12,000 crore will thereby be available per annum at the state and Central levels respectively.

State PESA laws are to be reviewed to ensure conformity with Central norms and efforts will be made to facilitate decentralized planning and decision making. Tribal culture and traditional knowledge are to be promoted and the legal and intellectual property rights of tribal communities suitably protected. Reservations will be continued and new forms of affirmative action explored. The scheduling and de-scheduling of tribes will be reviewed and measures initiated to take care of the special needs of nomadic tribes. Postings in tribal areas are to be made attractive through suitable incentives and administrative vacancies will be filled.

Making governors accountable

At the end of the day, however, the new National Tribal Policy can only be as good as its implementation. To this end, it will be monitored and periodically revised if necessary by a Union Cabinet Committee on Tribal Affairs. Nevertheless, the key lies in enabling governors to take a greater and more informed interest in the matter of over-seeing tribal affairs and for Parliament to insist on the presentation and scrutiny of their annual reports on Fifth Schedule areas and those of the Commission(s) for Scheduled Tribes (and Scheduled Castes). Consideration might be given to the desirability of issuing an Instrument of Instruction to all governors on their appointment in order that they are made fully aware of their responsibilities as guardians of the tribal interest. Further, it might strengthen the hand of governors were they to have suitably qualified tribal advisers in their secretariat to assist them quite independently of the State Tribal Affairs Departments.

An element of doubt with regard to the role and powers of the governor in the matter of Fifth Schedule areas persuaded the late President Narayanan to set up a Committee of Governors to study the matter in 2001. The Committee found that 'The present experience in all States is that the Governors have not exercised any significant role under the Fifth Schedule and wherever this has been so exercised it has been on the advice of the Council of Ministers'.

The Committee of Governors' sought the advice of the Attorney General who opined that in his view the governor in discharge of his functions under the Fifth Schedule is required to act on ministerial advice and not independently of it. The Committee of Governors appears to have accepted this view. The Bhuria Committee was, however, not convinced and argued that the Fifth Schedule is a specific and overriding constitutional safeguard for tribals and nowhere provides that governors may only act on the advice of the Council of Ministers. This view of the matter seems to be borne out by the Constituent Assembly debates on the Fifth Schedule. Article 163 provides that the governor shall act on the advice of his Council of Ministers 'except in so far as he is by or under this Constitution required to exercise his functions or any of them in his discretion.' Allowing for ambiguity in some cases, Article 163(2) further provides that 'if any question arises whether any matter is or is not a matter as respects which the Governor is by or under this Constitution required to act in his discretion, the decision of the Governor in his discretion shall be final'. This certainly is categorical.

The Bhuria Committee recommended a constitutional amendment to the Fifth Schedule. This would stipulate that after consulting his Council of Ministers and the Tribal Advisory Council where it exists, 'the Governor shall take such action as he considers necessary in his discretion.' However, the Bhuria Commission's report itself has been laid to rest and, with that, its finding that there have been many departures from the Samatha judgment in awarding mining leases.

It bears repetition that governors have a unique constitutional role that they have more or less comprehensively and consistently failed to discharge. Successive governments at the Centre, cutting across party lines, must be held culpable for this dereliction by forgetting or so casually violating the social contract that went into the making of the Fifth Schedule when the Constitution was framed. Bitter irony it is that the Maoists, born again Naxalites, who would wreck the 'bourgeois' constitution through revolutionary armed struggle, claim to champion a constituent tribal 'people' that 'We' seem to have so callously abandoned.

Future initiatives

According to official estimates, as many as 157 districts in thirteen states were said to be Maoist/Naxalite-affected in 2006. Of these, seventy-five districts are in the Central Tribal Belt of Middle India, and fifty-five of them are categorized as seriously affected.

Fortunately, all is not lost. Left-wing Extremism has forced some rethinking. There has been renewed exhortation to win back tribal favour through socio-economic development. Ideas are being woven together to fashion a coherent policy that it must now be for the state governments to implement with Central support. However, not much may be accomplished unless the administration of the Fifth Schedule areas is reorganized with a single-line administration, a robust panchayati structure and a cadre of dedicated officials.

Yet another Expert Group was appointed in May 2006 under Debabrata Bandopadhyay, a retired IAS officer who carried through Operation Barga in West Bengal in the 1980s, to suggest development responses to counter 'Causes of Discontent, Unrest and Extremism' and suggest 'an appropriate strategy for ensuring peace and life with dignity and for resolution of conflicts in areas of chronic unrest'. This too is struggling to find a balance between the development view and security concerns in view of the current Maoist depredations. Meanwhile, a significant reform has been initiated with the passage of the Scheduled Tribes and Other Traditional Forest Dwellers (Recognition of Forest Rights) Act, 2006. Basically, the Act seeks to give legal recognition to all rights of traditional forest-dwelling communities as they existed in December 2005. The definition of forest dwellers would include dalits and others living in so-called forest villages or in close proximity to forests and unclassified forests from which they derive their livelihood. A reciprocal duty to protect the forests is placed on the tribals in recognition of the symbiotic relationship that has historically existed between tribals and forests. Many rights have been made explicit. Fish and the produce of waterbodies have been defined as minor forest products and protection is granted to traditional intellectual, genetic and cultural knowledge. The conflict with wildlife conservation has been sought to be made more tribal-friendly by redefining 'core areas' under Project Tiger with a more comprehensive definition of 'critical wildlife habitats', with adequate safeguards. Problems of displacement and rehabilitation are also addressed.

The objects and reasons for the Act note that a purely management approach to forests ignored bona fide tribal interests while the modern conservation approach advocated entailed their exclusion rather than integration. Insecurity of tenure and fear of eviction have caused both physical and emotional alienation. 'This historical injustice now needs correction before it is too late to save our forests from becoming the abode of undesirable elements'.

According to the Ministry of Environment and Forests, a million hectares of forest land had been cleared for diversion to non-forest uses between 1980 and December 2005 for a whole range of development projects, large and small, and defence purposes. In addition, with effect from 2005, one-time clearance was granted to promote the development of public utility projects in underdeveloped areas entailing not more than one hectare of forest diversion in each case.

Nonetheless, forest cover registered an overall increase to 678,333 square kilometres countrywide and to 407,298 square kilometres in

187 tribal districts between 2001 and 2003, the percentage coverage in either case being a little over 20 per cent and almost 37 per cent respectively. (Forest Survey of India, 2003).

The Scheduled Tribes and Other Traditional Forest Dwellers Act (2006) was to come into force by July 2007, after the framing of rules by a technical support group. However, a rearguard action by the wildlife lobby has stalled progress, despite assurances that designated 'inviolate areas' were being demarcated in forests for the conservation of wildlife. The rules have been notified in January 2008.

Keeping all these factors in mind, it may be worth giving consideration to the Bhuria Commission's recommendation that there should be a Central Tribal Advisory Council to review and monitor the tribal condition and a secretary-level official in the Prime Minister's Office to keep track of tribal development. A separate Ministry of Tribal Affairs was created in 1999 and it is a moot point whether setting up another focal point would be advisable or efficacious.

Dileep Singh Bhuria, himself a Bhil tribal from Jhabua, sees the tribals as free spirits who were largely left alone until the British introduced the Permanent Settlement. This made them tenants at the mercy of rapacious intermediaries and the 'reservation' of forests subsequently excluded them as trespassers or, at best, concessionaires. The change wrought was cataclysmic. People with an oral tradition were made subject to written regulations and caught in the coils of legal procedures and ruinous litigation. The monetization of a barter economy brought debt and bondage in its wake. (Bhuria, 2007) Long years ago, Debabrata Bandopadhyay, too, wrote a moving piece about a tribal litigant entitled 'Indra Lohar and the due process of law'. Due process crushed and finally killed the wretched man in slow, relentless stages, as he lay clutching yet another impressively stamped and sealed court order, filled with grand words signifying nothing!

If the transition from hunter-gatherer and primitive agriculture to settled farming was not easy, every successive stage from agriculture to industry and urbanization, each eating into the forest and countryside causing displacement and alienation, has meant more trauma and uncertainty. The scaling-up of modern industry has led to an increasing appetite for land, water, minerals and other natural resources. This is further growing with the drive for markets and higher growth, the new reform agenda, the dictates of globalization and, above all, surging population increase. Development for the tribal and poor has meant displacement with or without satisfactory rehabilitation. On one estimate, a sum of Rs 100,000 crore has been spent in tribal areas since Independence without commensurate benefit. The money does not filter down and is siphoned away.

Until the British conquest, tribal homelands cut across kingdoms and principalities and the tribal people were largely left alone, though squeezed into narrower confines. Provinces were randomly formed and divided. Migration began to affect demographic geography. Partition and the integration of princely states created a new political geography. A further reorganization followed on the basis of linguistic states but the demand for the creation of tribal states like Jharkhand was feeble or ignored. The protective shield of the Fifth Schedule was rendered effete.

The rising discontent and disillusionment that followed gave birth to Naxalism. Problems were simply not addressed and refused to go away. Here was a situation ripe for revolution. The Marxist appeal to workers and peasants to unite and shed their chains was then taken over by more radical elements that found inspiration in Mao's dictum that power grows out of the barrel of a gun. Left-wing Extremism is not the answer. Nevertheless, it must be confronted not merely by recourse to law to protect the established order with its inbuilt structural violence and inequity but by a more imaginative process of development and change, reconciliation and fraternity.

{4}

Spring Thunder to Red Corridor

Jawaharlal Nehru heralded India's 'tryst with destiny' at the stroke of the midnight hour on 14–15 August 1947. India had awakened to 'a new dawn of freedom' which, he said, would only acquire true meaning when the country fulfilled Gandhi's call 'to wipe the tear from every eye'. Speaking on the adoption of the Constitution three years later, Ambedkar warned that political freedom would be incomplete and might indeed be lost without economic freedom and social justice.

The 150 years before Independence had witnessed a series of tribal and peasant revolts asserting the right of these oppressed classes to land, livelihoods and a life of dignity. In 1946 peasants in Bengal launched what came to be known as the Tebhaga movement, demanding a reduction in the landlords' harvest share from one half to one-third. The movement was spearheaded by an ascendant Communist Party and led to violent clashes as granaries were looted to relieve the landlords of their excessive exactions. Repression followed and the movement petered out within a year. Among those blooded in that battle was the principal party organizer in Jalpaiguri district, Comrade Charu Mazumdar, a fiery rebel within the ranks, of whom much more would be heard.

Meanwhile, the communist movement had also struck roots in pockets of Assam, Manipur and Tripura and in three to five of the eight districts in Telengana. There, feudal oppression by landlords and corrupt and rapacious *deshmukh*s and *patel*s, revenue officials of the Nizam's administration, bred increasing resentment. With the coming of Independence, the Nizam held out against accession, cobbled together an armed militia of Razakars, and lifted a 1943 ban on the communists who saw an opportunity of consolidating their position through a united front against what the CPI second congress of March 1948 termed as a capitalist-bourgeois government and imperialist lackey. This was something of a turnaround in the Party's stand and followed the dictates of the so-called Zhdanov line of armed, revolutionary struggle in February 1948 in the wake of the Cominform Thesis of the post-war international communist movement and the impending communist takeover in China.

The Indian police action in Hyderabad on 12 September 1948 put an end to the Nizam's pretensions. The Razakars fled, leaving much of their arms to the communists. The earlier communist movement had resulted in the withdrawal of the deshmukhs and patels and the creation of what were virtually liberated areas where *begar* or forced labour was abolished, debts cancelled, lands distributed and the sexual abuse of women ended. The Party claimed to have liberated 2500 villages and redistributed almost a million acres of land. All this, coupled with the return of the abhorred deshmukh-patel functionaries in the interregnum before Indian administration was established, won the communists sympathy and support. This was not to last. Stringent action to break their resistance by the military government resulted in a scattering of the communist armed cadres. Many were killed or arrested. The rest retreated into the hills and forests where they won over sections of Koya, Chenchu and Lambada tribals. The battle raged through 1949. The *dalam*s and higher-level armed formations of the Party put up stout resistance and despite inflicting grievous casualties, many of them on innocents, were forced out of the villages. Some took to individual terrorism while other elements infiltrated into the neighbouring areas of Madras Presidency (north coastal Andhra), Orissa, Bombay Presidency (Maharashtra) and the Central Provinces (Bastar).

A civil administration was established in Hyderabad state in February 1950. A Party pamphlet had months earlier described the Telengana struggle as 'the tocsin of the crumbling colonial order' and a 'warning of the advancing flood-tide of the people's democratic revolution'. Having lost its strongholds, the movement began to crumble, with the Party leadership bargaining for a conditional withdrawal of the struggle. This was rejected by the State. Some 8000 party cadres were arrested and 400 guerrillas killed in encounters. In October 1951, the armed struggle was called off. (Mullick,1972).

The Telengana movement saw interesting shifts in the CPI's ideological line. There was initial hesitation to endorse an armed peasant struggle as the dominant Soviet line placed the working class at the vanguard of the people's democratic movement. This was later modified to acknowledge the role of armed peasant struggle, which finally won both Chinese and Soviet endorsement for 'more Telenganas'.

An interesting offshoot of the Telengana struggle was Acharya Vinoba Bhave's campaign for an alternative, non-violent mode of redistributing land to the tiller by bringing about a change of heart among the land-owning class. This was through bhoodan or a land-gift movement under which more affluent farmers and landlords voluntarily agreed to donate land for distribution to marginal and landless cultivators. Land gifts were indeed made and the bhoodan movement spread and, in time, took on the more 'advanced' form of *gramdan,* or the donation of entire villages in trust for community management, under Jayaprakash Narayan in the 1960s and 1970s. A considerable part of the donated bhoodan lands turned out to be disputed or wastelands that would require litigation to free them from encumbrances or reclamation before being put to agricultural use. This was a lofty ideal that might have worked to some extent had energetic steps been taken to ensure meaningful follow-up. This was not forthcoming and the experiment was gradually relegated as a charade and forgotten, a sad ending to a brave moral initiative based on the Gandhian ideal of trusteeship.

Land to the tiller

The development process was launched with the First Five-Year Plan in 1952. In keeping with its long-standing commitment to vest land with the tiller of the soil, the Congress abolished zamindari and other intermediary rights and went on to legislate tenurial and other agrarian reforms, including ceilings on land holdings.

Landed interests and the feudal order fought back with tenacity and guile and the ruling political class and administration while willing to bark appeared unwilling to bite. Endless litigation ensued. In the hurry to extinguish zamindari, the authorities were careless or forgetful about taking over the records of rights, and new revenue settlements were not carried out, thus compounding the problem. The absence of proper land records delivered a fatal blow to the land-to-the-tiller promise, especially in 'permanently settled' areas where sub-infeudation, concealed tenancies, sharecropping and absentee landlordism made confusion worse confounded. Expectations of generating significant ceiling-surplus lands for distribution to landless and marginal farmers were belied. Legislative loopholes, litigation, delays in notifying and enforcing relevant sections and a general lack of political will resulted in benami transactions and evictions. The most successful and thoroughgoing land reform anywhere in the country was implemented in Jammu and Kashmir where the Big Landed Estates Abolition Act was swiftly enacted and enforced in 1951–2.

West Bengal's Estates Acquisition Act 1953 fixed a ceiling of twenty-five acres for farm land, fifteen acres for non-agricultural land and five acres for homestead land. Enforcement of the Land Reforms Act two years later was a signal for benami transfers and evictions by *jotedar*s. The All-India Kisan Sabha responded by organizing a peasant movement in 1959 to restore land rights and halt evictions.

Meanwhile, ideological conflict within the communist ranks intensified with the sharpening debate between the pro-Soviet and pro-Chinese factions. The ouster of the first-ever elected communist government in Kerala in 1959, the 1962 Sino-Indian conflict, China's maturing strategic partnership with Pakistan after 1963 alongside India's growing ties with the Soviet Union, China's cultural revolution, the death of Nehru, events in Vietnam, and the first challenge to Congress dominance with the election of several SVD (Samyukta Vidhayak Dal) governments in 1967 sharpened leftist ideological rhetoric and set the stage for what was to follow. The acute drought of 1966–67 was most harshly felt across the eastern Indian countryside and compelled heavy dependence on American PL 480 grain inflows. The thrust of policy imperceptibly shifted from agrarian reform to technological innovation to make a Green Revolution. The warning signs were there. The newly-created perspective planning division of the Home Ministry produced a paper arguing that in the absence of meaningful agrarian reform the Green Revolution might well turn red. The warning was ignored.

Rise of Charu Mazumdar

The Indian communist movement split in 1964 with the Communist Party of India (Marxist), the CPI(M), breaking away from the CPI in the wake of the great divide in the international communist movement between the rival Russian and Chinese lines. The CPI(M) followed the Chinese path. Che Guevera's 'hit and hide' guerrilla doctrine that was applied in Latin America also inspired some of its more radical leaders. Charu Mazumdar, with other radicals, was detained for a while for alleged pro-Chinese activities but on his release began to advocate the Maoist line of armed peasant struggle more forcefully, likening the Cultural Revolution to a 'moral atom bomb' that would spark other fires. The moderate wing of the CPI(M) thought it might be desirable to explore the parliamentary path in collaboration with other relatively 'progressive' elements. Mazumdar differed. He extolled the Maoist maxim that power comes from the barrel of a gun and published a series of eight letters or essays in which he analysed the current scene. He was not inclined to await the building up and consolidation of a mass movement of trade unions, students, peasants, intellectuals and cultural workers and had little hope that the parliamentary path would lead to a democratic people's revolution. Convinced that mounting contradictions merited a revolutionary response that should not be bartered for a gamble in the forthcoming 1967 general elections, he attacked the revisionism of those who compromised with armed struggle and argued that power could be captured area-wise by armed peasant groups as part of an unrelenting struggle against revisionism.

Charu Mazumdar's advocacy of a poll boycott in 1967 was opposed by some of his colleagues in the Darjeeling District Committee of the CPI(M) which thought that electoral participation could perhaps open the door for resolution of the agrarian question. He, however, forced the issue locally in Naxalbari, Phansidewa and Kharibari villages in Siliguri sub-division, near the India–Nepal–Bangladesh tri-junction at the head of the vulnerable Siliguri neck, where a largely SC and ST population of landless labourers, small peasants, sharecroppers (*bhagchasis*) and tea garden workers were organized to resist the jotedars and redistribute the land under the triumvirate leadership of Charu Mazumdar, Kanu Sanyal and Jangal Santhal. The peasants were also made to believe that a benign, newly-formed United Front government in Calcutta would look away. That was a miscalculation.

Peasant militia, including tribals with traditional bows and arrows, took the field, seizing land and stocks of grain from those denounced as kulaks. Tensions rose. Violence ensued. Hare Krishna Konar, the new land revenue minister, vainly sought to intervene. Ten persons were killed in police firing. A landlord was abducted and murdered. Arms were snatched. The situation steadily deteriorated over three months. On 5 July the United Front government ordered police action. The situation was soon brought under control. Top Naxal leaders and 700 rank-and-file members were arrested. (Prakash Singh, 1995) Unlike in Telengana, the upheaval was limited in time, area and bloodshed. The first Naxalbari uprising had been quite easily put down. But it had lit a spark and sent out a message that ignited minds elsewhere.

Beijing's *People's Daily* eulogized the uprising. An editorial dated 5 July 1967, proclaimed 'a peal of spring thunder' had swept across India with 'revolutionary peasants rising in rebellion'.

> In the past few months, peasant masses in the Darjeeling area led by the revolutionary group of the Indian Communist Party have thrown off the shackles of modern revisionism and smashed the trammels that bound them. They have seized grain, land and weapons from the landlords and plantation owners, punished the local tyrants and wicked gentry, and ambushed the reactionary troops and police that went to suppress them, thus demonstrating the powerful might of the peasants' revolutionary armed struggle.... The revolutionary group of the Indian Communist Party have done the absolutely correct thing and they have done it well. The Chinese people joyfully applaud this revolutionary storm of the Indian peasants, as do all Marxist-Leninists and revolutionary peoples of the whole world.
>
> It is an inevitability that the Indian peasants will rebel and the Indian people will make a revolution because the

> reactionary Congress rule has left them with no alternative. India under Congress rule is only nominally independent; in fact it is nothing more than a semi-colonial, semi-feudal country. The Congress administration represents the interests of the Indian feudal princes, big landlords and bureaucrat-comprador capitalists. Internally, it oppresses the Indian people without any mercy and sucks their blood, while internationally it serves its new boss, US imperialism, and its number one accomplice, the Soviet revisionist ruling clique, in addition to its old suzerain British imperialism, thus selling out the national interests of India in a big way. So imperialism, Soviet revisionism, and bureaucrat-comprador capitalism weigh like big mountains on the backs of the Indian people, first of all on the toiling masses of workers and peasants.

The editorial went on to speak of famine, and 'fields strewn with bodies of those who have died of hunger and starvation'. It saw this as a prelude to violent revolution by hundreds of millions of people across India.

What road then should the Indian revolution follow?

> The Indian revolution must take the road of relying on the peasants, establishing base areas in the countryside, persisting in protracted armed struggle and using the countryside to encircle and finally capture the cities. This is Mao Tse-tung's road, the road that led the Chinese revolution to victory and the only road to victory for the revolution of all oppressed nations and people.

The *People's Daily* likened 'Gandhism' and the parliamentary path as 'trash' and an opiate to 'paralyse' the Indian people and went on to rubbish West Bengal's United Front government.

This was the path the radical wing had already determined to take and here was glorious and ultimate endorsement from none other than Chairman Mao. However, ideological ecstasy had to contend with ground realities. A furious polemical battle ensued. The CPI(M) Central Committee meeting in Madurai later that year tore into Left deviationism, endorsed peaceful coexistence as a pathway to organizational growth and consolidation, faulted the Communist Party of China and denounced the Naxalbari line as anti-Marxist-Leninist. The radical wing was unbowed. It derided CPI(M) leaders as 'agents of reaction who masquerade as Marxists'.

Marxism-Leninism spreads like a 'Prairie Fire'

Charu Mazumdar was expelled from the CPI(M) towards the end of 1967. However, the Naxalbari idea, as in Bob Dylan's song, was 'blowin' in the wind' and had carried quite some distance. The members of the CPI(M)'s Darjeeling District Committee rallied round Mazumdar and he was persuaded to become convenor of an All-India Coordination Committee which was soon renamed the All-India Coordination Committee of Communist Revolutionaries (AICCCR), a compendium of revolutionary ideologues and experiments. Its mission was to promote revolutionary peasant and democratic struggle in furtherance of Mao Tse-tung Thought, which Charu Mazumdar proclaimed to be the highest form of Marxism-Leninism. Guerrilla tactics were to be employed.

The spark from Naxalbari lit prairie fires in Andhra, Bihar, Uttar Pradesh, Madhya Pradesh, Orissa, Punjab, Kerala and elsewhere in West Bengal. Srikakulam, an old Agency tract in the erstwhile Madras Presidency, was one of the first districts where the British had decreed that no hill tribal or *girijan* land could be alienated to a plainsman without the sanction of the district collector. With the opening up of the region, traders and moneylenders soon found ways and means of subtly alienating tribal lands by promoting indebtedness. There had long been a communist presence here. Peasant exploitation bred mounting resentment that a schoolteacher turned Marxist, Vempatapu Satyanarayana, mobilized to launch a struggle to secure better wages, restore lost lands, enhance tenurial rights and fight for tribal dignity. Confrontation inevitably led to clashes that found armed *dalam*s or guerrilla squads ready and able to give back more than they got. Landlords and moneylenders were terrorized. Word spread. Charu Mazumdar visited Srikakulam in March 1969 and was greatly enthused, calling for the creation there of 'India's Yenan' and building Srikakulams everywhere. Satyanarayana was killed in an encounter in 1970.

Meanwhile, T. Nagi Reddy of the Revolutionary Communist Committee of Andhra Pradesh rekindled the embers of Telengana in Warangal, Khammam and Karimnagar. Nagi Reddy was arrested but the movement continued.

Nearer Naxalbari, the movement spread to north Bihar in 1968 under Satyanarain Singh, with its epicentre initially located in twelve villages in Mushahari block in Muzaffarpur district, travelling from there to Samastipur and Vaishali and to Rohtas, Singhbhum, Gaya, Aurangabad and Bhojpur in south Bihar. Crops were harvested and lands seized. And so on to the Chota Nagpur Plateau (now Jharkhand), with tribal participation matching dalit involvement in the plains. It was here, in Singhbhum that an English girl, Mary Tyler, married to Amalendu Sen, a young engineer who had joined the movement, was arrested in a raid, jailed for some years and finally repatriated back to London. She wrote of her travails in *My Years in an Indian Prison* (1977).

If any state was ripe for violent revolution it was Bihar where social and political rot and economic regression had set in. Corruption and exploitation were endemic. The intermediate castes had gained from zamindari abolition and such land reform as had taken place. They were now emerging as key players in a caste-ridden society, eager to consolidate and enhance their new-found status and power and determined to fend off every challenge from below. Caste permeated politics, the administration and indeed every aspect of life. Ram Manohar Lohia had a decade earlier truly said 'Class is mobile caste. Caste is immobile class'. Now caste and class came together seamlessly in Bihar's revolutionary politics as well. Who owns the land is a question often asked. One answer to that, in Bihar at least, was 'He who captures it first.' (Pandey, 1985) The tribal belt in Midnapur's Debra and Gopiballavpur police stations along West Bengal's border with Bihar and Orissa, and in neighbouring Birbhum also witnessed Naxalite stirrings led by young, idealistic student intellectuals from Calcutta University, like Ashim Chatterjee and Santosh Rana.

Prakash Singh (1995) succinctly narrates the story of the extension of the Naxalite movement across other parts of India. Lakhimpur Kheri in the UP terai was an initial focal point but pockets of Naxalism developed sporadically in various other parts of the state. Punjab witnessed flashes of activity in Jalandhar, Ludhiana and Sangrur, and there were manifestations of the movement in Jammu and Kashmir, Rajasthan, in the tribal belt of Wayanad and elsewhere in Kerala, Tamil Nadu and Assam. There were more serious and persistent outbreaks in a core zone bounded by Bihar, Bengal and Andhra, in eastern Maharashtra around Gadchiroli, in parts of Madhya Pradesh, especially the northern and southern districts of Chhattisgarh bordering on Chota Nagpur and Telengana, and in Ganjam, Malkangiri and Koraput.

Among the foremost leaders to emerge during this period was Nagabhushan Patnaik, an Oriya working in Srikakulam, who fell under the spell of Charu Mazumdar and later spearheaded the movement in Orissa. He was captured and tried in 1970 and died in 1998 while serving a life sentence. Seetharamaiah was another leading figure who was later to found the People's War Group. Many of these and subsequent revolutionaries were highly educated and talented persons who could have done very well in life following their chosen vocations. But they were sensitive, committed, angry young men determined to change the world. Among them too were followers of the muse like Gummadi Vitthal Rao, better known as Gaddar, a balladeer, and Varavara Rao.

The political geography of Naxalism was soon discerned to extend through the central tribal belt and adjacent plains areas of Greater Dandakaranya, with tribals and dalits as the common victims of rapacious landlords, feudal interests and usurers.

CPI (ML) established

It was elements from many of these splinter groups that had come together under the banner of the AICCCR after Charu Mazumdar's expulsion from the CPI(M) in late 1969. On 22 April 1969 the Communist Party of India (Marxist-Leninist), CPI (ML), was formally established, dedicated to Mao Tse-tung Thought and revolutionary armed struggle, class annihilation and guerrilla warfare to liberate the Indian state and seize power for the people.

The Party's manifesto was adopted in May 1970, a document full of sound and fury. Past peasant revolts against British imperialism, it said, had failed for lack of scientific theory and revolutionary leadership.

> Beginning from the Champaran peasant struggle, the Gandhian leadership representing the upper stratum of the bourgeoisie and feudal class, with its ideology of ahimsa, satyagraha, passive resistance and charkha, sought to tailor the national movement to serve the interests of the British imperialists and its feudal lackeys.

Further, the Great October Revolution and the Chinese revolution were betrayed by the CPI after the 'sham (Indian) independence' of 1947. The new Indian leadership mortgaged the country to comprador-bureaucrat capital and US imperialism.

> In the name of 'national integration' these enemies of the people have been suppressing the genuine rights of all the nationalities and national and religious minorities. The right of self-determination is being denied to Kashmiris, Nagas and Mizos. Equal status to all the national languages is being denied and Hindi is being sought to be imposed on the people by them.
>
> Special oppression of the scheduled castes, including the lynching of Harijans reminiscent of the Middle Ages, is continuing unabated . . . . Semi-feudal land relations have transformed our country into a land of perpetual famine as a result of which millions of people die of starvation every year.

The semi-feudal character of India was further exemplified in its 'aggression against socialist China in 1962'. All these contradictions would be swept away by a new democratic revolution to establish a people's democracy through people's war, with China as 'a reliable base area for world revolution'.

Violence peaked in the countryside. In response to Charu Mazumdar's call to students and youth to join the revolution, what had largely been a rural, peasant-based revolutionary struggle saw a sudden eruption of urban guerrilla activity through 1969–70. Recruits were drawn from elite colleges and universities, Presidency College, Calcutta, and St Stephen's College, Delhi, among them. Calcutta and Jamshedpur were the principal storm centres of this mini and mindless Cultural Revolution. Red Guard squads were formed in schools and colleges as a precursor to the rise of a people's liberation army. Workers were instigated to rise against the capitalists. Terror spread. 'Class enemies' were denounced and an iconoclastic wave saw statues and portraits of the country's most revered and famed leaders desecrated and destroyed. Government offices were raided, gheraos and hartals were mounted, police personnel were attacked and property damaged. Lumpens and criminal elements infiltrated the movement. This was a premature and immature 'revolutionary' uprising.

The West Bengal government cast off benevolence and bemusement and ordered stern countermeasures. The Government of India too decided that it was time to act. The Army and police jointly mounted 'Operation Steeplechase' in July–August 1971, with the military manning an outer cordon to block off contiguous affected districts in Bengal, Bihar and Orissa while the para-military CRPF and police mopped up CPI (ML) cadres within the ring. Many top leaders and about 7500 cadres were arrested countrywide. China's taking up cudgels for Pakistan in the Bangladesh liberation war and its rapprochement with the United States caused incomprehension and disillusionment among the Naxal cadres.

Charu Mazumdar, always sick and now broken, was arrested in Calcutta on 16 July 1972. Twelve days later he was dead. There had been murmuring in the ranks earlier but now his critics were direct and often unsparing. For many, including some of the young left intellectuals who had answered his call, Mazumdar and his ideology was a god that failed. Reflecting on those heady times, Dilip Simeon (2006), one of those young men, who was introduced to Marxism by a fellow Stephanian, Arvind Das, had this to say:

> What caused me to shift from rebellion to reconciliation or perhaps from strife to reflection? . . . The transition . . . can better be described as a move from a nihilistic rejection of social reality to a critical dialogue with it; from the politics

> of violent 'overthrow' and 'seizure of power' to the politics of non-violent resistance and transformation. It is not often realised how powerful and widespread the attractions of extremism can be. The more radical the rhetoric the greater, supposedly, is the commitment to the public good; the more violent the suggested solution the more admirable the character of its proponent. Not for nothing has E.J. Hobsbawm named the twentieth century the 'age of extremes'. Radical discourse of all hues has been characterised by the assumption of a violently adversarial stance, of fierce polemic in the left tradition (polemos, incidentally, means strife in Greek), personal attacks on doctrinal opponents, the reduction of reason to dogma, a disdain for moderation and, above all, a glorification of violence in the form of the warrior cult.

Further, he found abhorrent the 'ruthless pragmatism' of the Chinese Communist Party:

> It was clear even then that they were motivated by nationalism and great-power ambition and not by world revolution. They had the blood of innocents on their hands. When the very ethical ground shifts beneath the feet of the foot soldier, it causes a collapse of morale. The loss of moral values made me lose the belief that the revolutionary project was feasible at all, and that the persons leading it had any ethical or even practical sense of what they were doing.

Others too found that the Party's doctrinal commitment to secrecy had led to absolutism, conspiracy and fragmentation.

Fragmentation and recrimination

After the suppression of the Naxalbari uprising, Kanu Sanyal had reported that 'ten great tasks' were achieved. Now he was more critical. In 'More About Naxalism' he noted a certain immaturity in grasping Marxism-Leninism and Mao Tse-tung Thought and its application in Indian conditions. (Prakash Singh, 2006) According to Punjab Rao, another leader, 'we thought of guerrilla warfare but forgot the people. The immature call for seizure of power soon turned into adventurism and ended with individual killings, destruction of statues and burning of schools and books.' (Pandey, 1985)

Flaws were exposed. Moreover, there was now a more attentive audience among the faithful. At the end of the day, the Naxalite movement was not for crops or land but for state power. Class annihilation had been mistaken for a higher form of class struggle leading to guerrilla war and the appearance of the New Man, creating what Mao had called 'red areas in white surroundings'. In retrospect, the truth appeared very different. Charu Mazumdar's reading of Indian reality was naïve. Nevertheless, he passed into legend and remains an icon for Left extreme groups. Naxalbari failed but it highlighted the urgent need to complete the unfinished business of meaningful agrarian reform and social justice.

Dissensions surfaced within the CPI (ML). The Party was banned during the Emergency and leading cadres and hundreds of rank and file were detained. With the election of the Janata government, Satyanarain Singh, who had earlier been drawn to Jayaprakash Narayan, offered it 'critical support', repudiating violence, only to be denounced by Kanu Sanyal and others. Before long, the Party had splintered, some of the divisions reflecting the wholly remote and irrelevant discords within the Chinese Communist Party.

Caste–class struggles in Bihar

In 1978 the CPI (ML) launched a rectification campaign but got caught up in polemics with Satyanarain Singh's new Provisional Central Committee (PCC) and Kanu Sanyal, who sought to revive the pre-CPI (ML) Coordination phase as a prelude to making a new beginning. Both were charged with 'liquidationist' tendencies by a third CPI (ML) group under Vinod Mishra, which rallied thirteen communist revolutionary organizations and went on to form a not very long-lived Indian People's Front (IPF) in 1982. This represented an important departure as it espoused the thesis of a united front to build a national political alternative to Congress rule and went on to advocate participation in elections, resolving 'to grasp peasant resistance struggles as the key link and to keep all our parliamentary activities subordinated to extra-parliamentary mass struggles'. (Vinod Mishra, 1999) The 1985 Bihar elections were the first to be contested by the IPF, setting a precedent for the Nepal's Maoists almost a quarter century later.

In 1980 two red stars, soon to be ascendant, were seen on the horizon. The Maoist Communist Centre (MCC)—already in existence in embryonic form as the Bengal–Bihar Special Area Committee—and the People's War Group (PWG), the former under Pramod Mishra and Sanjay Dusadh and the latter under Kondapalli Seetharamaiah. Both groups reaffirmed armed revolution.

Seven districts in central Bihar provided the main focus of activity that witnessed a 'resurrection of Telengana' in Bhojpur. What emerged was a pattern of class–caste peasant-landlord war of unbounded ferocity, with the dalits at the bottom of the heap. Every caste and formation had its own armed militia or *sena*s and the periodic massacres and torching of villages told only part of the gruesome story of murder, mayhem and vendetta that disfigured the calendar. Belchi, Arwal, Chauria, Pipria were some of the names written in blood at various times, only to be forgotten until the next savage killing. The Yadavs, Rajputs, Bhumihars and Kurmis had their own senas to confront one another even as they battled the dalit and lower-caste-based Lal Raksha Dal, Lal Sena and Mazdoor Kisan Sangram Samiti organized by the ML factions. The revolution had not come, but as the decade wore on, the state seemed to have effectively withered away despite periodic police action.

The struggle revolved around ensuring the payment and enhancement of minimum agricultural wages; the recording of tenancy rights; seizure of surplus, vested and homestead lands illegally occupied by landlords, mahants (temple trustees and priests) and rich peasants and their distribution among the landless and poor peasants. It entailed fighting corruption and dacoit gangs, pushing for village development works and relief measures, and asserting the social dignity of the dalits and backward castes.

Structurally, the CPI (ML) established consciousness-raising village committees at the grass roots, organized 'pockets' of 10–15 villages under a party unit, created peasant associations at the block level that held periodic conferences of tenants and middle peasants, set up village defence committees armed with spears, stiffening these with 'armed propaganda squads' and an intelligence network. It was Vinod Mishra's proud boast that for the first time, Indian communists 'had taken up all forms of (both caste and class) struggle, legal and illegal, extra-parliamentary and parliamentary, armed actions and mass struggles, and made serious efforts to combine them, without surrendering one for the other.'

The CPI (ML), like some other radical groups, also supported the struggle of various ethnic 'nationalities' and sub-national groups for self-determination. It was at the forefront of the struggle to achieve an autonomous district for the Karbis, Dimasas and others in Karbi Anglong and the North Cachar Hills in Assam.

People's War and MCC

In Andhra, a Central Organizing Committee was set up under Kondapalli Seetharamaiah following Charu Mazumdar's death in order to keep the revolutionary flame alive. He sought to procure arms, was arrested and detained for some time, before breaking away to form the People's War Group in 1980. The soil remained fertile for a Naxal revival in Telengana and Srikakulam as tribals and dalits continued to chafe under oppressive conditions. The authority and armed power of the PWG steadily increased and elements that argued in favour of Deng Xiao-ping's reformist line were purged, leaving Seetharamaiah in supreme command. He was once again detained, escaped from hospital but finally expelled from the party in 1992 on charges of authoritarianism. He was replaced by Muppalla Lakshmana Rao, better known as Ganapathy, who became general secretary and then president of the politbureau. Seetharamaiah was by now a sick man and died in 2002.

The PWG and MCC gradually emerged as the two most powerful ML formations with a steadily increasing number of militant cadres, more sophisticated arms and improved training and tactics. Arms and explosives were snatched, locally manufactured or possibly obtained through friendly sources such as other insurgent groups including the LTTE. The PWG held sway in Andhra, southern Chhattisgarh, and contiguous areas in Maharashtra, Orissa, Madhya Pradesh, Karnataka and Tamil Nadu, while the MCC was dominant in Jharkhand, Bihar and adjacent areas in Bengal, Orissa, northern Chhattisgarh and Uttar Pradesh. Success or dominance brought consolidation. In 1998, CPI (ML) People's War was formed with the merger of PWG and Party Unity. In June 2001, South Asian Left extreme groups joined together to form a Coordination Committee of Maoist Parties and Organizations of South Asia (CCOMPOSA). The Maoists in Nepal had meanwhile been steadly gaining revolutionary influence, controlling increasing areas in the countryside from which to encircle the towns and, ultimately, Kathmandu. Beyond the headlines and the political rhetoric of the day, Left-wing Extremism had taken hold across a considerable swathe of territory.

Ceasefire, dialogue and breakdown in Andhra

Gravely dissatisfied with the drift to disaster in Andhra, a Committee of Concerned Citizens took on the task of investigating the facts and seeking common ground for reconciliation and a resolution of the land question, tribal rights and social dignity in Andhra Pradesh. Led by S.R. Sankaran, a retired secretary to the Government of India, and composed of K.G. Kannabiran, president of the People's Union for Civil Liberties, and credible academics, jurists and media and political representatives, it made a sincere effort to negotiate a ceasefire and bring the Andhra Pradesh government and People's War representatives to the table. A detailed account published of the Committee's efforts 'to intervene in the climate of social turmoil and violence in rural Andhra Pradesh, especially in Telengana, in the interests of the common people of the State' has a story to tell. (Committee of Concerned Citizens, December 2002)

The first stage of the Committee's work through 1997 consisted of touring the Telengana countryside and conveying its assessment of ground realities to both the government and the CPI (ML). It next held detailed discussions with the CPI (ML) and the chief minister, Chandrababu Naidu, communicating its concerns to both and eliciting specific assurances from them. The next phase entailed documenting these efforts in Telugu and English tracts, 'In Search of Democratic

Space', which were made available for wider public discussion, and meetings with political parties. Having thus patiently prepared the ground, moving two steps forward and one step back owing to what it considered to be the obduracy of both sides, the Committee appealed for a ceasefire and dialogue in April 2000. The appeal was backed separately by a group of editors and academics.

People's War responded with eight demands. To break the logjam, the Committee once again approached both sides. It found no qualitative change in the attitude of either party. In consequence as many as 350 lives were lost in police encounters during 2000 and 2001 while 310 persons died as a result of Naxal violence. Most of the victims were from the weaker sections, including women and children, landlords, alleged informers and hapless villagers accused of harbouring extremist elements.

The Committee found a vicious circle of spiralling violence and progressive brutalization of state and society with the people reduced to passive spectators and victims. It kept pleading that the State must strictly abide by the rule of law for that alone gave the government moral and legal legitimacy. Equally, the Naxalites must adhere to higher standards of human rights and human values as this alone would provide moral legitimacy and justification for any revolutionary or transformatory movement, which would ultimately be judged by humane standards.

After further detailed discussions with political parties, trade unions, teachers and others, the Committee in 2002 offered a package of six suggestions to the government and People's War (PW) in order to create a climate conducive for dialogue. The State was asked to stop encounters and combing operations, to review all cases, and permit peaceful and democratic activities irrespective of political ideology. People's War was asked to stop all killings, including that of police personnel, stop attacks on police stations and end destruction of government and public property, desist from laying landmines and extortions, not interfere with democratic activities by other political parties or groups, and stop all activities calculated to obstruct administrative, development and welfare measures.

People's War responded positively and offered a ceasefire if the government responded and stopped combing operations and encounters. Another group, the CPI (ML) Janashakti, joined it. The government reacted favourably too but an encounter just at that juncture aborted the initiative. However, in May 2002 a ceasefire was announced and the chief ministers of Orissa, Chhattisgarh and Madhya Pradesh welcomed the prospect of talks. PW nominated Gadar and Varavara Rao, known cultural figures, as its representatives and the government designated two ministers from its side. Both sides put forward their cases strongly, but hopes were raised with a mutual commitment to strive to ensure no loss of life for at least a month pending a further round of talks. Unfortunately, another encounter killing vitiated the atmosphere and PW withdrew from the talks.

The Committee critiqued both sides. It regretted that the State continued to view the Naxal issue primarily as a law and order rather than a socio-economic problem coupled with the dignity and self-respect of the people. It accused the State of continuing with a policy of targetted custodial killings, euphemistically passed off as encounters, repression and harassment of ordinary people through illegal detentions, false cases and suppression of democratic activities. It described this policy as a systemic response of a state 'unable to comprehend a complex problem which is the result of inequity and denial of justice'. It warned that societal issues could not be solved by force and that to 'introduce terror as a component of governance' was to erode its very democratic essence.

It was equally harsh on the Naxalites whose thrust 'was more on military action than on mobilization of the people for social transformation, with indiscriminate force replacing democratic methods.' It accused them of indulging in brutal killing of 'converts'—and many hundreds of PW cadres had surrendered out of disillusionment and disgust—wanton destruction of public property, resort to extortion and landmines and other forms of arbitrary action, including death threats and a ban on political parties. It cited cases of 'infiltrators' who had joined the Naxal outfits, done their share of killings and then cynically surrendered to claim the police rewards on their head!

The Committee was strongly critical of mutual impunity on both sides that left no space for informed and meaningful debate, and condemned the reign of physical and psychological violence that prevailed. The land question to the Committee's mind was absolutely critical, with 9.5 million agricultural labourers and three million unemployed in Andhra seeking work. Telengana was backward and neglected and lacked irrigation. Altogether, the state was sitting on a volcano.

Both parties rejected the criticism. People's War was blunt. It scoffed at the Committee's 'bourgeois liberalism' in a 'bourgeois dictatorship' and called for realization of 'who constitute the people'. Some people are obviously more equal than others. On extortions, PW had earlier claimed that it had its own 'levy policy' and had been collecting money from rich individuals. For that matter, it said, 'every party collects donations and it is also a fact that nobody parts with money willingly . . . . These are all small issues'. It also admitted on another occasion that unintended killings had taken place at times. Losses had been serious and 'mistakes' had been made as a result of 'shortcomings in educating cadres'. These would not be repeated. Unfortunately such grievous 'mistakes' have been repeated. Collateral damage is regrettable but is obviously acceptable!

A second round

The general elections of 2004 offered a fresh opportunity to address the Naxalite issue. The Congress promised to open a dialogue if elected. Chandrababu Naidu, who had spoken of taking PW head on, was defeated. A new Congress–Telengana Rashtra Samiti coalition under Rajasekhara Reddy took office and approached the Committee of Concerned Citizens to assist in reviving talks. The Naxals declared a ceasefire; the Government said it would not use force. Wiser from past experience, the Committee laid down guidelines for the 'period of talks', a phrase that the government preferred to 'ceasefire'. There were to be no arrests or combing operations, no killings or laying of landmines. There was a good deal of discussion on whether moving 'without arms' meant disarming or not parading with arms. It was ultimately agreed to postpone discussion on this item, Clause 7, until the talks commenced. The PW and Janashakti delegates were offered safe passage to Hyderabad. Four ministers and four others represented the government. Both sides agreed to invite eight moderators, including some members of the Committee of Concerned Citizens (CCC).

There was discussion on whether a ceasefire on the Nagaland model might be appropriate. The Government was reluctant to use the term 'ceasefire' as this might suggest a law and order problem and also parity between two equal parties. With a legal ban on PW, the Government was also hesitant to sign on the same document and preferred an exchange of letters. The PW put forward its minimum demands such as withdrawal of cases and rewards and restraints on vigilante groups like the Cobras and release of detained cadres. Land issues were taken up, including enforcement of ceilings and validation of lands seized and redistributed by the Naxals. The PW also agreed to abide by Clause 7 relating to movement without arms. At this juncture the Government backtracked on all earlier understandings but agreed to a further round of meetings after a couple of weeks. Hope still remained as neither side wished to admit that talks had broken down.

However, violent incidents were reported from 4 December by both sides and the ceasefire was called off on 21 December despite pleas by the CCC.

CPI (Maoist) formed

Several explanations are offered for the Government's turnabout. Foremost was the announcement of the PW-MCC merger to form the CPI (Maoist) on 14 October, though this had actually taken place on 21 September. This at once altered the scope and dimensions of the Naxal problem. The government was also deeply concerned with reports that the PW was regrouping and consolidating its position on the ground and collecting money from contractors and others seeking favours or protection. PW had also gained immense publicity and propaganda mileage through press conferences and public rallies in Hyderabad and elsewhere that were drawing large numbers, and possibly not all of it out of idle curiosity. There was also anxiety in Delhi which felt dismayed at the turn of events with the formation of the CPI (Maoist). It was now obviously confronted with a new situation. Even while talking peace in Andhra, the PW had negotiated a wider coalition to wage armed struggle and establish a people's revolutionary government in Delhi. There was also apprehension that the Maoists would try and link up with their counterparts in Nepal to form a red corridor 'from Pashupati to Tirupati'.

The CPI (Maoist) does not believe in parliamentary democracy and the Indian Constitution on which it is founded. It upholds 'people's democracy' where the oppressed and exploited masses will in theory rule. Dedicated as it is to Mao's Thought, power comes out of the barrel of a gun and liberated zones in the rural hinterland must be enlarged and multiplied to encircle the cities and overwhelm them through a combination of peasant–worker power. The organizational structure consists of a twelve-member politbureau and, below that, a thirty-seven member central committee and state (Andhra, Maharashtra, Tamil Nadu, Karnataka, West Bengal, Punjab and Delhi-Haryana) and special zonal committees (the Dandakaranya, North Telengana and Andhra–Orissa Border SZCs). Below the state committees are regional, divisional, district and area committees. Estimates place the total Maoist cadre strength at 25,000. The CPI (Maoist) has been banned.

As a militarized organization, the seven-member apex central military commission commands the people's liberation guerrilla army (PLGA) and subordinate echelons and is responsible for training, intelligence and the procurement, manufacture and supply of arms and ammunition. At the base are seven-member armed platoons or dalams, supported by special guerrilla squads, militia and villager-based sympathizers organized in overground *sangams*. Weaponry and tactics have seen steady improvement and there has been widespread resort to landmines and improvised explosive devices. The mobile headquarters of the PLGA is believed to be located somewhere within the Dantewada district of Chhattisgarh in the Dandakaranya SZC area.

The Maoists run several front organizations and collect funds through regular levies on contractors, peasants (in the form of grain and labour), extortion and protection money. According to one account, kidnappings for ransom have been reported as well as operation of illegal mines, while opium cultivation has become a source of income in Chitrakonda in Orissa's Malkangiri district. (Nayak, 2006).

The CPI (Maoist) is a member of the Coordination Committee of Maoist Parties and Organizations of South Asia (CCOMPOSA), which it promoted in July 2001 'to hasten the world socialist proletarian revolution'. There have been four conferences since, the fourth in

August 2006, which was attended by parties and organizations from India, Nepal, Bangladesh, Bhutan and Sri Lanka. US imperialism and 'Indian expansionism' are seen as the common enemy.

In response to somewhat sympathetic though critical evaluations of the Maoists' record and programme in the *Economic and Political Weekly* (EPW) of 22 July 2006, there was a lively rejoinder by 'Azad', the official spokesman of the CPI (Maoist) in the *EPW* of 14 October 2006. It pooh-poohed criticism of Maoist violence, the killing of innocents and grievous collateral damage and argued that 'the violence of the Maoists, which is preceded and provoked by the violence of the oppressors, is not really the main issue; justice is'. Azad went on to speak of the structural violence in-built in India's feudally oppressive and caste-ridden society, cocooned in privileged enclaves, and reflective of the Maoists' own cult of conspiratorial secrecy. He was quite blasé about the liquidation of the mass of 'civilian informers', including several from among the poor who were employed by counter-intelligence to 'decimate' the movement. Nor were 'innocents' necessarily being killed in the crossfire, as 'people' are not a homogeneous mass within 'civil society' but consist of true masses and the ruling elite and their hangers-on. In a class society, 'where the ruling classes fiercely crush the oppressed at every step, real humanity entails fierce hatred for their oppressors. There can be no love without hate'. But why destroy soft targets such as schools or communication towers? This is because for Maoists 'it would be part of their long term aim to counter the enemy forces'.

Having defined 'people', Azad was also contemptuous of 'identity politics' and the idealization of backward tribal societies. Talk to the tribal women of Bastar, he says, and see what tribal culture gave them: 'forced marriages, witchcraft, superstition, forced drudgery, etc. Though not as bad as the Hindu patriarchal system, tribal culture is far from idyllic'. His take on the caste question was equally interesting. 'A class approach to the caste question demands an end to upper-caste oppression, brahmanical ideology and abolition of the pernicious caste system, including, untouchability. But "identity politics" only "emphasises caste and acts to ossify caste divisions".'

The formation of the CPI (Maoist) coupled with the course of the Maoist movement in Nepal, sounded warning bells. Levels of violence had risen across the country with major Maoist strikes: the 'liberation' of a jail in Jehanabad, Bihar, in November 2005; the hijacking of a main line passenger train with 300 on board in Jharkhand on the night of 6 March 2006; and the siege of a combined jail, police station and police training complex in Gajapati district, Orissa, on 24 March 2006, in quick succession. The prime minister said that Left-wing Extremism (LWE) represented the country's most serious internal security threat since Independence, with Middle India under siege along a long-neglected, exploited, underserved, ill-governed, poorly connected poverty belt of forest and hill country covering contiguous areas in nine states.

The Home Ministry traced the rising graph of Naxalite incidents between 2002 and 2005. The number of incidents had risen to 1,594; and 516 civilians, 153 policemen and 223 Naxals had been killed. Parts of seventy-six districts in twelve states or 509 out of 12,476 police stations in the country were affected. Among the worst affected was a contiguous region across Andhra Pradesh, Chhattisgarh, Maharashtra, Orissa, Jharkhand and Bihar. This dalit–tribal swathe of India could be said to define the geography of Indian 'Maoism'.

Chhattisgarh and the rise of Salwa Judum

At its heart lies Chhattisgarh, at the crossroads of Naxal-affected badlands in six states. Until 2000, this was a remote corner of Madhya Pradesh, one of the more backward states in India. Within Chhattisgarh, the former princely state of Bastar was a forgotten backwater, within which again Dantewada remains the most neglected of its three new districts. It partly incorporates Abujmarh (the Unknown Land) straddling adjacent parts of Andhra, Maharashtra and Orissa as well, a territory almost the size of Haryana, more or less constitutionally 'excluded' in British times and largely unadministered since, barring two forays—to settle East Bengal refugees in Dandakaranya in 1958 and to extract high-grade iron ore from Bailadila. This back-of-beyond region, rapaciously exploited for generations by feudal-caste oppressors with the connivance of successive governments of all hues, is inhabited by Primitive Tribes and is in the process of being properly surveyed virtually for the first time through remote sensing!

With pressure on the People's War Group and Maoist Communist Centre cadres in Andhra and Bihar/Jharkhand, before they merged, the Naxals sought refuge in the jungle fastnesses of Dantewada-Abujmarh, their first revolutionary liberated zone and secure base area for further expansion.

Chhattisgarh was a far away outpost of Madhya Pradesh and official policy was to 'live and let live'. The State did what it could where it could; for the rest the 'Dada-log' ran a parallel administration. The new Chhattisgarh state, established in 2000, abandoned the erstwhile policy of abdication to extend its administrative writ and promote development. Confrontation was inevitable. Casualties run to hundreds. The Naxals have mined the roads extensively and launched large-scale assaults.

The Naxals had first come to the tribals as friends and mentors but gradually assumed dominance, seeking enrolment of a male or female member from each family to their cadres, a grain tithe, the cultivation of distributed land to fill the Party larder, a levy on all traders and contractors and a bar on development, especially of roads, culverts and bridges, hand pumps, schools and *panchayat ghars*, so as to prevent connectivity and administrative penetration, which might threaten their patronage and supremacy.

The years 2004 and 2005 were ones of drought in Chhattisgarh. The Naxals insisted on a steep increase in tendu (beedi) leaf prices, which contractors found unviable. In the event, there was no tendu plucking and sale during April–May 2005 nor payment of the government bonus that follows final market sales, thus depriving the tribals of their main source of cash incomes from minor forest products in an otherwise subsistence–barter economy. Resentment sparked tension, spontaneous marches and meetings in Kotru in western Dantewada to resist further Naxal diktats. Politicians smelt opportunity and, under the banner of Mahendra Karma, Congress Leader of the Opposition and a tribal from the district, assumed leadership of Salwa Judum, or 'purification/peace hunt'. The Jan Jagran Abhiyan (citizens awakening movement) on similar lines had failed in the mid-1990s for lack of support. Now the BJP government readily clambered on to the bandwagon.

The narrative becomes murky at this point and the sequence of events is unclear. Much is anecdotal. However, clashes, reprisal killings and torching of huts created divisions among the people, some 45,000 of whom found refuge in miserable roadside camps as victims of a man-made disaster they could not fully comprehend. Fear and compulsion keep them there though some would have returned to their deserted villages if permitted to do so or given security.

Some among the 5000 or so Salwa Judum vigilantes, underage youth among them, were recruited as special police officers, given rudimentary training and placed alongside CRPF and other para-military units to provide camp security and man roadblocks to check movements. As of the summer of 2006 when the Independent Citizen's Initiative (ICI) and many other fact-finding groups visited Dantewada, they made an aggressive rabble and seemed under nobody's control.

On the best construction, a hapless government used an incipient popular upsurge to confront the Naxals but soon lost the plot, lacking a clear strategy. Official spokesmen were confused, defensive and defiant in turn. They insisted that the State had merely supported, not sponsored, Salwa Judum and denied any plan to clear the jungles to regroup villages. However, critics alleged that this could be a diabolical prelude to granting lucrative land leases for mega mining and industrial projects to be set up by large corporate houses without protest or squeamishness about land acquisition in tribal-protected Fifth Schedule areas within quiet woodlands. This seems a far-fetched theory. Significant investments, properly regulated, that open up the area in partnership with tribals could in fact be part of the solution to centuries of isolation, exploitation and neglect.

However, with the monsoon only days away in July 2006, the government was assisting a fluid camp population to construct semi-permanent mud-brick houses with better roofing and minimal services, to meet the threat of any epidemic. Beyond that, there was no official plan or thinking. Rations were being withdrawn and people were increasingly dependent on food for work, which was yet to be widely organized. The camps that were being 'consolidated', were ostensibly to be wound up by 2008, the unspoken hope being that the inmates would be able to return home by then. The new Counter-Insurgency and Jungle Warfare School in Kanker commenced training commando-type police jungle fighters. Whatever happens, great sensitivity and care will be needed if tribal life and culture is not to be torn apart in battling the Naxals.

A law and order approach by itself will not suffice. The Bastar and Sarguja Development Authority and a similar body for a scheduled caste development zone were set up under the chief minister and special funds sanctioned. A coherent approach and delivery system seemed lacking as the present administrative machinery is unable to cope.

Eight of Chhattisgarh's sixteen districts are Naxal-affected. The Salwa Judum is limited to part of Dantewada and not all among the political class, bureaucracy or ordinary people want it to spread. Its alleged misdoings need to be investigated. Policy too needs to be better concerted across states, and the Centre has to play a leading role rather than merely exhort from afar after tolerating and partnering rampant maladministration for decades.

The ICI forwarded its Report to the prime minister and the chief minister of Chhattisgarh, and to the CPI (Maoist) leadership. It condemned violence by all sides and called for a dialogue. (Independent Citizen's Initiative, July 2006) The CPI (Maoist) General Secretary, Ganapathy, replied in October. While he agreed that the well being and development of the adivasis should be paramount, the Party did not believe 'that their rights can be ensured more effectively through political, non-violent and open means, rather than through armed struggle'.

Ganapathy responded to the nine questions the ICI had posed to the Maoists but also asked whether its perception of the reality in Dantewada was not tainted by ideological biases against the Maoist movement and violent revolution. 'There is no level playing field in the merciless class war between the cruelly exploited, brutally oppressed majority on the one hand and the fatty upper five per cent of our society . . . on the other . . . . The truth of the oppressed is different from the truth of the oppressor'.

Specifically, Ganapathy said the Maoists were for dialogue but had been tricked and now demanded disbanding of the Salwa Judum, suspension of the ChhattisgarhPublic Security Act, and freedom for adivasis to return to their villages from the roadside camps. On their 'casual attitude' towards taking away life, he admitted and regretted 'mistakes'. *Jan adalats* (people's courts) had only punished paid special police officers and Salwa Judum 'goons' who had committed atrocities.

Landmines had been planted in self-defence 'to check the influx of hundreds of state forces and SJ goons who are creating a reign of terror'. The Party opposed using children in armed conflict. But, 'making a fuss over age makes no meaning in a situation where the enemies of the people are targeting children too without any mercy'. Schools were destroyed because they were being used by the CRPF as camps and 'transformed into torture chambers and concentration camps'. Education of adivasis had been affected essentially because 900 villages had been uprooted since June 2005. The Party was not opposed to development schemes 'if those really helped in ameliorating the lives of the people'. Essar and Tata would be opposed as well as 'the laying of those roads and railway lines that are meant for looting the wealth from the region and for enemy troop movement'. The Party had its own model of development that it was implementing. As for preventing voting, people had the right both to vote and to boycott the polls to a 'rotten system' and were instead electing their own *Janathana Sarkar*s.

Ganapathy cited 'one of the great founder-leaders of our Party, Charu Mazumdar' as stating that the 'People's interests are the Party's interests'. Therefore, 'it is better to die in struggle rather than by succumbing to hunger' as 'our armed struggle is to draw the curtain on the pre-history of humankind and herald the dawn of real history.' Finally, he agreed with the ICI that there must be a distinction between civilians and combatants.

In a separate mail to members of Chhattisgarh Net, a communications watch grouping, in March 2006, a Maoist spokesman claimed that through twenty-five years of armed struggle, the Maoists had formed people's governments at the village and area levels, 'leading to the formation of a government at the Dandakaranya level'. It also explained that it was not opposed to industry 'which was in the interest of the people, e.g., manual mines, or industry set up by Indian industrialists who do not have any foreign collaboration'.

Meanwhile, the Union government has strengthened the security presence on the ground, taken steps to upgrade police training and equipment, and permitted induction of civilian helicopters for aerial surveillance and medical evacuation. Various state governments have in turn announced surrender and rehabilitation packages. The Salwa Judum in Chhattisgarh unfortunately continues to enjoy official support despite coming under increasing Maoist pressure. Elsewhere, village self-defence groups have been established with varying success, with the Maharashtra government offering Rs 2 lakhs to any village coming forward to set up VDCs (village defence committees) with alarm systems, especially in Gadchiroli district. While there have been setbacks, many Maoist camps and cadres have been neutralized and the Union Government claims that the number of police stations affected came down by a quarter in 2006.

In Andhra Pradesh, the Maoist tide has been turned, especially in Telengana, where specially trained and equipped quick-response Greyhound police commando groups have achieved considerable success. Forty platoons have been raised and thirty more are being added. The State denies sponsoring the vigilante Cobra groups made up of former Maoists or their victims who are active in certain areas. Stress is now being laid on development and the training and employment of youth over and beyond the National Rural Employment Guarantee programme. The district development authorities have been earmarked special officers and funds provided to mount youth employment training and placement programmes in the public and private sector in construction, hotel management, nursing, security services and so on. This is yielding good dividends. A special Remote and Interior Areas Department has been set up to coordinate and monitor development activities in 300 villages for a start. Housing and irrigation are key elements. In one case, the police joined villagers in constructing a twelve-kilometre road that has improved market access and encouraged improved farming techniques that have resulted in considerable employment and income generation and rendered thoughts of armed struggle irrelevant.

Similar popular resistance is being reported elsewhere. In Bihar's Sasaram district armed villagers patrolled a 7.5 km access road under construction. Work had earlier been pending as Maoists reportedly insisted on a 5 per cent levy on a Rs 2.3 crore project. Development and the opening up of opportunities for income and employment generation can roll back Naxalism and neglect, and create hope for a better and more equitable future.

Despite admitted gains in certain areas, the Maoists have staged a series of daring strikes on SJ camps, police stations and industrial plants and infrastructure. An attack on a police outpost at Rani Bodli village in Dantewada district in Chhattisgarh on 15 March 2007 left fifty-five police personnel and SPOs dead. The Naxalite coffers are reportedly overflowing and some published though unconfirmed estimates place the income from levies at Rs 150 crores per annum in Jharkhand and mention a corpus of Rs 700 crores in Chhattisgarh.

More pertinent is the fact that the CPI (Maoists) reportedly held their ninth party congress in a 'liberated zone' along the Jharkhand–Bihar border in January–February 2007, thirty-seven years after their eighth congress in 1970. It was attended by 100 delegates from sixteen states, including fraternal delegates from Nepal, Bangladesh and the Philippines. The congress resolved to expand the Party's mass base and further strengthen the PLA. It reaffirmed its general line of democratic revolution with agrarian revolution as the key link and protracted people's war with dalit protests, struggles in support of self-determination for suppressed nationalities (Kashmiris, Nagas, Assamese, Tripuris, Manipuris), formation of separate states of Telengana and Vidarbha, jail-breaks to liberate imprisoned cadres, and protests against special economic zones. It recognized the role of caste in class war in the context of Indian semi-feudalism, which it held to be 'deeply interwoven with the caste system and Brahmanical ideology'.

Prospects for fresh dialogue

It is moot whether the government should enter into talks with the Maoists. One view is that the latter use these lulls to regroup, consolidate and propagandize, and thereby confuse and impact the morale of the security forces. The Orissa Government was open to dialogue in 2004 but expected the Naxalites to come to the table without any preconditions. Now, with the coming into being of a unified CPI (Maoist) state level negotiations may require wider consultation and a regional focus. Nevertheless, dialogue need not be ruled out, possibly with credible members of civil society as interlocutors, as earlier in Andhra. One approach that has been tried by UNICEF in situations of armed conflict elsewhere is to get agreement on declaring schools within a given area as 'zones of peace' with guarantees regarding the safety of children, their teachers, parents and others who support the system and possibly service school-feeding programmes and related activities. If it works, such zones and their activity content could be expanded so as to create space for meetings, confidence building and dialogue.

The Andhra Pradesh chief minister has said his doors are open for talks with the Maoists provided they lay down arms. This has been interpreted to imply not using or parading with arms rather than depositing arms. The Centre's policy is that the government is prepared to enter into a dialogue with any Indian-based militant group that eschews violence, as there is a contradiction between talking peace and waging war at the same time.

The country will have to await the reports of the special groups charged with formulating socio-economic programmes to wean away people from Left-wing Extremism and, more to the point, action on those recommendations. Land, livelihoods, (including forest rights), employment, dignity, self-respect and equity constitute the heart of the matter. Programmes, in turn, will not be worth the paper they are written on unless they are honestly and speedily implemented. Governments cannot deliver by themselves. Political will is necessary. All of society is involved and mindsets, die-hard traditions and attitudes will need to change. Participatory local governance, poverty alleviation, equal opportunity and social justice will eliminate the causative factors behind Left-wing Extremism.

One can perhaps take heart from the fact that some CPI (ML) factions have veered towards the parliamentary path though not totally abandoning armed struggle. Much more demonstrative of this trend has been the example of the Nepal Maoists who have laid down the gun in favour of the ballot paper and constitutional means. They have stalled the elections, stipulating preconditions that are not acceptable to their seven-party alliance partners in government. Whether they will stay the democratic course remains to be seen. But their joining the government does represent a major step forward in the context of both national and international revolutionary movements.

However, the objective situation in Nepal and India are dissimilar, the notable difference being that the seven-party alliance and the Maoists in Nepal found themselves in common opposition to an autocratic monarch in defence of the people's democratic rights. Nonetheless, the fact that the Maoists have laid down arms, joined the interim government and are in principle prepared to contest elections to a constituent assembly to frame a democratic constitution represents a huge gain for constitutionalism, democracy and peace.

Mao Tse-tung Thought has yielded to Prachanda Path.

Whether in Nepal or India, societal security alone can ensure individual and group security without which the security of the State itself could prove ephemeral. Naxalism has perhaps served to bring home this truth, howsoever painfully and at great cost.

{5}

An Ugly 'Social Democracy Deficit'

It was Ambedkar who coined the phrase and warned of India's 'social democracy deficit'. Moving the Draft Constitution for adoption by the Constituent Assembly in 1949, the law minister dwelt on the dangerous contradictions India would confront if it embraced political democracy while denying equality in social and economic life. That contradiction persists. It has even sharpened as disparities have widened. A few years earlier he had dedicated his book 'Who Were the Shudras?' to Mahatma Jyotiba Phule, 'the greatest Shudra of Modern India who made the lower classes of Hindus conscious of their slavery to the higher classes and who preached the gospel that for India social democracy was more vital than independence from foreign rule'. That was the weight he attached to it. Who will say that he was wrong?

Visit Incredible India and glimpse life for its 'Fourth World' citizens. Sample some recent headlines randomly selected. 'Dalit woman panchayat president auctioned for 2.16 lakh in TN Village' (19 November 2006); 'Dalit protests: Two trains torched, curfew in three towns, three killed, 60 injured in clashes' (Mumbai, November 2006); 'Untouchability like apartheid, says PM' (December 2006); '22 villages of Kendrapara tense: A day after Dalits entered it, rituals in temples were stopped' (Orissa, December 2006); 'Still bonded in Gandhi's Champaran' (Patna, February 2007); 'Still no justice for Periyar's people' (Tamil Nadu, February 2007); 'Caste bias unchecked here' (Madurai, April 2007); 'Dalits living in fear in Karnataka village' (Mandya, April 2007); 'Jailed for practising untouchability; with two separate pitchers used at a government employment guarantee work site for upper castes and dalits respectively, the latter were required to squat and drink out of their cupped hands while the former had tumblers' (Jaipur, April 2007). The indignities inflicted on women are worse. In Khairlanji, Bhandara district, Maharashtra, a dalit mother and daughter were stripped, paraded and gang-raped in the village in September 2006. 'Raising Khairlanji ghost: Dalit students "purified" with cow urine' (April 2007). This is a catalogue of disgrace abounding.

The pervasive sense of insecurity and inferiority fostered by caste oppression over time has begun to yield to anger and organized defiance. This has promoted new problems and anxieties in turn. As with other areas of discrimination and neglect affecting tribals, women and the marginalized, the root causes must be socially and politically addressed with due urgency, else the promise of a bold, new emerging India must unravel.

What is Caste

Megasthenes noted the existence of caste in the third century BC, but its origins possibly go back to Vedic times with the so-called Aryan coming. The Rig Vedic hymn, Purusha Sukta, describes the origins of the universe and how the *varna* or caste order, not unrelated to colour, came into being. The brahmins (intellectuals, thinkers and priests) came from the mouth of the Creator; the kshatriyas (warriors), from his arms; and the vaisyas (land and livestock farmers and merchants), from his thighs. These three castes might move up the ladder. Not so the fourth category of shudras (menials and artisans) and the most numerous by far. The whole complex of laws governing life and society were codified by Manu in the *Manusmriti* wherein it is stated that 'the Brahmin, the kshatriya, and the vaishya castes (varna) are the twice-born, but the fourth, the shudra, has one birth only; there is no fifth (caste)'. This clarification is important as it indicates that untouchables, were not part of the *chaturvarnashrama* and emerged as a distinct social category below the shudras only quite some time later, possibly in the post-Vedic age, placing them beyond the pale as pariahs and outcastes. Caste in some ways shaded into class. However, one important distinction remained. Caste was hereditary and pre-ordained whereas class in relation to status and wealth was based on merit and endeavour.

Increasing ritualism within the Hindu fold evoked reform, which followed in the shape of Buddhism and Jainism. These spread and gained great influence over the next one thousand years until eclipsed by a Hindu revival under Adi Shankaracharya. But it was the ensuing rigidities and encrustations that resulted in the ossification and hierarchical ordering of the caste structure as it obtains today.

The caste system has six attributes (Ghurye, 1957) These are: a segmental division of society determined not by selection or merit but by birth; regulation by caste panchayats, which has entailed stratification and the fragmentation of community; hierarchy or an order of social precedence; civil and religious disabilities and privileges leading to segregation; lack of unrestricted choice of occupations; and restrictions on marriage with endogamy within sub-castes (clans or *gotras*).

Caste was basically occupational, representing a division of labour within society, as in European guilds, with the hereditary passing of skills from father to son. It operated on a different plane from religion, and caste ties were in some ways stronger than those of faith. Castes could mutate, with the process leading to Sanskritization or a slow upward assimilation. Even tribes became castes as in the case of Kolis in Maharashtra, a section of Doms in UP and Rajbongshis (Rajbanshis) in Bengal.

Many have inveighed against the oppressive nature of caste and its inequities. But its origins are seen to have been benign and its practice efficacious. Abbe Dubois, the French Orientalist and Tamil scholar of the first quarter of the nineteenth century, had this to say:

> I am persuaded that it is simply and solely due to the distribution of the people into castes that India did not lapse into a state of barbarism, and that she preserved and perfected the arts and sciences of civilisation whilst most other nations of the earth remained in a state of barbarism. I do not consider caste to be free from many drawbacks; but I believe that the resulting advantages, in the case of a nation

> constituted as the Hindus, more than outweigh the resulting evils. (Dubois, 1906)

Another observer, J.H. Hutton, believed caste had integrated Indian society and 'welded into one community the various competing if not incompatible (occupational and religious) groups composing it.' He in turn quoted Gilbert as stating that 'India had developed a system of castes which, as a scheme of social adjustments, compares favourably with the European system of warring territorial nationalities.' Like Abbe Dubois, he too saw the flip side and cited P.N. Bose to the effect that 'caste has acted essentially to impose that attitude of mind needed to raise men from savagery but to stop them half way on the road to progress'. (Hutton, 1946)

In Sarvepalli Radhakrishnan's view, caste was neither Aryan nor Dravidian but was introduced to meet the needs of the time when different racial types had to live together in amity.'It was the salvation of the country whatever its present tendency may be . . . . India solved peacefully the inter-racial problem which other people did by decree of death'. In other words it was accommodative and made space for everyone. (Radhakrishnan, 1927)

Hindu protestant and reform movements had surfaced through the centuries from time to time as a reaction to high Brahmanical practices and rituals and caste divisions in society. In different parts of the country, the bhakti saints, Basavaraja, Jnaneshwar, Lalleshwari, Kabir, Sankar Dev, Mirabai, Tukaram, Surdas, Thyagaraja, a long line of Sufi and other Islamic mystics such as Sheikh Nizamuddin Aulia and, of course, Guru Nanak preached and sang of love and brotherhood and, sometimes, monotheism as the way to salvation. Emperor Akbar too sought to propagate his Din-i-Elahi in pursuit of inter-faith harmony.

Yet over the centuries, caste held society in a vice-like grip. It had acquired two striking and debilitating attributes. It became a system of graded inequality. And it subordinated the individual to the group. Lower castes, especially the lowest, found refuge in Islam and Christianity both of which did not interfere with non-ritual manifestations of caste in order to accommodate the converts. Perhaps this did not matter beyond a point until impacted by more modern trends with the advent of British rule. The Caste Disabilities Removal Act was passed in 1850 and the Special Marriage Act in 1872, which permitted inter-caste and inter-faith marriages, provided both partners disavowed adherence to any religion. Until 1923, Depressed Class (later designated Scheduled Caste) children could not sit in general classrooms in schools. That same year Madras Presidency threw open streets, wells and tanks to all members of the public if in any way financed by the exchequer. The decennial census began to enumerate castes and this, with the opening up of competition in services and other emerging opportunities encouraged the 'labelling' and 'pigeon-holing' of caste identities. At a different level, the British discovered that among the elements of the Bengal Army that had risen against them in 1857 were what had been thought to be loyal upper-caste Brahmin and Rajput units. Accordingly mixed regiments were now introduced with a lower-caste intake. The enactment of the Indian Penal Code likewise separated caste from the administration of justice. Winds of change were evident.

Social reform movements

Indian social reformers came on stage, influenced by the promise they saw in Western liberalism. India had begun to connect with itself and the world with the coming of the railways, the opening of the Suez Canal that foreshortened the long voyage to Europe, Macaulay's Minute and encouragement of the English language and learning, the founding of the three presidency universities, and the spread of Christian missionary activity. Raja Rammohan Roy led the movement against sati, a precursor to his founding the Brahmo Samaj, while Ishwar Chandra Vidyasagar campaigned for widow remarriage. Dayanand Saraswati founded the Arya Samaj, exorcising superstition and impurities and propagating Anglo-Vedic education and a puritanical Hinduism. He found no sanction in the Vedas for caste-*varna* gradations. For him, 'Arya Samaj was the Church Militant, India the chosen land, Aryans the chosen people, and the Vedas the chosen gospel'. (B.R. Nanda, 2004)

There were numerous regional reform movements, among them the Prarthana Samaj in Maharashtra, the Kayastha Conference in northern India, the Swami Narayana Movement in Gujarat, and Sree Narayana Guru's fight for temple-entry and the uplift of the Ezhava community in Kerala through the Sree Narayana Dharma Paripalana (SNDP). Syed Ahmed Khan endeavoured to rescue Muslim Indians from symptoms of withdrawal and despair through modern education imparted at what was to become Aligarh Muslim University. (De Bary, 1958)

The ferment was greatest in Bengal and Maharashtra. Ramakrishna Parmahansa's spiritual enlightenment was the inspiration for Swami Vivekananda, who became a missionary of Vedantic Hinduism and the idea that there was a divine spark in every individual. The fascination with everything Western had begun to wane and people began to look for a renaissance in India's own rich heritage. Vivekananda revolted against the poverty, other-worldly apathy and servitude to religious taboos he saw around him, inveighing against religion being reduced to 'the cooking pot' (diet) and 'don't touch me-ism'. The Vedas, he said, did not sanction the varna system.

At the same time he was critical of the Western ideal of competition. 'Competition—cruel, cold, heartless—is the law of Europe. Our law is caste—the breaking of competition, checking its force, mitigating its cruelties, smoothing the passage of the human soul through the mystery of life'(Philip Mason, 1967), a sentiment that Tagore was to echo later. Gandhi supported the varnashrama but fought untouchability and caste tyranny by advocating inter-caste marriage.

Social reform was aimed at removing inequities in society generally but was more concerned with ritual discriminaton against the depressed classes than the economic disabilities they suffered. Gandhi called the untouchables Harijans, a term Ambedkar and the dalits found patronizing.

In Maharashtra, the social reform movement centred around Poona and, for a while, Kolhapur whose enlightened ruler supported the cause of the Depressed Classes. In 1873 Jyotiba Phule, born to the *mali* (gardener) caste, founded the Satyashodhak Samaj that stressed the worth of man irrespective of caste. He was dedicated to the spread of education and in 1850 started a school for untouchables. Telang, Ranade and Gokhale followed and Maharashtra was for some years convulsed over the issue of raising the age of consent for girls from ten to twelve, a bill vigorously opposed by Tilak who felt Hinduism was in danger, but finally adopted in 1891 as an 'educative' more than an effective measure as it was non-cognisable as between husbands and wives. (Heimsath,1964).

There were political stirrings too. The Indian National Congress (INC) was established in 1885 in Bombay with the intent of debating both political and social reform as the twin pillars of rising Indian nationalism. However, opinion was sharply divided. Ranade and others were convinced that political and social reform must move in tandem; but others were of the view that while all nationalists were united on a common political platform in favour of self-governance ultimately leading to swaraj, there was insufficient common ground with regard to social reform. Given that, the issue was which should take precedence, social or political reform?

The second meeting of the INC, held in 1886 and presided over by Dadabhai Naoroji, tuned down the demand for a discussion on social reform on the ground that this would be an appropriate topic for a 'Class Congress' rather than the 'National Congress'. The apprehension was that such a debate would 'turn Indian against Indian, class against class.' Social reform was therefore to be regarded as a conspiracy against the unity and main thrust of the Congress. Surendranath Banerjea described the Congress as a common platform where (we agree) ' to bury our social and religious differences and to safeguard our (common) rights and reduce our common grievances'. (Ambedkar,1945)

In view of the impasse, Ranade devised a via media. It was decided in 1886 to establish an Indian National Social Conference with provincial units. This met annually between 1887 and 1895, immediately after the annual INC sessions, using the same venue and *pandal*. Many Congressmen attended both sessions. However, in 1896, Tilak organized the protest against social reform after which the Congress decided to detach itself from this platform.

The closing years of the nineteenth century saw a certain religious revival, one manifestation of which was a vigorous movement for cow-protection. The Viceroy, Lord Lansdowne, feared this was a potential source of mischief as 'disloyal' elements had found common ground 'on which the educated Hindus and the ignorant masses can combine their forces'. The year 1893 saw a communal riot in Bombay in which sixty persons were killed, the proximate cause being the playing of music before a mosque. Tilak went on to convert the joyful, family Ganapati festival into huge congregational and processional gatherings that acquired more than festive overtones. Social reform had subtly got enmeshed with communal issues.

Gandhi and Ambedkar

The Congress was a genteel debating society until Gandhi entered Indian politics in 1917 and took charge of the organization. One of its first actions thereafter was to engage the Depressed Classes who had met and resolved to seek separate electoral representation and social amelioration under the projected Montagu–Chelmsford reforms. By now there was another rising star on the horizon to champion the cause of the untouchables—Ambedkar.

Bhim Rao Ambedkar was born to a modest Mahar family and in the tradition of that community was commissioned into the army after graduation. He was soon called home following his father's death, won a scholarship to Columbia University, went on to the London School of Economics and was called to the Bar. He practised and taught law only intermittently as politics demanded his complete attention. It was not long before Ambedkar locked horns with Gandhi on the issue of separate electorates. A national crisis loomed with the Mahatma deciding to fast unto death on the British Government's award of separate electorates to the Depressed Classes in 1932. Ambedkar found himself in an impossible position and finally backed down to save Gandhi's life.

Writing to Ramsay MacDonald, the British Premier, Gandhi affirmed, 'for me this is a matter of pure religion'.

> The mere fact of the Depressed Classes having double votes does not protect them or Hindu society from being disrupted. In the establishment of separate electorates at all for the Depressed Classes, I sense the injection of poison that is calculated to destroy Hinduism and do no good to the Depressed Classes . . .

> I should not be against even over-representation of the Depressed Classes. What I am against is their statutory separation even in a limited form from the Hindu fold so long as they choose to belong to it. Do you realise that if your decision stands, and the (1935) constitution comes into being, you will arrest the marvellous growth of the work of Hindu reformers who have dedicated themselves to the uplift of their brethren in every walk of life?

Ambedkar saw Gandhi's statements as cosmetic, including his renaming untouchables as Harijans and extolling scavenging. In India, retorted Ambedkar, 'a man is not a scavenger because of his work. He is a scavenger because of his birth, irrespective of the question whether he does scavenging or not' (Ambedkar, 1945). That argument took place seventy-five years ago. Scavenging and the terrible caste stigma on scavengers remain.

The Dravida movement

Meanwhile, another wave of protest hit the South. The Dravida movement began as a non- or anti-Brahmin manifestation in Madras. Though the Presidency had no more than a 4 per cent Brahmin population, this coterie of educated elite dominated the government services and professions. Not since the rise of Buddhism and Jainism had the country witnessed such a social and political tide. The Dravida movement was initially not confined to the Depressed Classes but embraced the non-Brahmin upper castes, Muslims and Christians as well, all of whom felt envious of and marginalized by Brahmin ascendancy. This echoed corresponding trends in Maharashtra. In the North, Mughal rule had displaced Brahmin privilege and the Kayasthas had emerged as prime recruits to the civil services. There was no such competition in the South. (Sattanathan, 2007)

The South Indian People's Association issued a Non-Brahmin manifesto in 1916. The concept of special seat reservation for occupational and caste groups had already been introduced. Nevertheless, anticipating the Minto–Morley Reforms, the Association expressed anxiety about any premature Home Rule as this must result in Brahmin overlordship. This prompting for prolonged British tutelage by a significant native population was not unwelcome to the government.

A broad-based Justice Party was born in 1917 and immediately met with electoral success. By 1926, dissensions had surfaced in the party. Not finding the Congress sufficiently giving in matters of social reform, E.V. Ramaswami Naicker, or Periyar (Great Leader) joined the Justice Party and broke away in 1938 to found the Dravida Kazhagam, a lower-caste, partly atheist, self-respect movement, with black shirts as its livery. The drive to promote Hindi as the country's lingua franca saw the makings of a North–South rift, with EVR pitting Dravida pride against Aryan dominance. In 1939 he put forward a demand for Dravidistan about the time the Muslim League was advocating Pakistan. The slogan did not find much resonance elsewhere in the South.

A Tamil cultural renaissance and an element of Tamil chauvinism marched hand in hand, until another rupture brought Annadurai, Periyar's chief lieutenant, to the fore with the formation of the Dravida Munnetra Kazhagam. The Dravidistan plank was softened and later abandoned. By 1972 the DMK had again split but the Dravida parties had come to power and remain the dominant political force in Tamil Nadu to this day, establishing what Sattanathan (2007) was to term 'Shudra raj' under the fourth caste.

Caste is in some ways more deeply ingrained in the South than in the North, possibly on account of the Peninsula's insularity beyond the coastal strip, whereas the North was more exposed to conquest and foreign influences. With the landowning Brahmins and some other upper castes taking to government and the professions, Sanskritization and conversion to Christianity provided vehicles for upward mobility among the lowly Padiyachis, Vanniyas and Nadars. These castes, along with the Kallars, Maravars and Agamudiars further south, ranked above the untouchables, the latter group counting among their ranks some influential princelings like the Rajas of Ramnad and Puddokottai. The Padiyachis, for instance, styled themselves Vanniyakula Kshatriyas and, in league with others, organized the Toilers and Commonweal

Party, growingly influential caste lobbies in an electoral age, demanding representation for the backward classes.

The classification of backward classes in Madras goes back to 1885 when the question arose of how to make grants-in-aid to backward communities. Lists were devised and periodically revised and expanded through the years with school fee concessions becoming an added item of state patronage. The non-Brahmin movement resulted in the proclamation of a Communal Government Order of 1921, an elaborate preferential system of rotational caste appointments to a variety to government services. The Other Backward Classes had announced their political arrival.

Whether in Madras or Bombay, the untouchables remained at the bottom of the pyramid, inert, unorganized, exploited and disadvantaged in every way.

A disillusioned Ambedkar proposed in 1935 that the Depressed Classes abandon Hinduism and convened a Mahar conference to discuss the issue. The announcement caused a stir. Though he initiated some discussion with Sikh spiritual leaders he devoted time for an intense study of comparative religion and finally adopted Buddhism twenty years later. He toyed with the option of leading a movement to convert to Christianity or Islam but finally turned to Buddhism because of its cultural affinity to the roots of his own people.

The Muslim League's Pakistan resolution in 1940 caused Ambedkar deep concern and he formed the Scheduled Castes Federation following the Cripps Mission in order to be able to stake a claim for the community in any new power-sharing arrangement. (Rodrigues, 2002) There followed a period of polemical writing to educate people on the condition of the untouchables but, having opposed the Congress and getting little quarter from the British, he chose to make his peace and joined Nehru's Cabinet to become Law Minister and chairman of the Constitution drafting committee. He won great laurels for his erudition, lucidity and sagacity and was generously applauded for his seminal contribution towards the making of the Constitution. He resigned from the government in 1951 for a variety of reasons and was subsequently disappointed that orthodox opposition precluded a more radical Hindu Code Bill that might have moved decisively in the direction of reform that he had advocated over a lifetime.

Ambedkar's Constitution

The Constitution that Ambedkar was so instrumental in framing was democratic, liberal, secular and broadly socialist. The welfare component was located in the chapter on Directive Principles rather than under Fundamental Rights. Yet Article 14 provides for equality before law; Article 15 bars discrimination on grounds of caste and religion; Article 16 enjoins equality in matters of public employment; Article 17 specifically abolished untouchability and made its practice an offence under law. Article 19 enumerates fundamental rights, including those of speech and expression, movement and residence, while Article 21 stipulates that no person shall be deprived of life or liberty except according to procedure established by law. This Article has since been broadly interpreted as implying more than mere animal existence. It constitutes an assurance of dignity and rights concomitant with enjoyment of the fullness of life in terms of health, education, work privacy, protection from sexual harassment, speedy trial, legal aid, and public interest with regard to common property resources. Article 23 prohibits forced labour and human trafficking while Article 24 bars child labour in factories, mines or in hazardous conditions.

The right to freedom of religion is guaranteed by Article 25 which, however, permits the State to intervene in all secular manifestations of religious activity and to provide for social welfare and reform or the throwing open of Hindu religious institutions of a public character to all classes and sections of Hindus.

The Directive Principles are not enforceable in law but are 'fundamental to governance' and the State is enjoined 'to apply these principles in making laws' to secure a social order in which 'justice, social, economic and political, shall inform all institutions of national life' (Article 38). The State is particularly called upon to adopt policies that ensure all citizens adequate livelihood. It must see that ownership and control of material resources subserve the common good; that the economic system does not lead to concentration (Article 39). Other articles provide for the organization of village panchayats as units of self-government; the right to work, education and public assistance; a living wage; a uniform civil code; provision of free and compulsory education for children; more specifically, the promotion of the educational and economic interests of the Scheduled Castes; the raising of nutritional levels; and linking prohibition of cow slaughter to the organization of agriculture and animal husbandry on scientific lines.

Taken as a whole, the constitutional scheme envisions an egalitarian India with a bias towards the protection and well being of the weaker and more vulnerable sections of the population, with due regard for gender equity, care of the environment and the well being of children. In crafting something that approximated to his ideal, Ambedkar did his best to preserve and promote national solidarity while addressing the uncertainties, insecurities and identity aspirations of all of India's variegated people. While he despised the localism, petty tyrannies and stratification of village life he doffed his cap to Gandhi on panchayati raj but on the premise of genuine empowerment of all.

More than any other, Ambedkar stressed Fraternity and the dignity of the individual. For him, these were inseparable, the jewel in the crown, without which political and economic liberty and the ideal of equality must falter and fail. In this, Nehru and some others may have been with him, but for the most part he was alone. The very word *Fraternity* has since been lost and all but forgotten in the otherwise overblown political rhetoric of the day.

Ambedkar's conversion to Neo-Buddhism was emulated only by a section of Mahars in Maharashtra. His political party, the Scheduled Castes Federation, made little headway after his demise and the successor Republican Party of India kept splintering and was soon co-opted.

'The Dalit Panthers'

The late 1950s and 1960s were sad years. The economy faltered under famine and the foreign exchange crisis. Unemployment and debt paralleled increased pauperization and atrocities, with signs of upper caste Hindu revivalism. EVR's visit to Bombay, however, fired the imagination of his Depressed Classes audience.

Across the world, the Black Panthers showcased the rise of militant Black power in the United States. That change of mood was reflected in India too. The untouchables cast off the sanctimonious Harijan label and proclaimed themselves Dalits, the Oppressed. A rising dalit middle-class elite in Bombay felt the time had come to reject separate wells and tumblers, boycotts and indignity. Many Mahars had joined the army and had acquired independent views. Raja Dhale and Namdeo Dhasal represented a new genre of dalit writers who came together at a Dalit Literary Conference in 1970 preaching a counter-culture. If Black was now Beautiful, to be a dalit was a badge of pride. And thus the Dalit Panthers were born in 1972, a grouping of angry young men with an aura of militancy that proved to be more Buddhist and literary than revolutionary.

The Dalit Panthers had no clear structure or programme. They were emotionally committed to Ambedkar's ideals, practised a collegiate leadership that never quite gelled, were wooed by the socialists, communists, Satyanarain Singh's Marxist-Leninist faction, and the Congress. The organization was racked with internal dissension and split in 1974. The Left urged class not caste struggle. The Panthers were trapped between Ambedkar's constitutionalism, Buddhist non-violence and revolutionary slogans. There were street-corner meetings and processions, and counter-threats were issued against atrocities on dalits. The lurid language used by the Panthers against the Hindu pantheon offended liberal Hindu opinion that might otherwise have supported the dalit cause. At the end of the day, Neo-Buddhists alone could not be a force and no dalit movement could succeed if it ignored 75 per cent of its rural base. (Murugkar, 1991) The only other cause it fought was on renaming Marathwada University after Ambedkar.

Dhasal lost credibility during the Emergency when he eulogized Indira Gandhi and her twenty-point programme. He finally dissolved the Dalit Panthers in 1997 to form a so-called mass movement to fight caste disabilities. That too faded away. All that remained was the poetry.

How long must we endure this terrible tyranny?
Must we live like prisoners of war until we die?
My soul has roared out Zindabad

Innumerable suns lit with blood
Go now from city to city setting them on fire

(Namdeo Dhasal, 1975)

Mirage of land reform

If the Scheduled Castes are to win real emancipation, then education, equality of opportunity and employment hold the key, apart from the enforcement of legal prohibitions against caste disabilities and atrocities against them. The dalits officially constitute a little over 15 per cent of the population but the vast majority live in the countryside, the bulk of them landless or at best small and marginal farmers. Their high dependence on agriculture therefore merits a look at what has happened in the farm sector. The slogan during the freedom struggle of land to the tiller was premised on the abolition of zamindari, subordinate intermediaries and rentiers. Land ceilings were to be legislated and surplus lands redistributed. However, very little had been accomplished during the pre-War tenure of the Congress ministries. Earlier, Gandhi had led a movement against the exactions of European indigo planters in Champaran in North Bihar and there had been other non-tax campaigns in Bardoli, Gujarat, and elsewhere. These were primarily aimed at reducing the State's revenue demand on landholders, a relief measure no doubt but not quite land reform.

Few have described the feudal nature of the Indian agrarian structure as lucidly and candidly as Daniel Thorner (1973) after an extensive state-by-state village survey in the early 1950s. The unique feature of Indian agriculture, especially in the permanently settled (zamindari) areas, was that those who owned the land in accordance with a layering of rights did not cultivate it. They exercised their superior position to exact rent from their sub-infeudators, leaving the actual peasant at the bottom of the heap with a crushing burden of grinding labour, much risk, little reward, probable debt or, worse, cruel bondage. In Thorner's words:

> The superior right-holders typically found it more profitable to rent out their lands than to manage them personally. As members of higher castes, they preferred not to think in

> terms of undertaking the 'degrading' fieldwork themselves. The primary aim of all classes in the agrarian structure has been not to increase their income by adopting more efficient methods, but to rise in social prestige by abstaining as far as possible from physical labour . . . (serving) to produce an effect which I should like to call a built-in 'depressor'.

In other words, caste was a 'depressor', militating not only against equity in land ownership but in farm productivity, income generation and employment. The lower the caste, the greater was the loss, with the devil of debt and bondage very literally taking the hindmost.

Zamindari abolition was to be the first radical law in the name of peasant emancipation. Thorner traces the 'life-cycle' of zamindari abolition legislation. The various stages from first consideration, to drafting, legislating, notifying and implementing the enactments, ranged from four years and a half in UP to eight years in Bihar and six years in Madras, progress being blocked at every stage by vested interests within and outside the system, and endless litigation that provided ample time for falsifying records, making bogus partitions and transfers, and intimidating sharecroppers into describing themselves as farmhands rather than cultivators. The intermediaries were deprived of their right to collect rent on lands they neither owned nor cultivated and for this loss were assured of compensation from the peasants. In other words, the victim compensated the landlord for grudgingly giving up his age-old parasitic ways only to find the latter back in the guise of new tenure holders. 'Zamindari is dead. Long live the zamindar', may well have been the cry! Thorner's report card on agrarian reform on the ground is not flattering to many states. Bihar was and possibly remains the worst case. Secretariat employees and bar associations protested against measures to 'proletarianise the middle classes', indicating the nexus between the bureaucracy, the legal fraternity, the feudal interests and the political class.

Exceptions and delays in fixing and implementing land ceilings similarly provided ample scope for legitimizing various appropriations (for self-cultivation, orchards, etc.) and effecting wholesale evictions, as in Punjab. The top Congress leadership, barring some elements, clearly did not have its heart in anything more than cosmetic land reform. Only Jammu and Kashmir acted boldly and differently. In course of time, the argument veered in another direction. Technological change for higher productivity required larger or more economic holdings—a theory conclusively disproved by the Green Revolution that showed that the new technology was neutral to scale.

What was possible in 1950 or 1960 or even in 1970 may not be possible in 2007. A great opportunity was lost to innate social conservatism, often posturing under the cover of radical or pious rhetoric. Radical land legislation was sometimes adopted but never honestly implemented. The difficulties in the way should not be minimized; but the will was lacking. Amending the Constitution to incorporate a new Ninth Schedule to place land legislation beyond judicial challenge turned out to be a disingenuous exercise in camouflaging masterly inactivity under the garb of protecting 'radical' legislation pertaining to land and, increasingly, other matters. The Supreme Court properly ruled against this charade only to have the DMK in Tamil Nadu ask whether the time might not be ripe to rewrite the Constitution, a preposterous suggestion irrespective of the grounds indicated—the protection of the State's 69 per cent reservation against an ordained 50 per cent.

Bihar's long night

Sixty years after Independence, tillers remain bonded in Champaran according to the chairman of Bihar's Land Reforms Commission. Thousands of acres are in benami possession and local influentials still control vast estates with political patronage. Despite widespread sharecropping, only five disputes have been registered in all these years as none dare raise his voice. The situation is no different from that which prevailed in 1917 except in one respect. Gandhi no longer strides across the countryside; Maoists stalk the land.

Yet what did Gandhi do for the kisan? Writing in *Young India* on 18 May 1921, during the height of the first non-cooperation movement, he said:

> The kisan movement must be confined to improvement of the status of kisans and the betterment of relations between

> zamindars and them. The kisans must be advised scrupulously to abide by the terms of their agreement with the zamindars, whether such is written or inferred from custom. Where a custom or even a written contract is bad, they may not try and uproot it by violence or without previous reference to the zamindars. In every case there should be friendly discussion with the zamindars and an attempt made to arrive at a settlement.

Gandhi's advice to the propertied classes in turn was to treat their wealth as a trust and it is on this concept of trusteeship that Vinoba Bhave developed the idea of bhoodan and, later, of gramdan. The results are known. It was a heroic effort in some ways, but did not succeed. It failed to address the basic rights of asset-less dalits and sought instead to tap the wellsprings of the landlords' better nature.

Thorner concluded that ceilings and redistribution of land had failed. He therefore suggested the more practical and simpler measure of conferring on the tiller the exclusive or improved right to work the field he cultivated, thus separating ownership from control of the land. The programme, in his words, must be then to 'leave the land alone; redistribute the proprietors'. That in fact is perhaps what is beginning to happen today as rentiers relinquish the land (or are bought off), leaving the actual tiller to cultivate the soil. Is the day of the dalit tenant-cultivator finally at hand?

Bihar in many ways represents the dark side of misgovernance and feudalism in India. Its human development ranking, agrarian record, demographic profile and rate of growth are poor. Poverty and corruption are rampant. A survey conducted twenty-five years ago showed that agricultural labour made up over 90 per cent of all rural households, almost a third of the agricultural labourers were bonded and there was heavy out-migration. The Scheduled Castes and tribals make up the vast bulk of this impoverished and desperate rural proletariat and it is no wonder that a section of it has got radicalized and come under Maoist influence especially around Bhojpur, which the Marxist–Leninist leader Vinod Mishra once described as the flaming fields of Bihar. Land records continue to be in a sorry mess. The current Bihar Land Reform Commission represents the latest effort to put things right. Its terms of reference include examining the feasibility of contract and cooperative farming, modernizing and updating of land records, measures for the speedy resolution of land disputes and measures to prevent encroachment on and the illegal occupation of public assets and resources.

The late Arvind Das wrote with despair about the abysmal situation in Bihar (1992). Though a lapsed Naxalite himself, he paid tribute to the Indian People's Front for enabling the traditionally disenfranchised dalit, tribal, landless and women voters to cast their ballots in the 1990 Bihar polls by forming voter protection committees to prevent booth capturing.

There are faint signs of a turnaround in Bihar under the present Nitish Kumar administration. Some bold measures have been taken. A large number of schoolteachers have been appointed; the idea of common neighbourhood schools is being canvassed as a means of promoting both equality and quality. Panchayats are being revived and a new thrust is being given to agriculture. Private levies on trade and business have been curbed, creating a positive climate for investment. This has been manifested in the negotiation of investments worth Rs 25,000 crore in eight mega sugarcane- and maize-based ethanol plants with facilities for cogeneration of electricity and production of alcohol, the ethanol being used as a 5 per cent mix with petrol. To achieve this target, cane acreage will have to be increased from 230,000 hectares to 1.5 million hectares with cane production rising from 13 million tonnes to over 84 million tonnes by 2015 in large sugar complexes. This will entail expanding the gross area under irrigation from 8.4 million hectares to 11.5 million hectares, with the cropping intensity rising similarly from 112 per cent to 200 per cent alongside crop diversification so that cereal and other crop production does not suffer. The potential for fruit and vegetables is to be exploited through contract farming.

It must be hoped that Bihar will stay the course in building an inclusive and more egalitarian democracy with an expanding agro-industrial base that curbs unemployment and ends increasing out-migration. Social justice and development are the two instruments that, with education and empowerment at the grass roots, will mitigate caste conflict and roll back Maoism.

Sad official and political neglect

What is the nation's record on caste? There has certainly been considerable progress in some ways over the past sixty years but nothing commensurate with the shame, urgency and sheer magnitude of the problem of continuing caste discrimination. Indeed, this has in a sense actually sharpened. What was largely a dormant mass of maybe forty million people is now a socially and politically conscious community of around 160 million who are rightly insistent and impatient about claiming their constitutional and human rights and will not be denied. The bulk of liberal Indian opinion is with them and so is the world, which is becoming increasingly intolerant of internal colonialism or slavery anywhere. India's treatment of its Scheduled Castes and Tribes has been taken up at the World Social Forum and is increasingly coming on other international agendas. These are issues that can no longer be evaded or allowed to drift. They must be confronted and cured.

It is easy, where inequalities or differentials in the provision of amenities exist, to create separate facilities for the dalits as for instance in the case of providing wells or hand pumps. While this may be necessary in many cases on account of locational compulsions, the danger is that it could lead to and harden segregation and ghettoization. 'Separate though equal' addresses needs but not attitudes, rights but not dignity and self-respect. India cannot reject the two-nation theory at one level and practise it at another.

In November 1988, the Commissioner for Scheduled Castes and Tribes, Dr B. D. Sharma, submitted his Twenty-eighth Report to the President for the years 1986 and 1987, after an unpardonable lapse of seven years during which this constitutional position had remained unfilled. It was a moving and anguished document and merited urgent and earnest attention. On the contrary, it received the most leisurely and casual attention. It took six years for the 1986 Report to be placed on the table of Parliament in 1994 as it was mandatory to file with it an Action Taken Report (ATR) that it had taken all these years of mock-strenuous effort to prepare! When debated, the minister was vague and the discussion desultory. None cared to inquire about the progress of a status paper that the government had promised in 1990, as recorded in the ATR itself. Writing later, Dr Sharma (2000) lamented that the only action was inaction and the record 'an unbroken record of broken promises'. Large amounts of special Central assistance remained unspent. The Commissioner raised a number of pertinent issues relating to land reforms, sharecroppers, ceilings, minimum wages, leather workers, traditional *dais* (birth attendants), education, stipends, policies to promote positive discrimination, developing a principle of non-lapsable funds, employment, doing away with scavenging, and other matters. The responses were routine though it must be acknowledged that some action did follow along the road. However, this is simply not good enough.

The Commissioner's post was 'upgraded' to that of a full Commission through a constitutional amendment. The change has made absolutely no difference, as lazy, uncaring mindsets remain unchanged. The Sixth Report of the erstwhile Commission for SC/ST for 1999–2000 and 2000–01 was presented to Parliament in 2004 and the Seventh and Eighth Reports (of the bifurcated SC Commission) for 2004–05 and 2005–06 and a special half-year report for 2006 have been sent to the President but were yet to be submitted by the government to Parliament with an ATR as in mid-2007. Why this appalling indifference? The answer is that very few in the power hierarchy or media are genuinely interested. The Commission for Scheduled Castes has become a sinecure and for the officials a chore and a bore. Many of its members, like all too many SC MPs, have been co-opted into the system. Having 'arrived', they have little interest in the community except as a political constituency. Others are unconcerned or content to let matters rest.

The other problem is that the dalits are not an undifferentiated mass but a highly stratified group with their own hierarchy and order of precedence. The benefits of reservations and other ameliorative measures have largely gone to the upper bracket and not filtered down as intended. The Elaya Perumal Commission that reported on this matter some decades back made the point quite forcefully and argued in favour of measures to ensure a more even flow of benefits to those in the lowest tiers. It does not appear that the situation has changed materially.

The educational dimension

The criticality of unversalization of education and quality education was reiterated by a Group of Ministers set up by the UPA administration in October 2006. It noted that though the literacy gap had been reduced between 1991 and 2001 the SC and ST literacy rates stood at 54.69 per cent and 47.1 per cent respectively against 68.81 per cent for the general population. It accordingly recommended the establishment of 136 Special Navodaya Vidyalayas (SNVs) or upgraded residential schools in SC-dominated villages and seventy-two SNVs for STs. Midday meals, the provision of uniforms, special attention to the girl-child and improving the quality of teaching and textbooks are among major thrust areas and incentives to attract and keep children in primary school. The Sarva Shiksha Abhiyan is a national programme to ensure universal elementary education in the 6–14 age group by 2010, a goal that the founding fathers had set for 1960.

A recent report estimates that there are 9503 no-teacher schools in the country while another 122,355 primary schools have only a single teacher for the five classes they run. As many as 42,000 government schools have no buildings and over 100,000 schools have only one room. Investment in school infrastructure and staff requires enhancement. While the education budget has indeed been increased, it remains no more than 3.5 per cent of GDP as against a recommended 6 per cent. The priorities are not right. Yet, money is not the retardant as much as organization and political will. Years ago, the American sociologist, Myron Weiner, wrote perceptively that in India schooling is a 'right' but unlike in many other parts of the world, it has not been made a 'duty'. Thus the burden of action is on the citizen, not the State. So, much of Indian social legislation rests with a mere statement of intentions. 'Government officials are fully aware of the international embarrassment that comes with having the world's largest population of child labourers and adult illiterates, but they ascribe the failure to achieve universal education as a result of the county's poverty rather than the government's failure'. (Weiner, 1991)

Under the Eighty-sixth Amendment of the Constitution, all children between six and fourteen years of age are now entitled to free education. About 200 million children qualify. Only a certain proportion gets the benefit for one reason or the other. Those needing and deserving it most are the poor and among that category the dalits would be most numerous. The largest educational failure, as in all aspects of human development, lies mainly in the northern, Hindi-speaking States. Whatever politicians and bureaucrats may say or think, there is ample evidence that the rural and urban poor place a high value on education and pay handsomely to send their children to private and English-medium schools in order to get an education that they expect will give their wards a better start in life.

Contrary to common belief, the Scheduled Castes are not confined to Hindus alone but are found among Sikhs, Muslims and Christians, especially in the ranks of the more lowly converts among them. Ritual aspects of caste may have been discarded with conversion but the social manifestations sadly remain even within the adopted faith. The 1901 Census identified 133 castes as completely or partially Muslim. It noted four categories of Muslims: ashraf or noble, high-class persons with Arabic, Persian, Turkish or Afghan blood; converts from upper-caste Hindus; aljaf, or those converted from among lower-caste Hindus; and arjal or those converted from the lowest of low castes. (Ali Anwar, 2005)

These people need special attention, as do Christian SCs who again are low-Hindu converts. But whether they need reservation, as pleaded by the Church, is a moot point. It is for the community to take care of the educational and social well being of its disadvantaged members who may nonetheless claim entitlements, with others, on grounds of poverty and historical neglect but not on grounds of (change of) faith.

Given the opportunity, dalits can and will rise to the top. The late Bismillah Khan of Banaras, the great *shehnai* maestro, was a Muslim dalit who received the Bharat Ratna. K.R. Narayanan became India's first dalit President after a distinguished career in diplomacy, education and politics. And today the country can be proud that Justice K.G. Balakrishnan, another dalit from Kerala, is the Chief Justice of India, while Mayawati is the chief minister of India's most populous state. There is space at the top. But the path must be cleared for getting there.

Other Backward Classes

The Other Backward Class (OBC) question has now superimposed itself on the dalit issue. In the hierarchy of castes, the lower order of shudras, though facing no ritual discrimination like dalits, have suffered social and economic backwardness. Taking due cognisance of this, Article 340 of the Constitution provides for the appointment of a commission to investigate the conditions of 'socially and educationally backward classes . . . and the difficulties under which they labour, and to make recommendations . . . to remove such difficulties and to improve their condition'. It is noteworthy that the reference is not to backward castes, but to socially and economically backward classes, a terminology that could include but is obviously not limited to backward castes.

The first Backward Classes Commission under Kakasaheb Kalelkar reported in 1956. It identified 2,399 backward classes on the basis of certain economic, social and educational criteria and suggested measures to remove these handicaps, including a system of reservation of posts in government. However, the report of the Commission came to naught as the Chairman himself signed the majority report and simultaneously rejected it wholesale in his letter of transmittal to the President on the ground that the remedy of caste reservations could be worse than the disease in perpetuating social divisions. He specifically set his face against reservation in government services as 'the services are not meant for the (civil) servants but they are meant for the service of society as a whole'. In other areas his formulation was 'no reservation but generous preference', especially for women, subject to an overall limitation on 'reservations' to 49 per cent of the total number of seats. He was also clear that in a democracy, the government must not recognize intermediate groupings between the individual and the nation as a whole in the interests of national solidarity. Nonetheless, the Commission advocated that the 1961 Census elicit information on caste and sub-castes in order to provide a better factual basis for future deliberation. Five other members wrote minutes of dissent. In the light of a totally fractured verdict and in the absence of objective criteria for classifying OBCs, the government set aside the Kalelkar Report.

Following the abortive Kalelkar Commission, as many as ten States had set up their own Backward Classes Commissions when the appointment of the second national Backward Classes Commission under B.P. Mandal was announced in 1978. This time there was no ambiguity and the Commission proceeded to determine social and economic backwardness on the basis of caste. The Commission was not without its critics. None other than the chairman of its technical committee, the anthropologist Roy-Burman, described its research findings as 'specious' and it was argued that projections of backward classes on the basis of the last caste census conducted in 1931 were unscientific and inflated. However, the Commission replied that to treat unequals as equals would be to perpetuate inequality and deny social justice. Caste ranking and prejudices had vitiated the principle of equality of status and opportunity. The rationale made out for reservations in government service was that such appointments connoted both prestige and power and served as a corrective to the status quo.

The Mandal Commission identified 3743 OBCs, making up as much as 52 per cent of the population, in addition to the 22.5 per cent SCs and STs. In view of a Supreme Court ruling that reservations under all heads must not exceed 50 per cent, it suggested that OBC reservation be limited to 27 per cent so as to keep overall reservation within the prescribed limit. Notwithstanding that caveat, reservations for SC/STs plus OBCs in certain southern states in particular pierced that ceiling to touch as much as 69 per cent in Tamil Nadu. This was challenged but was pending before the Supreme Court for years and has only recently been listed for hearing.

Reservation or Affirmative Action

Consistent with the principle of equality of opportunity enshrined in Article 14, independent India's first Parliament attempted to accord preferential treatment to socially and economically backward sections of the population. This was struck down as discriminatory in the Champakam Dorairajan case and resulted in the First Amendment to the Constitution in 1951. This amended Article 15, pertaining to non-discrimination, and added a proviso permitting the State to make special provision for the advancement of any socially or educationally backward class of citizens. Many states took action under this protective umbrella. Later, another constitutional amendment permitted reservations in promotions for SC and ST officials in government services if they were found to be under-represented.

The proposal of the Gujarat government to raise OBC reservations from 10 per cent to 28 per cent in 1985 triggered a wave of anti-reservation riots by forward castes. The decision by the National Front Government under V.P. Singh to implement the Mandal Commission recommendations in 1990, a decade after the Commission had reported, was met with an even greater storm of opposition, especially from professional students already confronted with the problem of being crowded out of preferred colleges and faculties despite attaining high marks. The argument turned on merit versus social justice, with passionate advocacy on both sides. The government stayed the course and 27 per cent reservation for OBCs was upheld in principle, though super-speciality institutions and centres of excellence, like the Institutes of Management and of Technology, were exempted.

The issue, highly charged as it was, was further politicised with the BJP–VHP rhetoric about building a Ram *mandir* on the site of the Babri Masjid rising to a shrill crescendo as L.K. Advani's rath yatra rolled across an increasingly tense countryside. The issue was posed in terms of Mandal versus *Kamandal*. Hindu consolidation under the banner of Hindutva was posited against secular, liberal forces out to break high-caste hegemony and deliver social justice and opportunity to the lower castes and classes of an upwardly mobile, modernizing India. It was a searing experience and it took a while for the country to adjust to a newly emerging social and political reality.

Prudence demanded that the new dispensation be allowed to work itself out and that steps be taken steadily to expand the base of educational and social opportunity bottom upwards by not merely reiterating old promises but by implementing practical and imaginative programmes on the ground to ensure delivery of good-quality universal elementary education. This could lay the foundation for further measured progress through vocational and higher and technical education to specialized institutions and centres of excellence. The object should have been to assure a progressively expanding base at all levels in the arts and sciences and emerging, cutting-edge areas of research and technology. Such expansion would accommodate the swelling numbers knocking at the door and enable the country to man and deliver an 8–10 per cent rate of growth. No deserving student need be turned away at any level, given stipends and scholarships, including loan scholarships, supplemented by systems of open and distance learning, coaching facilities, evening colleges (of the genuine kind) and workers' education.

Instead, without adequate thought, consultation or preparation, the government rushed to announce that all higher and specialized institutions, including the Indian Institutes of Management (IIMs) and Indian Institutes of Technology (IITs), shall forthwith admit 27 per cent OBC students across the board from the new academic year commencing July 2007. This was said to be in conformity with the recently adopted 104th constitutional amendment sanctioning the enhancement of educational quotas up to 50 per cent. Could it be that the announcement was in the nature of a crude election ploy to position the ruling coalition on the side of the angels? An expansion of this order requires additional infrastructure by way of classrooms, laboratories, hostels, libraries, teachers and textbooks. Can these be funded and put in place in good time without diluting standards? Indeed the problem could be even bigger than may appear at first sight as the general intake is not to be reduced and the additional 27 per cent OBC intake will need to be absorbed within the ordained 50 per cent overall reservation quota, excluding those OBC, and SC/ST candidates admitted through the merit list.

The danger of 'backwardness' becoming a crutch is ever present. The second Backward Classes Commission identified 50 per cent more backward communities than the first. Since then many more communities have been added to the list and some OBCs have been transferred to the SC list, which has also been otherwise expanded alongside the ST list. Thus, more and more Indians are competing to be declared 'backward' in order to move forward, not by dint of hard work or merit but through a questionable and even dishonest labelling process with official connivance and blessing in the expectation of garnering votes. Job, representational and educational preferment is even driving re-tribalization in certain cases. From being exploited by society on account of caste, some have begun to exploit society on grounds of caste in a turnaround that can only be viewed with dismay. The numbers in this particular category may be small, but the trend should sound a warning bell.

The Supreme Court has stayed the government's fiat and has declared that it needs better evidence, possibly through a regular Census survey, to get a handle on the facts as there is no hard evidence after 1931 of OBC numbers, only informed or interested guesses. It has also drawn attention to the amazing contradiction in a country proudly aspiring to be a world leader and economic superpower of ever-larger numbers agitating and being officially aided to proclaim themselves 'backward' in a race to the bottom! There is also need for an exit policy as suggested by the Court and others at various times so that that available benefits move down and are not captured disproportionately or even entirely by the 'creamy layer' on top. Surely the better answer would be that the State and society encourage affirmative action at every level, including recruitment by the private sector, not under compulsion but as a social investment. Such programmes can be backed by incentives such as tax and other benefits and through special coaching and training programmes.

Distress migrants, the nowhere people

No one is opposed to social justice but there must be qualms about political gimmickry. The school base has been grossly neglected. To erect a huge superstructure suddenly on that shaky foundation is to ape Marie Antoinette. When told that the people were clamouring for bread and there was none to distribute, her cryptic response was, 'Then let them have cake'!

Overall, it is not just the OBCs but all the deprived and wretched of India, among whom the SC/ST population are the most numerous, that must be mainstreamed in every sense. Planning and development must ensure inclusive growth. Whether it is raising HDI indices or meeting the Millennium Development Goals (for the provision of basic services) the target group primarily includes the dalit castes and tribes. Whether it is a disaster or technological change or globalization, the dalits are among the most vulnerable, and women and children among them most of all.

Most people cite an address to establish their identity. An address implies belonging and at least a right to entitlements even if these are denied in practice. Slums and irregular shanty settlements are often neglected; but since their residents render some local service and are potential voters, they get provided for in howsoever limited a measure. This is not true of vagrants and street children, even pavement dwellers, who lack an address. They miss out on schooling and BPL (below the poverty line) ration cards and do not find their names on voters' lists. Nomads suffer the same handicap, as do itinerant workers and herdsmen who practise transhumance. They are marginalized for lack of a fixed address and are vaguely somebody else's responsibility.

Worst of all are those that migrate seasonally as a coping mechanism in times of drought or crop failure when they must travel long distances in search of work, either on their own or in work gangs marshalled by contractors who feed the labour market from distress areas. There are both push and pull factors. Some leave on their own to seek greener pastures. True distress migrants have few or no assets other than their labour and move for their very survival. Occasionally, only the men may go, but in many instances whole families migrate, including children who cannot be left behind without care. Labour contractors cunningly count children as part of the family work unit, incidentally helping along. They are given small and then increasingly burdensome tasks on family piecework, without payment or recognition. This cruelly robs them of their childhood. Their work is harsh, often hazardous, and at the cost of their education, health and basic nutritional needs. Women and the girl child suffer extreme deprivation and are subject to sexual abuse. The migration of able-bodied males for work has additionally led to the feminization of affected villages. In Garhwal in the 1970s, women led the famous Chipko (hug-the-trees) save-the-forest movement as the men had either joined the army or gone down to the plains to earn a living in the absence of any development or work opportunities in their places of abode.

Distress seasonal migration is widely prevalent but the migrants remain 'invisible' as there is none to assume responsibility. The sending villages and local functionaries write off the migrants, ignoring their entitlements as they are not physically present for much of the time. On the other hand, recipient villages see these seasonal migrants as visitors who do not belong and will sooner or later return to their permanent abode. They live dreadful lives in temporary work camps put up by the contractor or 'employer'. They live beyond the law, neglected by State and society.

There are an estimated 30–40 million distress seasonal migrants of which some nine million are children under fourteen who should be in school. Most of these are expectedly SCs, STs and OBCs 'who produce wealth but are excluded from its benefits'. (Smita, 2006) The migration cycle starts post-monsoon and continues until the next summer, spanning six to eight months. It is spurred by dire need and becomes mandatory because of debt bondage through cash advances, piece rates in defiance of labour laws, and contractual obligations. These 'missing citizens' have no rights, no entitlements, no security, only pain, suffering and endless indignity. In the process they lose all sense of identity. They are not enrolled in electoral lists, have no representation and are most often excluded from the Census count. They are disempowered in every sense. Nowhere People are Non-People. Distances traversed extend over several hundred kilometres across state boundaries and linguistic and cultural divides. The contractors determine the destination and specific worksite.

The tragedy is that unless these children receive education they are condemned to repeat the hopeless and barren lives of their parents. Efforts have been made by dedicated NGOs to provide schooling at the 'destination' but then continuity is lost when the worksite changes. So schools and hostels are being provided at the original places of residence so that the children can stay behind in safety and good care. The task has just begun. Essentially a huge national effort is needed basically to prevent distress migration by providing gainful employment in situ through the National Rural Employment Guarantee programme (100 days work in 200 plus another 113 backward districts) and other means. For these millions, a 10 per cent rate of growth is meaningless if they are excluded.

Relief ameliorates disasters. But discrimination follows here too. The experience of the aftermath of the Bhuj earthquake in Kutch and the tsunami in Nagapattinam and elsewhere along Tamil Nadu's

Coromandel Coast shows that there was reluctance on the part of some to share with and care for dalits. Again and again one comes back to the centrality of empowerment.

Panchayati Raj

Decentralized governance has long been seen as one way of empowering people. The constitutional amendments mandating panchayati raj in Chapters IX and IXA as the third tier of government was a giant step in that direction. It also provided for one-third reservation at all levels for women in addition to reservations for SCs and STs in proportion to their population. One can scoff at instances of manipulation and misuse and cavil at the reluctance of the bureaucracy and upper political tiers to share power, but the fact is that the hitherto disempowered are gradually coming into their own, admittedly more slowly in some states than in others.

Gandhi spoke of purna swaraj through gram swaraj but only lip service was paid to this in the initial drafting of the Constitution, partly on account of Ambedkar's aversion to village localism. In 1959, a process of democratic decentralization was introduced by activating panchayati raj. But this had no legislative backing and was largely unreported and soon scuttled by the bureaucracy and MLAs who feared a loss of political power and patronage if devolution worked. Rajiv Gandhi put both rural and urban local self-government back on track in 1989, with constitutional backing for both panchayati raj institutions and nagar palikas. The amendment was narrowly defeated in the Rajya Sabha, underwent revision during the tenure of the ensuing National Front regime, to be finally adopted as the Seventy-third and Seventy-fourth Amendment under Narasimha Rao's Congress administration in 1992. In the twenty years since then, some states have dragged their feet. However, the government has now determined to forge ahead after countrywide consultation and a review of progress.

The third phase of panchayati raj now programmed has within it the makings of a major social revolution and empowered governance at the grass-roots. (Panchayat Raj Ministry, November 2006). The Prime Minister has graphically described the envisaged rural transformation as the creation of 'seven hundred million opportunities'. It is no less, and also holds the promise of regenerating Indian politics from the bottom up in the bargain. The opposition to any such development will surely be no less formidable.

The principle of subsidiarity is now being emphasized in the three-tier panchayati structure, with each level entrusting upwards only that which it is unable to perform adequately at its own level. This is intended to make 'the people' truly sovereign, with the gram panchayat being the kingpin of the system for delivering basic needs and social justice. State Finance Commissions have been at work but the process of financial devolution will receive considerable impetus from 'activity mapping', which defines budgeted action along the precise contours of matters that have been devolved. Kerala and Karnataka have done this, with Kerala devolving 40 per cent of its development budget. Thus financially empowered, it has also initiated the formulation of district plans. District planning will also make it possible for the Centre to devolve grants to these bodies and to encourage implementation of national programmes such as the employment guarantee scheme, Sarva Shiksha Abhiyan and rural health mission through them.

Consideration has been given to the preparation of a devolution index to measure comparative empowerment and thereby induce laggard states to do better. A Panchayats Empowerment and Accountability Incentive Fund that is under consideration will hopefully enlarge the Central financial kitty and thereby persuade states to bid for a larger share by doing more. In addition, 250 less developed districts will benefit to a larger degree from a Backward Regions Grant Fund that will give them 'gap filling' assistance to the extent of Rs 15 crores each on the basis of specified criteria. This kind of consensual grass-roots planning will make for transparency, accountability and closer monitoring, reinforced by a regular process of social audit. However, several weaknesses will have to be plugged. There is, for instance, good reason for concern about the 'dangerously slow and incomplete manner' in which PESA (Panchayat Extension to Scheduled Areas) is being implemented in Fifth Schedule areas that have a tribal concentration, as addressed in a previous chapter.

Among planned innovations are the introduction of *nyaya* panchayats for local dispute resolution and establishment of cyber connectivity not only to promote e-governance but also electronically to tag and track the transfer of funds and their utilization in real time. A rural business hub programme is also being readied for launch to develop local enterprises related to needs and resource and skill endowments. All this is going to require training and retraining of personnel and changing bureaucratic and political mindsets. Maybe that could turn out to be the hardest task of all. Nevertheless, a new foundation for social and economic and, indeed, political progress has been laid. The work must go on.

The panchayats described above must in no way be confused with the oftentimes retrograde and feudal caste panchayats or *khap* panchayats that rule over and sometimes terrorize sub-caste communities, especially on matters of caste protocol and ritual in relation to social and family matters such as marriage. These bodies have been prone to violence in upholding tradition and dead habit and have conducted vicious 'honour' killings, ordered boycotts and practised excommunication.

Towards Bahujan Samaj

Another powerful tool for empowering the people has become available with the passage of the Right to Information Act. This is making for greater transparency and accountability especially in the matter of development, entitlements and poverty alleviation programmes.

However, there are signs of change. After a period of quiescence, the late Kanshi Ram, a Scheduled Caste government employee, hit upon the idea of banding together SC, backward and adivasi officials as well as those drawn from the minorities, all of whom he believed shared a sense of vulnerability and could provide leadership in an organization he called BAMCEF, the All-India Backward and Minority Communities Employees Federation. The purpose was to lobby, network and build awareness. In due course this evolved into the Bahujan Samaj Party, which has developed political muscle in certain states. There is a growing dalit middle class. At the same time some caste taboos, not all, are fading with mobility, migration, urbanization and education. The National Dairy Development Board village milk unions, starting with Amul, saw men and women of all castes lining up in a single queue twice a day to pour milk into the same cans for weighment and processing. In Punjab, vegetarians learnt about non-fertilized eggs, which it was permissible to eat, resulting in the gradual loosening of this once strict food taboo in many households. Likewise, a study of marriage advertisements over the years show a trend towards more inter-caste, inter-regional marriages with 'colour no bar'. Many prohibitions linger but the bar is coming down in many areas, albeit all too slowly. The politicization of caste for electoral gain through vote-banks remains and must continue to cause concern.

Elsewhere, organized dalit groups are setting the pace as in the matter of temple entry and fighting for their rights and entitlements and demanding action under caste disability laws such as the Protection of Civil Rights Act, 1955, and the Prevention of Atrocities Act, 1989. Even so, impunity and non-prosecution for crime are reflected in very low conviction rates on account of inherent biases in the system.

Long years ago, in a prayer for India's awakening to full freedom, Rabindranath Tagore exhorted his countrymen to build an India 'Where the mind is without fear, and the head is held high'. A century later, public opinion and public policy must strive relentlessly to end a thousand years of caste servitude and Fourth World indignity in all its manifestations if India is to make the desired transition from the Third World to the First.

{6}

Changing Living Spaces and Livelihoods

How much land does a man require? Ultimately, only as much as the Count in Tolstoy's story needed for his burial. So it is for all of us; perhaps even less. Yet people are closely bonded with land, which vests them with identity and assures them a home, a sense of security and livelihood. This is truer of traditional, pre-industrial peasant and tribal societies where communities tend to live more intimate lives and closer to nature, which is what makes agriculture and pastoralism for many a way of life. Urban living is different, being more impersonal and, sometimes, liable to cruel loneliness amidst the crowd. Whatever the context, for most ordinary people 'homeland security' at the micro level is a basic concern.

India is fast changing, with burgeoning numbers and growing pressure on land and traditional livelihoods. As numbers rise and expectations increase, per capita land availability must necessarily shrink and there is no way land can be stretched except through enhanced productivity. The normal progression in developing societies is for people to move from the countryside into non-farm and urban-industrial occupations. This should not be seen as either unnatural or necessarily undesirable, though transitions can be difficult and must be handled with care.

Lewis Mumford traces the history of the city. In the subcontinent, this goes back thousands of years to Mohenjo-daro and even earlier elsewhere and, in his view, preceded the village that had its origins in the domestication of animals by hunter-gatherers and the coming of a more secure age. With the growth of the market economy, the village *haat* or weekly bazaar, gave place to the commercial hub, the industrial and port city beyond the ancient walls and gates to make the global village. The progression has been universal though the pace has obviously varied. (Mumford, 1961)

Population scenario

Some numbers will help set the scene. India's population at the time of Independence was around 336 million. It is now three times that figure and could rise to 1350 million by 2025 and may only stabilize around 1600 million or more by 2050. The good news is that Kerala, Tamil Nadu, Andhra Pradesh and Karnataka, accounting for 200 million people out of India's 2001 population of a billion, have completed their demographic transition. This means that the total fertility rate (TFR), or the number of children born to a woman, has dipped below 2.1 or replacement level. In other words, married couples in the South merely replace themselves and do not add to overall numbers. Further, the nation as a whole is likely to reach replacement level by 2015 despite some laggard states in the North. The population problem is by no means behind us. Nevertheless, the evidence is that the country is turning the corner and can look forward to a period of 'demographic gain' when a predominantly youthful working population can give significant impetus to economic growth over the two ensuing decades until around 2035, if they are given the jobs and necessary tools.

However, there remains an important 'but'. The translation of this impeding demographic gain into tangible human and economic benefit depends on a simultaneous improvement in the quality of the nation's human resources. The population must be imbued with the skills and capacities required to effect the potential economic transformation. A sustained 9 per cent or more growth rate, that adds great allure to so many economic prognostications of future prospects, is not going to be realized without a range of critical manpower necessary to give India the competitive edge in manufacturing industries and in the knowledge and service sectors. This is where educational and employment policies need to be thought through carefully instead of being hijacked by misplaced, short-term, vote-bank populism that could ultimately harm the disadvantaged by injuring the larger good.

The experience of the four states in the South offers several illuminating insights. (Leela Visaria, 2007) The greatest fall in fertility has occurred in the age group above twenty-five. This suggests a higher age of marriage among women, reducing their child-bearing span to a brief six to seven years, and greater use and availability of contraceptive services, generally ending in the terminal method of female sterilization. The pattern of social development in Kerala has spurred its human development, based as it is on widespread female education, a more egalitarian social structure both gender and class-wise, land reform, enhanced minimum wages and easy access to good public health services. Tamil Nadu, with lower female literacy and higher infant mortality than Kerala, has had a different set of drivers. Ramaswami Naicker's social reforms rejecting caste, invested women with a higher status and encouraged widow remarriage. How far this led to diminishing son-preference remains to be measured. But there is no doubt that education propels social and economic advancement even as more offspring work to the detriment of farm families because of greater fragmentation of landholdings.

Andhra and Karnataka were somewhat late starters within the southern quartet. But, as in Tamil Nadu, the role of the mass media and cinema has been significant in building awareness and projecting role models. Regional variations in Andhra show that work participation among women, rice subsidies to the poor, widow pensions, and implementation of the Integrated Child Development Scheme did impact on attitudes and trends in respect of childbearing. In Karnataka, the coastal districts, with their higher literacy and female work participation and good rural communications, have fared better than the more backward northeast plateau. Goa has outdone Kerala and is now at the top of the league.

There are lessons here for the low-performing northern states, especially Bihar and Uttar Pradesh. Apart from the obvious importance of human development, feudal attitudes towards male domination and son-preference and its murderous obverse of female foeticide and heavy dependence on female sterilization as the preferred contraceptive choice carry high social costs. Punjab has run out of brides and confronts new problems of family life. There is a dire warning here. Female sterilization in Tamil Nadu and Andhra has led to the spread of HIV-AIDS, for once a wife is sterilized she cannot negotiate with her husband to use a condom. The demographic transition together with more rapid economic growth has also resulted in the influx of more migrant labour from Orissa and elsewhere while more traffic along the transport corridors brings AIDS riding on trucks.

There are also some negative consequences of Kerala's demographic success. With numbers in the age-group 0–9 actually shrinking, about 1000 schools are having to shut down for lack of pupils and may be converted into day-care centres for the growing number of ageing elderly, especially women. Pension and long-term health care bills have gone up and 30 per cent of the population live on (Gulf) remittances. Resultant stresses have caused mental health problems reflected in the highest suicide rate in the country, apart from the highest road accident rate in an increasingly crowded and ageing countryside. Reverse migration is increasing on account of very high unskilled wage rates and in order to fill the gap in the labour force because of ageing and out-migration in search of more lucrative skill and knowledge opportunities in other parts of the country and the world. This in turn poses new health threats and lifestyle diseases (diabetes, heart, cancer, malaria) and dangers from pollution and biomedical and domestic waste. The shift from public to private health care could also affect access to and the quality of medicare for the poorer segments of society. All these are certainly a cause for worry and call for fashioning new strategies. But progress and change always present ever-new challenges. This is no reason to flinch. Rather, we must continue to progress, learn from experience and anticipate the future.

Land policy and prospects

According to the National Bureau of Soil Survey and Land Use Planning, India is spread over 328 million hectares (m ha) though the reporting area is 306 m ha, allowing for areas under foreign occupation. The net cultivated area is 142 m ha, falling somewhat in a drought year, with per capita land availability declining in keeping with population growth. Land ownership is important because productivity is invariably higher when the land title is clear. A little over 67.8 m ha is classified as forest (in addition to areas under random tree cover) of which

29 m ha is degraded, with a crown cover of under 40 per cent. About 40 m ha is under reserved forests and another 23 m ha constitute protected forests. According to the Forest Survey of India, between 2001 and 2003, the area under forest increased by 0.28 million hectares.

The forests were brought under working plans in the late nineteenth century in the interests of scientific forestry and enhanced revenue. This continued under various national forest policies even after Independence until ecological alarms compelled rethinking and forests came to be regarded primarily as an ecological rather than a commercial asset, with the passage of the Forest Conservation Act in 1980. By then much damage had been caused not only by population growth and reckless and clandestine felling by timber mafia but on account of carefree diversion for a variety of developmental and infrastructural purposes, submergence under dams, refugee rehabilitation, agricultural and urban expansion, industrialization, unsustainable *jhuming* cycles, the survival economics of the poor, man-made forest fires and heavy livestock pressure. The *terai* forests were cleared in the 1950s and Dandakaranya, in the wilds of Middle India, was opened up for mining and a grandiose refugee-cum-resettlement programme that was fortunately only partially implemented and would otherwise have created a country-sized habitation with an economy based on blue pine plantations feeding giant pulp and paper mills. In furtherance of the objective of conserving forests as an ecological resource, natural game parks and sanctuaries and biosphere reserves have been created and special steps taken to protect and preserve endangered species of animals and plant biodiversity, Project Tiger being one such effort. Human and, particularly, tribal exclusion has, however, resulted in a denial of rights and has affected livelihoods, matters that are now sought to be corrected through implementation of the recently adopted Scheduled Tribes and Other Traditional Forest Dwellers Act and the older Panchayats (Extension to Scheduled Areas) Act. Everything said, forest productivity remains low and requires serious attention and concerted action, towards which objective joint forest management is one pathway.

One aspect of failure of forest policy has been the exclusionary regime applicable to degraded forests and wastelands. Large tracts of forest, including degraded forests, are owned by the State and denote jurisdiction rather than biotic status. While policy has appropriately been directed towards making the poor the primary beneficiaries of reforestation, corporate and other forms of collaboration have needlessly been kept at bay. Reclaiming wastelands and upgrading degraded forests require organization, management, investment and technology that poor rural and tribal communities are not necessarily able to provide and which State partnership through forest departments has been unable to make good. In the result, standstill has in some cases meant sliding back and losing out on available employment and income generation opportunities. It would certainly be desirable and entirely feasible to lay down guidelines for private or corporate players ensuring stakeholder participation for local communities together with a say in species choice, training of local personnel and participation in downstream processing and related benefits. Cooperative–corporate partnerships could also be fashioned. Unfortunately, none of this was earlier attempted on misplaced ideological considerations even as contract tree farming has flourished on private farms in some parts of the country, an indicator of wider possibilities.

Much wasteland is owned by panchayats and by government agencies, especially the Railways and Defence Ministry. Most of this remains non-productive and unused and is part of the larger tragedy of the commons, with powerful caste and feudal interests usurping common property resources for private gain to the detriment of rural livelihoods and employment. Fortunately, wiser counsels are coming to prevail and the government would now like to invite private investment in degraded forest lands. This will, however, require a new forest policy and enabling legislation in place of the prevailing old-fashioned inspector raj with its built-in disincentives. There are many contradictions in the present system, not least those stemming from certain blanket court rulings and judicially-determined structures such as the Central Empowered Committee, that perhaps served an ad hoc purpose but now sometimes appear to have become a fifth wheel in the coach. Wastelands and degraded forest lands can be reforested by eco-development brigades, as has indeed been successfully tried out, and through the National Rural Employment Guarantee (NREG) programme, utilizing local landless, tribals and idle poor along with others, subject to the condition that they will enjoy title to the assets they create in accordance with agreed terms and conditions. The

Companies Act was amended in 2002 to permit the creation of producer companies with a membership of registered primary producers as a variant of cooperative societies. One suggestion mooted is that a fraction of the National Rural Employment Guarantee Act (NREGA) wage (Rs 58 per day) might be converted into a shareholding and that the usufruct or revenue be distributed in that proportion or in relation to the quantum of labour invested. The balance could go to the producer company or 'owner', be it a panchayat, the Railways or Defence Ministry, provided that the 'producer' enjoys freedom of choice regarding land use, whether it be growing trees or livestock farming on pastures or whatever. Women could be given separate pattas or titles so that gender rights are secured.

One among several initiatives is the Poorest Areas Civil Society (PACS) Programme, supported by the UK government and managed by Development Alternatives, an internationally-recognized development agency in India. A seven-year programme, now in its sixth year, PACS focuses on 108 of India's poorest districts in six states and presently covers nearly 16,000 villages in eighty-nine districts through a network of 562 civil society organizations (CSOs). Under the leadership of Action for Agricultural Renewal in Maharashtra (AFARM), a group of CSOs is working in 240 villages in Marathwada among 6,000 dalit families, helping them to convert barren, encroached lands into productive fields. Experiments such as these could provide gainful livelihoods while healing the land, within a legislative frame, and with a little organizational support. Collectively, the result could be transforming.

Policy implications of the agrarian crisis

Tackling the agrarian crisis in India offers a far greater challenge and opportunity than even wastelands and land degradation. Among the most authoritative pronouncements on this is the Report of the National Commission on Farmers (2006) chaired by Dr M.S. Swaminathan, doyen among the country's agricultural scientists. Its findings are stark. Its draft national policy for farmers' states:

> Agricultural growth has decelerated during the last decade. This has led to a decline in real per capita incomes in rural

> India in comparison to the rapid growth in urban incomes . . . . No wonder a recent NSSO (National Sample Survey Organisation) survey revealed that nearly 40 per cent of (India's) farmers would like to quit farming, if they have the option to do so. Unfortunately there is little option for them except moving into urban slums.

By one count, over 8,200 debt-ridden farmers committed suicide up and down the country between 2003 and February 2007, though largely in the cotton belt. Further, with increasing distress migration, there has been a feminization of agriculture.

India's agricultural growth declined from 3.2 per cent in the 1980s to 1.7 per cent per in the 1990s and has fallen further since, along with farm investments and profitability, though a welcome upturn has been lately reported. One does not have to look far to discover the reasons for this trend. Agricultural research has stagnated, with a large number of posts remaining unfilled, even as the national extension service has been allowed to run down, thus weakening the technological support base available to the farmer. Only 0.4 per cent of the country's agricultural GDP is invested in R&D as against a world average of 1 per cent, and 3 per cent in the United States. Over and above this, for the first time since Independence, the net area sown fell by as much as 8 m ha between 2002 and 2003 and the area under irrigation has not seen any real quantitative or qualitative increase. (Alagh, 2006) The first green revolution has long exhausted itself and the next green revolution is awaited. With the annual growth in foodgrain production falling below population growth there is reason to believe that hunger has increased.

About 70 per cent of India lives in the countryside, with almost 60 per cent of its workforce engaged in farming, the actual numbers increasing annually by 1.84 per cent. Meanwhile the share of agriculture in GDP fell from 31.3 per cent in 1991–2 to 19.6 per cent in 2005–6. Whereas India's reform process saw services and industry account for the largest chunk of its GDP growth in that order, China's reform was initially led by agricultural growth. Now, in order to attain a projected 10 per cent growth by the end of the Eleventh Plan, the calculation is that Indian agriculture must grow by at least 4 per cent per annum, and manufacturing and services by 12 per cent each. Doubling the agricultural growth rate is going to be a formidable challenge. But this by itself will not prevent a further widening of income disparities between the farm and non-farm sectors unless 10 million farm workers are diverted to gainful non-agricultural pursuits. Thus non-farm employment must increase by 6 per cent per annum; else the perceived demographic gain could turn into a demographic and social disaster. (Planning Commission, 2006).

The strategy for this has to be increased agricultural research and a technological leap forward, more irrigation with improved water use efficiency, diversification to higher value and more labour-intensive crops, improved credit, storage and market linkages and the promotion of agro-processing. The transition to new crops and systems will call for safety nets and employment generation for those temporarily displaced, through the NREG programme and other means. The old slogan of self-sufficiency in foodgrains is dated and needs to be discarded. Agricultural subsidies and minimum price supports favour the paddy–wheat–cane cycle. This has led to 'overproduction' and procurement well in excess of the requirements of the public distribution system. Food stocks at one stage rose above 60 million tonnes. The burden of transporting and storing this grain and the inevitable wastage and losses incurred in exporting some of this grain at unfavourable prices entailed huge unrequited costs that the farmer bore.

As per the High Level Committee on Food and Public Distribution, 2001, expenditure on maintaining these stocks was by 2001 greater than public expenditure in agriculture, irrigation, flood control and rural development combined!

Part of the reason for the low offtake was that the food habits and household expenditure of upwardly mobile families changed from cereals to other high-value items like vegetables, fruit, fish and meat, dairy products and spices, flowers, herbs and medicines, niche items and organic foods. On the other hand, the poor lacked the purchasing power to augment their meagre rations, underlining the terrible contradiction of hunger amid an overflowing larder.

Land, labour, capital and enterprise are basic factors of production and land certainly is in short supply with increasing demands on a fixed stock. How well do we use this asset? The National Commission on Farmers notes that the policy of farm subsidies in Punjab and Haryana invoked in the name of the poor has recoiled. It has resulted in distortions in land use and fertilizer consumption and promoted the reckless mining of groundwater, causing salinity in certain areas. The heavy subsidy given to nitrogenous fertilizer has come in the way of balanced fertilization and encouraged a disregard for soil micronutrient deficiencies. Factor productivity is consequently falling, adversely affecting production costs. In Punjab agricultural indebtedness in 2003–4 was estimated at Rs 24,000 crore (and increased by Rs 1000 crore by 2005–6) or more than the state's gross annual earning from agriculture. The state's agricultural growth rate, once the envy of others, has correspondingly witnessed steady regression since the 1990s and now ranks below the national average, a major reason for its overall economic decline. (Witsoe, 2006).

According to informed estimates, an acre of wheat in Punjab fetches a net income of Rs 17,000 whereas tomatoes cultivated in Hyderabad under the aegis of ITC, which has led corporate investments in agri-business, give a net return of around Rs 1 lakh per acre. The latter crop is also land saving and labour intensive thus delivering a handsome employment-cum-income dividend that is just the tonic Indian agriculture requires. World wheat output has peaked at around seven tonnes per hectare and has plateaued at four tonnes in north-western India. Further increases will not come easily and will call for greater investments and superior husbandry. Contrast this with the huge untapped potential for wheat (and rice) production in eastern India where productivity hovers around two tonnes per hectare. The existing cropping pattern is soil-exhausting and highly water-consumptive. In Maharashtra as much as 67 per cent of irrigation supplies go to water just 3 per cent of the farmland that is under sugar cane.

The obvious strategy that suggests itself is that the next green revolution should focus on eastern India (given flood control, technological inputs and some agrarian reform) while north-western India must diversify and go in for high-value, demand-driven crops, and backward and forward linkages along the entire food chain, led by a vigorous agri-business thrust which holds high promise. Even within the ambit of major cereals, special varieties for special culinary purposes command a market and even a premium well above official procurement prices, basmati rice being a prime example. Cold chains and rural road connectivity are particularly important to prevent spoilage of perishables and enhance market access. One of the major drivers in making and sustaining the strategy for agricultural-cum-rural revival must be a retail revolution in a departure from the familiar mom and dad *kirana* (general merchant) store to the establishment of modern retail chains with a reach and management skills that enable them to ride the market, trading larger volumes at lower prices. Displacement of friendly family minders, who can be retrained and absorbed in the new rural economy, will be more than compensated by the direct and indirect employment generated by the new marketing structure, though many may be only marginally viable for some time. This will open up the countryside, which is where savvy entrepreneurs see the next great business opportunity with not just the great and the rich but a rising multitude of upcoming, beyond-subsistence median earners eating and living better.

All innovation tends to attract opposition. Not unexpectedly, middlemen who stand to lose their superior bargaining power over hapless peasants have organized physical attacks on retail food chains, such as Reliance Fresh in Ranchi and Indore, behind a front of local vegetable vendors. They too can be retrained and absorbed. There was similar scepticism and motivated opposition when Verghese Kurien launched the Amul cooperative dairy and when Delhi's Mother Dairy started its vegetable kiosks.

Land and water being scarce, there is no alternative to increasing their productivity. With the growth in population, per capita availability of arable land fell from 0.24 hectares in 1979–81 to 0.10 hectares in 1997–9, and continues to fall. The median size of holdings has shrunk with passing generations and the unit of cultivation has fallen further with increasing fragmentation, despite periodic but essentially desultory efforts at consolidation. This has led to marginalization of large sections of the peasantry and rising landlessness and distress migration. Agrarian reform remains a necessity, not so much in terms of acquiring and redistributing ceiling surpluses—though this should not be excluded—but in updating and maintaining accurate records of rights and ensuring security and equity for tenancy, even while noting the distinction between ownership and cultivation. Professor D.C. Wadhwa has tirelessly emphasized over the years that the absence of clear land titles has been a major economic depressor and a fertile cause for endless litigation that must cost the country some percentage points in annual growth and a great deal more by vitiating national tranquillity. More recently, McKinsey and Co. has in a consultancy paper made the same point and put mind-boggling numbers on what this costs the nation as a prime rural and urban growth retardant.

Excessive field partitions also entail loss of land in boundaries and access paths and have a clear time and efficiency cost in providing irrigation and drainage and in pest management. Other than consolidation, where feasible, the answer lies in aggregation of holdings. Cooperation was once the great hope but has by and large not worked for a variety of reasons except in the case of processing units, most notably in the case of dairying, sugarcane and possibly fish. Lack of land titles bars pooling and its use as collateral. However, land can be leased in and leased out, and this is increasingly happening in a crowded countryside as marginal farmers lease or sell their holdings and either migrate or join the army of agricultural labourers. The ushering in of producer companies under the Company Law now makes it possible for groups of farmers to organize themselves to scale-up operations and negotiate strategic partnerships with corporate players. Tentative and informal arrangements of this kind that have come into being can now be properly rooted and enjoy the benefit of technological support and value addition through large-scale corporate processing, marketing and branding. A supreme example of this, though through the cooperative route, is the National Dairy Development Board. This mothers a large number of district and state-level federations of milk-marketing unions, themselves made up of many thousands of small grass-roots dairy farmers.

A variant of this that has come into vogue is contract farming. Here, a corporate house organizes farmers in given areas to band together to grow stipulated produce under close extension supervision and with a guaranteed buy-back arrangement and the possibility of additional downstream benefits. Particularly with regard to new crops or new varieties, contract farming can serve as a mechanism for transferring risk from small, individual farmers to more powerful and stable corporate entities. At a far humbler level, but not to be despised is homestead farming or kitchen gardening as it is appropriately called. In this case, householders tend these mini-compound farms literally plant by plant whenever time allows, raising a variety of crops or plants both for domestic consumption and exchange or sale. In Kerala, as in other parts of South-east Asia, homestead farming is very popular and many families make up a good part of their food basket from this source. In the erstwhile Soviet Union and earlier in China, private homestead farms provided valuable nutrition supplements and kept a large part of the population alive during the roughest periods of collectivization and the communes. Homestead farming, including poultry, duck and fish rearing, has considerable potential in many parts of the country but needs extension support. All these many variants of farm organization or aggregation can be means of enhancing production, productivity, employment and incomes especially during periods of transition from one level of farming and cropping to another. These are useful coping strategies and provide much-needed safety nets.

The insistence on total self-sufficiency in foodgrains is archaic and perhaps a throwback to the famine days when India lived 'from ship to mouth' on PL 480 wheat supplies. Autarky is unwise and constricting. Nevertheless, to prevent over-dependence on the global market, India must certainly produce a sufficiency of grain, for its population constitutes a sixth of mankind and international grain surpluses are shrinking. Though there is enough land globally to augment production, even a modest Indian or Chinese deficit could send global grain prices soaring. In any event, WTO rules and globalizing trends preclude a closed Indian market. India has to open up to world trade, even while fighting dumping of highly subsidized European and American agricultural products, if it is to market its own produce abroad. Even so, India now has a sufficiency of foreign exchange reserves and a growing trading capacity to import a few million tonnes of grain, sugar or oilseeds to tide over a bad season. Strategic reserves must be maintained; but over and above that one can already see a trend towards reducing grain consumption in favour of more balanced diets, including vegetables, fruit, milk and other produce. With rising living standards, balanced diets, not hunger, will be the major issue with regard to food security.

Punjab was one of the earliest states to take to contract farming as the government linked Pepsi's soft drink entry into India to its making a commitment to go in for agro-processing as well. This resulted in the establishment of a very large Pepsi tomato processing plant in Hoshiarpur in Punjab alongside the sale of its Colas. Feeding this plant and a subsequent unit for potato chips entailed augmentation of tomato and then potato production through contract farming. Superior varieties were introduced and, with improved tillage practices and guaranteed forward prices, production and productivity rose, assuring farmers a good return. The plants changed hands and other players entered the market but contract faming had come to stay and showed that crop diversification paid. At that time acerbic critics had argued that India needed integrated chips, not potato chips. They failed to understand the employment and income benefits of an integrated farm-food chain. Few will use that argument today, though the product and venue of political agitation has shifted to Tata's small car project in Singur in West Bengal and elsewhere.

Punjab's agricultural workforce has shrunk as a more prosperous and better-educated farmer does not want to dirty his hands if cheap migrant labour from Orissa and Bihar is readily available. The size and class of holdings favour medium and large farmers who constitute the majority of the farm population and cultivate the bulk of the land. The Punjab Agro-Foodgrains Corporation plans to diversify cropping over 2.5 million hectares of land and has found an instrumentality for doing this through contract farming especially with larger farmers. They are engaging in reverse tenancy (by leasing in lands from those who have migrated abroad) to expand the size of their holdings to many times above Punjab's 17-acre ceiling, or otherwise coming together as contiguous plot-holders where possible. Sunflower and seed potatoes are among the crops grown under collaborative arrangements or growers' associations. More and more corporate houses are entering the field, Hindustan Lever, Bharti Enterprises (with Rothschilds) and Chambal Agritech (a Birla enterprise) among them. Pepsi is the technical support partner to the Punjab Council for Citrus and Agriculture that is spearheading a programme to bring 100,000 acres under superior varieties of citrus, including *kinnow*, by 2012. It is already half way there and yields are up by 400 per cent while water use is only a couple of percentage points of that required for paddy. Reliance has launched a massive Reliance Fresh retail project linking farmers with consumers through a countrywide supply chain infrastructure. Others are doing likewise. Pieces of the new agriculture infrastructure are beginning to fall in place. But there is no room for complacency.

While irrigated agriculture must expand, there are gains to be made in rain-fed farming, which accounts for the larger part of the arable acreage. Here again, a package of R&D, extension and technological improvements in relation to seeds and water use efficiency will be necessary. There is no reason to fear properly evaluated genetically-modified seeds while keeping in mind the need to maintain an adequate and sufficiently varied gene pool of indigenous and traditional varieties. BT cotton has hugely augmented production. A new tillage practice, the SRI method (system of rice intensification), has shown promise in terms of water saving, a lower seed rate and higher yields in Indian field experiments. Watershed management is critical. Sprinkler and drip systems are beginning to be employed but are best used for high-value crops. The new National Rainfed Areas Authority could be an apt vehicle, imaginatively used, to concert action in this sector. Reports of a cheap desalination process if translated into a viable technology could benefit the coastal belt and possibly also be used to desalinate or upgrade northwest India's saline aquifers and salt lakes for growing salt-tolerant varieties or for water blends appropriate for industrial and municipal uses.

Rural Employment

An agricultural revival is, hopefully, on the cards. But this must be underpinned and can be fortified by large-scale employment generation in agro-processing and in rural hubs, backed by short-term distress-mitigating safety nets in the form of the NREG programme. Such work schemes, however, can be productive and need not be ad hoc if woven around longer-term programmes for the construction of rural infrastructure and land reclamation and improvement. Experiments with land armies and national social service have been tried but all too fitfully and peripherally. The task is indeed massive and urgent. Certain projections suggest that a net additional 110 million persons are likely to enter the labour force between 2005 and 2015, or 11 millions (or half an Australia) per annum. (National Institute of Rural Development, 2005)

The National Sample Survey (NSS) Report on the employment situation in India during 2004–5 sets the scene. About 56 per cent among rural males and 33 per cent among rural females belong to the labour force, the corresponding figures for urban India being 57 and 18 per cent respectively. The unemployment rate, measured in terms of the number of unemployed per 1000 persons in the labour force, is 17 and 15 in rural and urban India respectively, unemployment among females being higher than that among males. An evaluation of the NREG programme during its first year of implementation in 200 backward districts shows that it generated 729 million person-days of employment in 668,000 works, just over 40 per cent of which were availed of by women. As many as 18.3 million households had been provided with employment until February 2007, a significant number drawn from SC and ST households. Coverage is still modest and many shortcomings and imperfections have been revealed as may be expected in such an ambitious and gigantic programme. Nevertheless, a start has been made and lessons learnt. Several best practices and innovations have been adopted. The scope of permissible works has been expanded, including those that may be taken up on lands of individual beneficiaries and an additional 130 districts will now be covered. The main thrust has been on water conservation and land development, including drought proofing, afforestation and tree planting, water harvesting, irrigation, de-silting of traditional waterbodies and tanks, flood moderation and drainage works, and road connectivity. Such programmes, carefully planned and executed, can help build farm capital assets, enhance land productivity and mitigate erosion and land degradation. The cultivation of bio-fuels such as jatropha is also being propagated for wasteland development (preferably in good rainfall areas) and extraction of oils that can be blended with petrol (as an alternative to ethanol produced from cane, maize and other crops).

The Constitution provides for national social service under which rubric it should be possible to mobilize and organize young people and ex-servicemen with an appropriate reward system in national volunteer corps brigades tasked to promote education and health for all, ecological and heritage conservation, disaster management programmes and so forth. The feeble and faltering efforts made in this direction in the past cannot be a guide to the latent possibilities, quantitatively and qualitatively, as exemplified by programmes like the Peace Corps and National Volunteer Service in the United States and the United Kingdom.

Self-help groups supported with micro-credit have shown the way for unemployed and under-employed groups, especially women, to launch small, productive enterprises ranging from poultry keeping to broom making. These have provided a valuable income supplement and have fostered a rudimentary base for rural processing, tiny industries and marketing. India's vast and varied artisanal and craft tradition waits to be tapped and rejuvenated and given a new functional reach to serve modern needs. This will call for technological and design inputs, marketing and organizational skills, finance and possibly some training in the use of newer and more productive tools. Some of this is happening by happenstance or piecemeal; it needs to be transformed into a mission mode around emerging concepts of rural hubs. Many crafts have in fact become arts and are no longer affordable or utilitarian, as they have to compete with cheap, novel and, often, tawdry manufactures. There is an 'arts' market for certain crafts, both domestically and abroad, and the tradition should additionally be preserved in museums as a tribute to our forebears. But retaining them exclusively as they are would be ultimately to kill them, stifled by nostalgia. The handloom industry marks a beginning of what can be done through sensible and sensitive modernization, with fabrics being designed, woven and tailored in keeping with current trends and uses, ready-mades and accessories. Unfortunately, this has by and large not been the case in the khadi and village industries sector. This barely survives as a heavily subsidized and ritualized ideology that serves both its producers and consumers poorly when it could be restored as a vibrant business prospect for millions. The Khadi and Village Industries Corporation (KVIC), covering khadi and some twenty-two village industries, employs millions of workers and has over 40,000 outlets that could be an immensely powerful market network if imaginatively employed.

India is industrializing, as it must. Yet it would be unwise and counterproductive to ignore small and medium enterprises (SMEs) that can, like the garment industry, generate hundreds of thousands of jobs and ancillary activity, capture niche markets and compete with the best worldwide. The Prime Minister, Dr Manmohan Singh, has warned against crony capitalism and emphasised the role of SMEs in industrializing backward regions and making growth more inclusive. A multiplication and qualitative improvement in the pattern of vocational education and industrial training are necessary and this is something that industry could adopt both regionally and sectorally. Relocating people on off-farm employment will not be possible unless there are decentralized opportunities for such side-stepping as there is no way that capital-intensive large and mega industry and big cities can alone absorb and manage the numbers involved. There are numerous small towns that can host such enterprises as they have the infrastructure and are reasonably well connected but the necessary land will have to be found.

Industrialization, development and environmental compulsions

Land for development: this is where the argument is joined. Where is the land unless it is diverted from agriculture or forest? Wastelands are often owned or are common property. This being so will not land acquisition, as and when required, cause displacement? This could be problematic. Then what about the availability of water supply and energy? What is likely to be the environmental impact of providing such infrastructure as well as of resultant emissions and effluents? These are valid questions and tend to arouse antagonisms on account of cumulative grievances born of past thoughtlessness and neglect. There is sufficient reason for this. The past record combines errors of omission, when the country was far lower down on the environment-development learning curve, to mistaken policies, broken promises, poor implementation and corruption. Estimates of displacement on account of development since Independence range from 40 to 60 million and more but these are difficult to verify, may entail double counting in certain cases and are largely based on anecdotal evidence.

Nevertheless, what they underline is the large and growing magnitude of the problem with more rapid and widespread development superimposed on population growth. Figures of forest diversion since the Forest Conservation Act, 1980, are better documented. According to the Ministry of Environment and Forests, about 12,535 development projects had been granted forest clearance in the twenty-five years ending December 2005, entailing diversion of a little over a million hectares of forest. This included special one-time clearances of a hectare each for social infrastructure and utilities in underdeveloped and underserved areas.

There are certain myths and fallacies about development, displacement and the environment that should be dispelled. Certain caveats are in order. There is invariably a cry that whatever area is surveyed or selected as a possible project site is uniquely special and must not be touched. This started with the movement in 1973 to preserve Silent Valley in Kerala, that had some justification; but it has since been exploited exponentially from the mistaken belief that all of nature is and must remain inviolate. The fact is that nature is constantly changing, and not only in the long run. The entire Indo-Gangetic Plain was created by the filling of the Tethys Sea and even today the silt carried to the ocean by the Indus, the Ganga and the Brahmaputra is overwhelmingly on account of natural mass wasting and erosion and not on account of man-made factors which, however, can be incrementally ruinous and must therefore be mitigated if not avoided. Agitations about 'losing ground' and floods can be needlessly alarmist unless placed in context. Then there are hardy arguments about the environmental and financial costs of doing something and building therefrom cost-benefit scenarios based on what can be doomsday scenarios. These could result in do-nothing decisions or policies, which can be ecologically and financially damaging. There is a cost for doing nothing and non-decision can be a painful decision. There is often also a high opportunity cost of delay and lagged or foregone benefits and their multiplier are not something that the poor should be asked to bear by the relatively well-heeled. Then of course one must factor in the enormous ecological burden of population growth and the demand this makes on space and resources. Simple comparisons recalling a happier situation 'even ten years ago', let alone 'when I was a child', cheerfully ignore the generational population increase of 100 to 300 million during the intervening years. And what about livestock? Who factors in the huge unrequited burden of scrub and useless cattle let loose on the forests, commons, fields and streets of India?

It is argued that development displaces people. It admittedly does so. But that is the story of civilization—people moving from distress to opportunity. Otherwise, too, it can safely be said that whatever the figure placed on displacement, the numbers involuntarily displaced by poverty and want, products of non-development, is far, far greater. Some 30 to 40 million distress migrants or Malthusian refugees are estimated to be on the move annually. And the notion that these peasants move exclusively from land to land and to other agrarian occupations, and that therefore rehabilitation can only be meaningful if they are resettled on the land, does not square with the facts or, literally, with ground realities. There is simply not enough land.

This is not for a moment to suggest that compensation and rehabilitation are side issues and that non-performance or non-compliance with rights and equity are acceptable. Clearly not, as failure here can turn sullen resentment to explosive anger, as we know to our cost. Equally, failure to develop and meet basic needs and legitimate aspirations of the underprivileged and poor can be very costly—socially, economically, and politically. Individuals and groups may do so but no responsible government or state can in justice and equity take a uni-focal view and ignore the bigger and more holistic picture. Wangari Maathai, the Kenyan Nobel laureate and renowned ecologist, summed up the situation well during a visit to India in 2007. She noted that humankind is part and parcel of the eco-system and so 'in undermining our ecosystems, we are undermining our own lives'. Asked about the challenge and environmental cost of massive infrastructure building, her response was that 'This is difficult for people in charge of management and development because you always have to make a choice. There are times when you have to cut trees and take over the land for development; but it is always a matter of making right choices and finding the balance . . . . Many people don't have that sense of balance'. One of the best definitions of rehabilitation derives from the root meaning of that term, namely, to invest with dignity. Those are key words: choice, balance, dignity.

Is it not necessarily true that every villager wants land? Some 25,000 of the country's most deprived dalits and tribals from eleven states marched in October 2007 from Gwalior to Delhi to represent their case for land redistribution before the powers-that-be. The government responded by setting up two land commissions to examine the situation and speed up or de-bottleneck processes to transfer disputed lands, deal with *benami* holdings, confer land titles and so forth. But what was interesting is that random newspaper interviews of these very unfortunates indicated that many marginal cultivators had to migrate annually to sustain themselves during the lean season and that they would prefer a job to farming if they had the option. Most tellingly, some stated that they would sell their land, given the good prices being offered these days, in order to invest in the education of their children. For many therefore, education, not land, is the avenue to better living.

Having said that, it must be admitted that the record on land acquisition has not been altogether happy, though it is certainly improving by the day as knowledge and awareness grow. Environmental awareness was never altogether absent from Indian society, not merely as a coping strategy but as a way of life. This is evidenced in the sacred groves, age-old water harvesting practices and the Bishnoi care for life of earlier tradition and in many scriptural texts. Gandhi was close to nature, but modern environmentalism came to India in the 1970s with the World Environmental Conference and the Chipko movement. Population planning came on the agenda and India told the world that poverty is the worst polluter, making a pitch for accelerated Third World development with international assistance. The Club of Rome had earlier published 'Limits to Growth' which was dismissed as alarmist but was perhaps ahead of its time in making the case for sustainability.

Nehru had, of course, rejected the Gandhian path of decentralized development and was more taken with the Soviet model of planning that aimed at 'capturing the commanding heights of the economy'. The thrust on building the 'new temples of modern India', major river valley projects like Bhakra, Hirakud and the Damodar Valley Corporation (DVC), foremost among them, was a product of this outlook. Priorities were misplaced insofar as balance was lacking and there was a fugitive hope that the trickle-down effect and an economic 'take off' with accelerated growth would resolve all problems. Indira Gandhi brought ecology on the national agenda with the establishment of an environment ministry and the Forest Conservation Act, but environmental pressures kept mounting.

Development and displacement

The Sardar Sarovar Project evoked both strong support and protest led by the Narmada Bachao Andolan. The clash of rhetoric mistakenly posited a crude choice between 'development' and the 'environment or displacement'. Delay led to shifting goalposts, swelling numbers, sequential rehabilitation packages that generated envy and new expectations, court interventions, time and cost overruns and the creation of ever-new 'facts'. The Tehri Project suffered a somewhat similar experience with overblown arguments about dam safety related to seismic hazards and violation of the holy Ganga. In both cases ideology triumphed over reason. The slogan of land for land, on which the World Bank also insisted, has been unreal as both the Narmada Valley and Garhwal have seen distress migrants move involuntarily to non-land and urban occupations.

The administration too has often been wooden and callous. The Council for Social Development, Delhi, sent a team to look at rehabilitation and other problems concerning the Utkal Alumina International Ltd (UAIL) plant in Rayagada, Orissa, a Fifth Schedule area, in 1999. It reported a lack of information or dialogue, violation of legally ordained procedures under the Panchayats (Extension to Scheduled Areas) Act, PESA, multiple displacements in the case of some of the affected population, and an improved compensation package only after hard bargaining—something that should have been conceded *ab initio* as a right and as part of an inclusive process. On the contrary, the team found that the tribals were mystified that they were required to pay a royalty of Rs 180 per quintal for forest grass traditionally collected by them for the manufacture of brooms, whereas UAIL was being asked to pay a royalty of around Rs 30 per tonne for the bauxite they planned to mine. This recalls the throwaway rates at which some paper and pulping plants were sold bamboo in the past, resulting in the devastation of rich bamboo forests at the cost of the forest ecology and tribal interests.

Agragamee, an NGO working with Kondh and Jhodia tribal women in and around Kashipur in Rayagada, a major bauxite–aluminium hub, takes the story back in time to the construction of the Upper Indravati dam. It narrates the sufferings of the women who bore the brunt of the multiple encounters this tribal community had with development and industrialization: first the road, then the dam, then the mines, and now the factories. Negotiation and dialogue were lacking. The industries are extractive and the local communities got little while they had to cope with effluents and emissions. Ultimately, they have been compelled to migrate to brick kilns in Andhra Pradesh, to Raipur as rickshaw pullers or to industries in Surat. (Agragamee, 2004) The investments made are seen by the displaced as having largely created enclaves or islands of prosperity amid an ocean of poverty and neglect.

A series of revised industrial policies formulated and announced from time to time have perhaps succeeded in improving the investment climate but have not focussed equally on the impacts and, indeed, opportunities presented by industrialization for simultaneously improving the lives of the ordinary people. Such criticism is linked to globalization without adequate safety nets resulting in emerging regional and sub-regional disparities with attempts at 'forced inclusion of the local in the global'. (Mehor, 2006) In the result there has been marginalization of the poor, ecological degradation, cornering of mineral wealth and plant bio-diversity, and an immensely profitable even if speculative land and real estate market favouring a rising urban middle class Everything said, at the end of the day there has been a deficit of trust. This has to be made good patiently and confidence established through transparency, consultation, true generosity and compassion.

Displacement is traumatic at any time and for any person but most of all for simple people whose lives, livelihoods and memories are inseparably linked to the forest, fields and streams in and along which they and their ancestors have lived for as long as they can remember. Who cannot but be deeply moved by the lament of the Chief of the Seattle Indians to the American President in 1854: 'How can you buy or sell the sky, the warmth of the land? The idea is strange to us. If we do not own the freshness of the air or the sparkle of the water, how can you buy them? Every part of this Earth is sacred to my People'. Is anybody listening or taking time to explain why some things will change? Sadly, some of those displaced long back still face an uncertain future. Questions are suspect and there is intolerance of protest. The brutal murder of Shankar Guha Niyogi who organized workers in the Dalli Rajhara–Bhilai mine–steel belt in Durg district (now in Chhattisgarh) in 1991 signalled the high stakes involved.

What is displacement and who are 'project-affected people'? Displacement concerns geography. A landless person has no land to lose and his habitation may be unaffected by, say, submergence behind a dam or land acquisition for a factory or mine. But if he is denied access to resources and territory where he earned his livelihood, he is affected and deserving of compensation. The test is that a good Resettlement and Rehabilitation (R&R) policy should leave an affected person (and indeed the community as a whole) at least as well off and, preferably, better off, as a result of the intervention causing the displacement in the first instance. The issue then is to minimize dislocation and injury and ensure that apart from adequate compensation and R&R, the benefits arising from the project in question are shared as far as possible so that the local community becomes a stakeholder in the enterprise. The Land Acquisition Act of 1894, as amended in 1984, vests the state with unilateral powers to acquire any private property for a 'public purpose' under the doctrine of eminent domain. Market value must be paid, but very often this is a depressed price as people do not register the full value of the transaction in order to minimize stamp duty. Going by the average registered value of similar land recently sold in the general areas may not therefore give the owner a fair price for his land. These are among the aberrations that recent policy modifications have sought to overcome. Simple people living in a subsistence–barter economy are unable to understand or handle big money and have in the past been relieved of their cash compensation by 'relatives' and 'friends', not to mention liquor contractors and bauble-sellers, including motorbike salesmen these days. They need to be assisted to manage sudden bounty.

Vasudha Dhagamwar, a sensitive scholar, looked at the debate going on around the acquisition of land near Paradip for an ancillary port for the proposed giant twelve-million tonne POSCO steel plant. She speaks of the tendency on the part of some NGOs 'to insist on preserving the old lifestyle, the rice pounded by foot (*dheki*), the bajra ground by hand (*chakki*), and the water fetched from the river (all by women, of course) . . . The harsh truth is that India is changing . . . . Life is rapidly becoming non-land based'. Yet even absentee landlords are counted in for land-for-land compensation. (Dhagamwar, 2006)

A new national R&R policy, under consideration over the past several years has finally been announced after undergoing many changes and refinements. The controversy over a crop of large steel plants and mines and Special Economic Zones through 2006–7 around the country had reopened the issue leading to the formulation of a more liberal and comprehensive policy document. These developments had climaxed in twin agitations surrounding land acquisition for a low-cost automobile plant in Singur near Kolkata and an SEZ for a chemical hub at Nandigram near Haldia in West Bengal, triggering an impassioned national debate.

Singur and Nandigram

The southern part of West Bengal today has probably the highest population density anywhere in India. In response to mounting pressure on the land, the Department of Land, Government of West Bengal, published a paper on the Status of Land Use. This provides the framework for the Left Front's new industrial policy. The total reported area in the state is 8.687 million hectares (one hectare equals approximately 2.5 acres), of which 63 per cent is sown, 1 per cent is fallow, uncultivable or under pasture, 13.5 per cent is under forest, mostly in the north and west, and 3.7 per cent is urban, mostly concentrated in the south. Strong demands for land are coming from and for industry, infrastructure, housing and urbanization and can only be met by diversion from existing uses. The challenge portrayed is to protect and consolidate agriculture at higher levels of productivity, diversify agricultural production and promote rural development while yet moving firmly on the path of industrialization and urbanization. In so doing, current land use efficiency must be weighed alongside the social cost of diversion, including environmental costs and the satisfactory rehabilitation of those affected, together with the stimulus given to employment and income generation. The state hopes to be able to complete a scientific and consolidated land use database by about 2013 and compile a land bank listing all vacant lands currently available for diversion.

After decades of de-industrialization and stagnation for a variety of reasons, West Bengal now needs to change its occupational and habitation pattern from farming and rural livelihoods to industry and urbanization. Agriculture has done well since the mid-1980s, riding on successful land reforms and administrative decentralization. Both production and productivity rose but the trend weakened as Operation Barga was not carried to a conclusion, with the CPI(M) co-opting upwardly mobile medium and small peasants glad to reap the advantages of joining its cadres. The process stopped short of being inclusive, which explains some of the current resentments that are evident. Be that as it may, two generations after land reform, holdings have fragmented and are no longer viable for those at the bottom of the agrarian pyramid. Two trends have followed. Marginal farmers have sold their lands and have migrated with the landless to the cities in search of a living. Alternatively, marginal farmers have leased their lands to those desirous of making up a viable holding and joined the ranks of agricultural labour.

The message is clear. Bengal, like other states, must industrialize and urbanize as it strives to fashion a second green revolution through diversified agriculture, further agrarian reform and value addition through food processing and improved market access. This will necessitate selective land diversion from agriculture. The argument that this will endanger national food security is totally ill informed. Land, like water or forests or anything else, must be used efficiently. Intensive farming at higher levels of productivity is possible and can release land currently being used sub-optimally for other and more productive purposes. The West Bengal Chief Minister, Buddhadeb Bhattacharjee cannot be faulted for adopting what is basically a sound and sensible strategy given some fine-tuning that seems to be under way.

The state government came in for much motivated criticism for strongly supporting Tatas' bid to set up a greenfield 100,000 unit small car plant in Singur, Hooghly district, forty kilometres from Kolkata by partly acquiring and partly leasing 997 acres of land for the purpose. Rather than look at the matter rationally, the whole issue was politicized and hijacked by a motley coalition including various opposition parties, the Maoists and other Naxal groups, eco-fundamentalists, Left dissidents and sundry others. Several questions were agitated and, as the dust rose, reason was eclipsed by emotion. The chief minister explained that the state had wooed the Tatas to site the project to Bengal in order to trigger re-industrialization after years of depression and disinvestment and the collapse of the old jute and engineering industries. Investors had multiple options, national and global, and needed to be attracted on terms in keeping with the state's best interests. Tatas selected Singur in preference to other sites offered, possibly on account of its proximity to Kolkata. Looking for a wasteland site may not have been entirely infeasible but could have added to costs and start-up time and called for a lot more secondary investment in infrastructure. Singur therefore was seen as a turning point with a dynamic brand investment signalling a new chapter in Bengal's economic regeneration.

Something over 1,800 unrecorded *bargadars* and others left out in the first count are being granted appropriate compensation for the Singur lands. The compensation package is Rs 6–8 lakh per acre of single-crop and Rs 8 lakh per acre or more for double-crop land. Sharecroppers are to receive at least 25 per cent of what the owners get and improvements were being negotiated. According to State officials, a farmer investing his compensation in a fixed deposit will probably earn more than the net value of the crop he used to cultivate. In addition, Tata Motors are training the displaced and other locals for employment in the Rs 1500 crore motorcar plant and ancillary units in which its associates are investing another Rs 500 crores. A considerable multiplier will come into play and any consideration of the project must take all of this into account. Tatas estimates the creation of 10,000 jobs in the next few years, direct and indirect. To the extent that local youths are unable to avail of the newer industrial opportunities, a twofold strategy could be put in place. First, the NREG programme should be used as a safety net for the unskilled. Second, more Industrial Training Institutes and vocational institutes must be set up in the Singur area or wherever required together with the establishment of higher secondary schools and colleges to graduate young people to the next higher level of employment in technical and managerial positions or in the services that industrialization fosters.

If anything went wrong in Singur, it was the process rather than the substantive policy decision. Surveys and consultation could have been more meticulous. The resort to political force to settle arguments was misplaced and the use of police powers to quell unrest was, typically, unwise and excessive, leading to firing, deaths and charges of rape and molestation of women. This fanned emotions and distorted the issue. This was more apparent at Nandigram, in East Midnapur, selected as a Special Economic Zone (SEZ), for a chemical hub in collaboration with the Indonesian Salim Group. This was to be enlarged in further stages to embrace a petrochemical complex and a multi-product SEZ within a projected Haldia mega-SEZ with an ultimate spread of 62,500 acres. Consultations were to commence on moving forward on the first-stage Nandigram SEZ proposal when on 3 January 2007 the Haldia Development Authority, on its own, wrote to the BDO, Nandigram, to initiate a preliminary study to earmark areas for possible acquisition of land. Protests erupted and this led to violence and firing. The government apologized for the lapse in regard to the premature land survey and stated categorically that there would be no SEZ in Nandigram without the informed consent of the local populace. But by then disparate political, ideological and lumpen elements had got into the act. Nandigram was sealed from the world outside. CPI (M) members or supporters of the area were set upon and had to flee. Culverts were broken and all roads blockaded, preventing any ingress. State functionaries were prevented from entering and Nandigram was for months a republic within the republic under the aegis of the Bhoomi Uchchhed Pratirodh (Land Eviction Resistance) Committee in which the Trinamul Congress, as in Singur, assumed a leading role. The Nandigram SEZ proposal was formally withdrawn by the state government, which has said the chemical hub contemplated will be established elsewhere. On 3 May 2007, the Calcutta High Court observed that the people of Nandigram had prima facie been deprived of their fundamental right to life and liberty and called upon the State to restore basic services to the hapless villagers trapped in a political conflict not of their choosing. Nevertheless, strife continued, manifesting strong political rivalries more than economic or social issues. There have been clashes and deaths and in November 2007, CPI(M) cadres went on a brutal offensive, evoking concern and protests from the other side and indeed the entire nation as the grim story of party terror unfolded.

Meanwhile, Nayachar, near Sagar Island, has been chosen as an alternative site south of Nandigram for the chemical SEZ, but controversies continue.

The Singur project, unlike the Nandigram proposal, is not linked to an SEZ. In both cases the issue that has triggered agitation concerns acquisition of agricultural land, livelihoods and compensation. That loss of farmland will threaten food security is absurd. The 60,000 acres West Bengal plans to acquire for industrialization over the next few years for ports, steel plants, petrochemical complexes, thermal stations, expressways et al. adds up to no more than 0.44 per cent of the area under cultivation in the State. As far as possible, farmland, especially fertile, irrigated lands, will not be acquired but there will be some diversion here too as significantly large and contiguous areas with clear titles are required. This is one reason why utilization of derelict or sick industry premises in the state are not necessarily suitable locations.

The related argument about real estate/housing development critically diverting farmlands and threatening agriculture is equally fanciful, except in very limited, specific contexts. It is livelihoods rather than Indian agriculture that might be affected.

The SEZ debate

The larger debate in the country has turned on the drive to set up a number of SEZs up and down the country, many as specialized hubs or parks for electronics, biotechnology, petrochemicals, pharmaceuticals IT and IT-enabled services and so forth. An Export Promotion Zone (EPZ) was established at Kandla in 1965, the first in Asia, followed by another at Santa Cruz in Bombay and then others in Noida,

Madras, Cochin, Falta and Vishakapatnam. Encouraged by this experiment and spurred by the need to attract foreign investment and related technology, the foreign trade policy of 2000 announced a more ambitious plan to establish Special Economic Zones with quality infrastructure and a package of Central and state fiscal incentives and minimal regulatory constraints. An SEZ Act and Rules came into force in February 2006 after wide consultations. These provide for simplified procedures, single-window clearance for both SEZ developers and individual unit investors through a Board of Approval and relaxation of some labour laws, and seek to promote employment and exports.

Within a year, 234 formal SEZ approvals had been granted in nineteen states with a land requirement of 34,400 hectares (86,000 acres), much of this already in the hands of the state governments or the corporate houses involved. State industrial development corporations are among those bidding for SEZs as a means of promoting industrialization and investments. In respect of the sixty-three SEZs that have come up after February 2006, the total investment expected by December 2009 is Rs 58,459 crore that will in turn generate 890,000 additional jobs. If all the 234 SEZ approvals fructify, the anticipated investment and employment is expected to be of the order of Rs 300,000 crore and four million additional jobs respectively. The response has been very satisfying, with several world brand leaders like Nokia, Motorola, Adidas and others setting up shop in India.

Some SEZs, such as those proposed at Maha Mumbai–Raigad (35,000 acres) and Jhajhar, Haryana, (25,000 acres), have met with resistance on account of their size and the quantum of displacement involved. The land allocated for an SEZ is segmented into a processing area of 25 per cent, a warehousing or trading area and a non-processing area for other economic (roads, water supply) or social infrastructure. The social infrastructure must include housing, office space, shopping and recreational facilities, hotels, and medical and educational facilities. This explains the need for substantial non-processing areas, which are not intended for real estate profiteering. Some would ask why SEZs should provide these facilities. If they do not, the entire burden of housing and providing for the accommodation, schooling, medicare, transportation and other social overheads of and for the SEZ population must fall on the municipal or state authorities. Bangalore, for instance, is in a mess because the IT companies located there have spanking and spacious premises without housing. Therefore tens of thousands of their employees (around 18,000 in the case of Infosys alone) have to commute through municipal roads causing traffic jams, interminable delays and pollution. The new SEZ policy wisely seeks to prevent entrepreneurs transferring such social costs to the state and community.

Fallacies abound on all sides. The regulation size of SEZs or individual processing units should not be so small as to deny economies of scale nor so large as to affect investment optimality. Insistence on a large unit size of processing area in Hyderabad led Hewlett-Packard to withdraw its approved application and go elsewhere. Wiser for the experience, the government is now inclined to be more flexible. It is not correct that SEZ enterprises enjoy exclusive tax benefits. Export-oriented units and software technology parks are also entitled to tax breaks until 2009, under provisions of the income tax law, or in some cases for up to ten years. In the circumstances, the net tax exemptions allocable to all other SEZs will be far less than otherwise assumed.

The price at which land has been acquired from farmers and compensation offered has been a matter of considerable controversy. Many factors come into play, especially when land is acquired in bulk and then sold to individual enterprises at different times with an element of capital appreciation at each stage, as has happened in Kalinganagar in Orissa. Land values appreciate with development and use. In the Mundra SEZ in Kutch, barren saltpans were acquired for Rs 5000 per acre; but with a port, airport and rail and highway connection planned, the value of adjacent lands has shot up astronomically. Near Sriperumbudur in Tamil Nadu, Nokia purchased farmland at Rs 5 lakh per acre. A recent random check made just a few kilometres away in a neighbouring village, indicated that land prices here had rocketed to Rs 80 lakh per acre. A local farmer with a holding of 2.2 acres told an interlocutor that he planned to sell an acre of his land to finance the education of his children and would retain only the remaining 1.2 acres for farming. Social values and aspirations are fast changing and the past is no more a reliable guide to the future. With training, new underprivileged sections of the population, including women, are joining the industrial work force. At Raigad, there will be no displacement from any of the forty-five villages whose lands are to be acquired. Reliance is offering affected persons various options, the basic package including land compensation at market rates, assurance of a Rs 4,000–5,000 per month job after a two-year training period, sustenance allowances at the rate of minimum agricultural wages for the landless, an investment of Rs 90 crore for upgrading the infrastructure of the affected villages and the allocation (at a price to be determined by the state government) of developed land equivalent to 12.5 per cent of the land acquired. This is by no means an ungenerous package; but some farmers remain resentful about losing traditional livelihoods and being denied a choice of whether to sell and to whom. Standard rates of compensation are not possible across the country or even within states as local circumstances, locations and opportunities vary. But comparisons keep being made and those displaced want their compensation to match the best being offered elsewhere. There is more than one aspect to keeping up with the Joneses.

Critics argue that China has only a limited number of coastal SEZs, including Shenzen opposite Hong Kong, whereas India is planning hundreds of SEZs, or more than the rest of the world. Such comparisons are invalid. China observers believe that virtually all of China is in effect an SEZ. Beijing is only just beginning to legislate to protect private property.

Objections have been raised in many quarters to proposed SEZ tax breaks that, according to the Finance Ministry, will cost the country Rs 100,000 crores by 2010. The Commerce Ministry is, however, confident that the investments and returns on them in terms of revenues, employment and the multiplier effects will be considerably greater. A leap in India's overall exports to $500 billion and an additional 2 per cent to GDP from SEZs over the next six years is forecast. The sceptics are not impressed and snide references keep being made to the return of the East India Company and a second Permanent Settlement under a new class of zamindars.

Land for industry

Land acquisition for any purpose is being resisted and not for SEZs alone. Objections have been raised to land acquisition in coastal areas on the plea that this will affect fisheries; to thermal and hydro projects and mining, to forest diversion for wind energy farms and so on. Yet land use patterns must and will change and land acquisition must be done with consent and compassion. The State has the power of eminent domain under the Land Acquisition Act and may take over private lands for 'public purposes'. But employment, income generation and poverty alleviation are public purposes. In response to protests, the government decided in January 2007 to freeze all SEZs not already approved pending the formulation of a new and more liberal rehabilitation policy. While this was prudent, it must be kept in mind that any irrational hiatus can cause uncertainty and affect timelines and cost estimates.

Before considering the options for a better compensation package it would be useful to look at some other mega projects and the controversies surrounding them, as well as the approach to growth and industrialization adopted by the Central and state governments. In keeping with the country's projected growth trajectory, the Government of India has projected a massive 40–60 million tonne increase in steel capacity to 120 million tonnes by 2020, coupled with a policy of processing rather than simply exporting iron ore. With a buoyant international steel market and with China's steel investment having peaked, India is a favoured destination for steel investments. The Mittals, South Korea's POSCO, Essar, Tatas, Jindals, Larsen and Toubro, the Indian public sector units in steel industry and others are queuing up to build large new capacities. Orissa, like Jharkhand and Chhattisgarh, is extremely mineral rich and understandably looks to exploit this abundant resource endowment to pull it out from the depths of poverty. At the same time, a transformation is envisaged in the social development, agricultural, fishery and forestry sectors, with irrigation and crop diversification in the tribal highlands as much as elsewhere. These objectives inspire the 'Orissa Vision 2020' that sets out a road map for the future.

Kalinganagar in the predominantly tribal Jajpur district of Orissa was selected as a major new metallurgical hub in 1992 when 13,000 acres of private and government land was progressively acquired. Compensation was paid only to patta (title) holders. With the last land survey having been done in 1928, errors and omissions were alleged. As industrial activity only picked up gradually, acquired lands not taken over were left in the possession of the original landholders. In November 2004, Tata Steel signed an MOU for a six-million-tonne steel plant in Kalinganagar and paid the Orissa Industrial Development Corporation Rs 3.35 lakh per acre for 2400 acres released from its land bank. Original tribal landowners who had received not more than Rs 35,000 per acre on the basis of depressed 'registered' sale values immediately questioned the transaction. With the development of infrastructure and other industries coming in, land values had greatly appreciated. The state government accordingly enhanced the compensation in two further instalments after 1996, to Rs 1 lakh per acre. However, the agitation gathered momentum and organized protest groups, originally pro-job but now anti-industry, sealed off the site, preventing any further surveys or construction of a boundary wall or other activity. An effort to level the Tata site on 2 January 2006 under police escort led to a fracas and firing after a policeman was beheaded in the melee. Twelve tribals were tragically killed and several others injured. Thereafter an ex gratia of Rs 1 lakh was paid to all Project Affected Families (PAFs). Nevertheless, anger and defiance mounted.

The 679 families to be displaced were enumerated as 1,400 extended families, with a change in the R&R policy that designated each major son and unmarried sister or daughter above thirty as a separate family unit. They are being offered a generous compensation package. Each family will receive a 10 cent homestead plot with services, Rs 24,000 as a twelve month maintenance allowance, a Rs 1.5 lakh house-building allowance, training for future employment and a job per family or cash assistance in lieu thereof. Special attention is being given to training women and the creation of employment opportunities for them. Each family is to be given a smart identity card and will be 'tracked' for five years to ensure proper rehabilitation. To ensure compliance, an annual independent social audit is proposed as was done in the case of Tata Steel in Jamshedpur on three occasions between 1980 and 2002–3. The Tatas' concept of corporate social responsibility has steadily expanded from looking at shop floor standards, product quality, procurement and sales, and labour relations to township and community management, welfare activities and a variety of social services. Other major corporate houses and chambers too are making corporate social responsibility integral to doing business.

South Korea's Pohang Steel Company (POSCO) signed an MOU with the Orissa Government in June 2005 to set up a twelve million tonne integrated steel plant in three phases at Jagatsinghpur near Paradip with an investment of Rs 52,000 crore. The project encompasses a township, related ore mines and a connecting highway, a power plant and a captive port to handle the thirty million tonne iron ore swap trade (swapping low alumina ore imports for high alumina Indian ore exports). Some 4,004 acres of land, 436 acres of this privately owned, have been sought for the project, spread over five villages and displacing 467 families. As much as 1,135 acres of government-owned land have been encroached upon while other locals are using the non-encroached land for growing betel vine and cashew as well as for aquaculture. Although POSCO has paid out compensation at the rate of Rs 25,000 per acre, locals look on possession of the land as different from its ownership, and the encroachers are resisting eviction. Livelihoods are involved. As in Kalinganagar, protestors sealed off the project site and no member of the administration or representative of POSCO was being permitted to enter the area.

In May 2007, three POSCO officials who visited the site to discuss land acquisition were taken hostage by the agitators who demanded that the steel plant should be located elsewhere. Were that to happen, what would it mean? POSCO offers 467,000 jobs during the construction phase and 48,000 direct jobs on completion of the third phase of the project. Training programmes are under way and a corporate social responsibility charter is under preparation. In view of the large benefits expected from POSCO, the project has been granted the status of an SEZ. Some forest and mining clearances remain but the project authorities were hoping that with strong state and Central government backing everything would fall in place before long. With the passage of time, however, POSCO has hinted that unless they are enabled to proceed soon they may have to look for a more congenial site.

Consistent with the Orissa government's new industrial policy and R&R policy, a dedicated high-powered committee has been set up by the government to ensure the progress of POSCO and other mega projects. A single-window clearance committee has been established to short-circuit delays and cumbersome procedures. Each project has been assigned a 'nodal officer' who is a focal point for all queries and clearances on behalf of the government. The May 2006 R&R policy mandates environmental sustainability and social justice and provides for mandatory consultation and approval from gram sabhas in Fifth Schedule areas. The policy provides that where any person opts for one-time cash assistance in lieu of the mandated employment, the individual may be given the option of converting 50 per cent of this amount into preference shares or secured bonds. Encroachers who can show ten years' continuous possession prior to a notification for land acquisition may, if not challenged, be granted compensation for one standard acre. The government shall also appoint a state level council to review and monitor R&R, with social activists, academics and experts among its members. In order to encourage displaced persons to implement and monitor their own R&R, the government may also constitute a Rehabilitation-cum-Periphery Development Advisory Committee. The concept of ensuring the development and welfare of those on the 'periphery' of projects is an innovation that can be creatively used to promote the idea of wider area development as part of corporate social responsibility in partnership with government and in consonance with the thinking underlying the Samatha Judgment discussed in Chapter 4. This would be facilitated if, say, 5 per cent of the net profit of a corporate were returned to the affected community as a 'royalty' for its social and economic development.

The story of Vedanta Aluminium, a former subsidiary of Sterlite Industries Limited headed by Anil Agarwal and registered on the London Stock Exchange, is similar. This Rs 4000 crore, one million tonne per annum, aluminium refinery in Lanjigarh, Kalahandi district, will mine bauxite in the Niyamgiri Hills in collaboration with the Orissa Mining Corporation (OMC). A MOU was signed in 1997 and land acquisition commenced in 2002 for some 3,625 acres at the two sites for the smelter and mine respectively, in roughly equal proportions.

The forest and environmental clearances were challenged and matters taken to the Supreme Court. The project is moving forward against local opposition and the refinery was planning trial runs at the end of 2006. The 120 extended families displaced from three villages have been handsomely compensated and resettled and employment training of Kondh tribal youth has commenced. The compensation money has been banked and the beneficiaries are being encouraged to utilize only the interest earned. In addition, eighteen peripheral 'focus villages' have been earmarked for social and livelihood development by Vedanta and a further fifty-four 'outreach villages' are being given assistance on demand.

Similar problems of land acquisition, compensation and R&R have come up in respect of other projects in Orissa, Chhattisgarh, Jharkhand and elsewhere. Wiser for the experience gained, Orissa is scouting for government land for potential industrial clusters where water facilities and rail, road, port and airport connectivity will be available or could be conveniently provided. The Dhenkanal–Sambalpur corridor is slated for coal-and-gas based power projects with a possible overall capacity of 25,000 MW. A port-based cluster around Paradip will be a steel and petrochemical complex with related ancillaries or downstream units. Kalahandi-Koraput is seen as an aluminium-bauxite cluster and Sundargarh as a cement complex using fly ash and blast furnace slag. Gopalpur, where Tatas hold lands acquired earlier, could be another port based cluster and possible SEZ.

The area around Bhubaneshwar is planned to become a Knowledge City and IT and ITeS complex. Vedanta is committed to investing one billon dollars in a world-class university with an international faculty, centres of excellence and an Olympic-standard sports complex on 8,000 acres of land given to it along the Puri–Konarak Highway. Four states had bid for the university. The project has been criticized by some as a devious land grab. But the state authorities see a nice fit with their ambitious development goals that will require an expanding pool of specialized talent and trained manpower. Kharagpur IIT would like to build a campus around Bhubaneshwar where the state is endeavouring to attract a new National Institute of Science as well.

The building up of a government land bank will make it possible to attract industry. Following recent controversies, many favour leaving it to individual entrepreneurs to acquire private land when and where necessary through direct negotiations with landholders rather than have the State exercise its power of eminent domain. This is unobjectionable but for the difficulty that arises when significantly large contiguous areas are not available through aggregation or on account of islands of resistance by those holding out unreasonably for more or on ideological or political grounds. But proper, computerized land records and scientific land use planning with environmental safeguards will avoid multiple displacement and ecological harm. Andhra Pradesh and Tamil Nadu have established land banks while Karnataka is offering incentives to those willing to go to backward areas. Older industrial estates are being refurbished. The opening up of land markets without excessive State interference would ensure that land is optimally, and therefore, more productively used as a factor of production. When land was plentiful and populations small inefficient land use was a tragedy but not a catastrophe. This is no more the case. Managing the 'commons' has to take on a new and deeper meaning.

Innovative ideas and corporate social responsibility

Various proposals have been made to reduce the trauma of land acquisition and displacement. The concept of 'public purpose' is being redefined to include strategic purposes vital to the state, infrastructure development and public facilities and projects beneficial to the general public. Many problems have arisen because of faulty land titles and delays or staggered development that entails differential prices and benefits at different times or stages of project implementation. This has been met by raising compensation benefits in response to pressures or by making ex gratia payments and by guaranteeing employment in the project to at least one member of each affected family. This is where training comes in to make simple villagers or tribals employable at higher skill levels. There is the further uncertainty of discontinuity should the chosen job-beneficiary die or retire prematurely. In view of these considerations an argument has been made for converting

land acquired into a shareholding or annuity, thereby making every landholder a stakeholder. But this still leaves out the landless and those not displaced but indirectly affected by a loss of livelihood or income. Anyway, should not all those affected gain something from the expected stream of future benefits from the project? In other words, how can the concept of 'compensation' be expanded and extended over time and place to cover those directly and indirectly affected both in the core area and the 'periphery', not merely as individuals or families but as communities. This idea has been sought to be incorporated in the Government of India's new R&R policy.

It has been suggested that a certain percentage of net profits of any commercial venture, like a hydro or industrial plant, mine or port, be returned for local community development in and around the project site. This too will give the locals a stake in the project and build partnership. Orissa is also proposing that a small cess on power sold outside the state go to an environment management fund to stem local coal-fired thermal pollution. The process of skill development could also be broadened and carried to a higher level in stages so that those displaced are enabled to rise steadily up the employment ladder. A group of economists have made out a case for the state to capture windfall gains for and on behalf of the community. They have suggested compensation in the form of inflation-adjusted monthly pensions combined with savings bonds that can be sold as and when necessary, or investment of some of the compensation amount in mutual funds tied to real estate valuations in the affected area. (Banerjee et al., April 2007). There can be different packages or options from which individual families might choose to suit their circumstances.

Some of these concepts are already being implemented on the ground in different ways by business houses in terms of their corporate social responsibility (CSR) which Gandhi termed trusteeship. Tatas for example have long been ahead of legislation and have sought to uplift communities around its plants, going beyond the welfare of its immediate workforce. Ashok Leyland has similarly set an example in pioneering sound environmental practices. More recently the IT giants Wipro and Infosys have, like many others, devoted time and resources to promote education and health.(Mitra, 2007). The good Corporate Citizen has an increasingly important role to play as India industrializes. Public–private partnerships, not excluding civil society, have to assume wider responsibilities in promoting good governance.

Middle-class lifestyle issues

In maybe twenty-five years from now, current demographic trends will have accelerated to a point where a majority of the population lives in urban India. Agriculture must thrive but cities will grow as more people move off the land. India has 5161 towns and over thirty-five million urban agglomerations as against 638,346 villages (2001). Of these villages, over 91,000 have a population under 200 and another 127,500 are populated by less than 500 persons, many of these in tribal-forest and mountain areas. Villages of this size are scarcely viable and a process of regrouping in larger units, evident in some places, is likely to gain momentum with the growth of agri-business occupations in emerging rural hubs. Industrialization and SEZs will also spawn townships and there are a whole host of district headquarters and capitals of former princely states that have development potential. The Integrated Development of Small and Medium Towns programme formulated in 1979 and the more recent National Urban Renewal Mission are aimed at upgrading infrastructure and housing stock in smaller towns. In all of this, decentralized local government, rural and urban, seems the way forward in order to ensure more focused and participatory governance.

The urban drama will, however, be largely played out in the mega-cities as metropolitan areas grow and new urban agglomerations develop along transport corridors. The metro cities are fast expanding and there are plans for a Greater Bangalore with five new satellite cities in addition, a Greater Hyderabad, and five more Noidas. A large proportion of metro city populations live in noisome slums and shanty towns and there are huge problems of provisioning essential services, many of these aggravated by inadequacies of urban governance and spatial planning. Nevertheless, urban India is a melting pot in which a large and growing middle class is being cooked and seasoned. According to a news report, the management consultancy firm McKinsey sees the Indian middle class (defined as households with an annual disposable income between Rs 4,380 and Rs 22,000) growing from fifty million at present to 580 million by 2025, given the projected high rates of economic growth. This would make India the fifth largest consumer market, from twelfth place now, overtaking Germany. (*Indian Express*, 5 May 2007)

Even assuming this happens, what kind of India will that be? For one, it should be one India and not markedly two as at present, Bharat and India. It is unlikely to be an Arcadian India of pastoral tranquillity that Gandhi envisaged. The latest data on expenditure and employment presented by the National Sample Survey Organization suggests that expenditure on food has declined since 1972–3 and that consumption is diversifying into white goods and other consumables and services whether for reasons of better living or for status. A great new rural market is opening up.

This is going to throw up issues of lifestyles, the environment, sustainability and limits to growth. Climate change will dictate many adjustments. Disparities may well widen between the rich and poor. But with abject poverty eliminated, an important safety valve will be found in the process of levelling up and upward mobility. However, this could be countered by widening regional disparities that would put a strain on Indian federalism and political tolerance. The next thirty to forty years will witness the full flowering of India's diversity, a good part of which still lies disempowered and submerged. The transition, as the old order yields place to new, will expose many insecurities as socially and economically upwardly mobile cohorts jostle and clamour for a place in the sun. The negotiation and management of this complex and dynamic process will be a huge challenge. We must be prepared to understand and ride the suppressed energy and creativity underlying this trend rather than feel threatened by it and get locked in confrontation.

The new debate: past versus future

There is a furious debate raging across India. The headlines talk of and variously juxtapose SEZ, land, infrastructure, farming, modernization, food security, dams, compensation, rural–urban, public–private, 'jobs' versus 'employment' (a distinction little understood), agriculture versus industry, labour versus capital, mother tongue versus English. Translated, the dialogue is essentially about tradition versus modernity and the past versus the future. What the debate is not about, as mistakenly projected, is 'us' versus 'them'. We are all in this together. And again, posing the question as this *versus* that is to proclaim a false dichotomy. The choice is not this *or* that but this *and* that, in somewhat different proportions.

Many tend to hug the country's shameful poverty in the strange belief that it exemplifies simplicity and virtue. At another level, people are afraid of change. Every established status quo gathers around it a body of vested interests that fears anything different. This is what the Luddites believed at the commencement of the Industrial Revolution in England. Neo-Ludditism confronts India today. We must of course also heed Goldsmith's lament: 'Ill fares the land to hastening ills a prey; where wealth accumulates and men decay'. The human and social decay we have permitted over the years must be corrected. But the prospects are grim if we wilfully disregard this other truth that India will be undermined and its prospects dimmed if it does not accumulate wealth to sustain its burgeoning numbers. We must promote equitable growth or let men decay. Landed farmers commit suicide, children remain unschooled, beggars abound and millions go to bed hungry.

Meanwhile, to decry industry, urbanization and private enterprise as pandemics, corporate India as a vector of some dread disease and globalization as evil—though India has always been a globalized society except under colonial rule—is to betray a fevered imagination. Some might argue that colonialism itself integrated local economies into the global economy, though on unequal terms. This was only partly true as the nexus was utterly one-sided. Today, it is the balance that matters.

{7}

Community and Culture: Towards Fraternity

India's incredible diversity embraces a multiplicity of languages, faiths, communities, regions and cultures, each distinctive yet subtly blending one into the other in an intricate multicultural unity. This mosaic is made up of several traditions, great and small, that have competed for space and attention over the ages but have also learnt to live and come together despite periods of strain and conflict. This conclusion may be challenged. Nevertheless, there has been no apocalyptic clash of civilizations; rather a sufficient spirit of tolerance and accommodation to mend the rifts and antagonisms that surfaced from time to time. Transient insecurities of communities as might be expected on this count have seldom led to politically-driven migrations to other lands, as from Europe and West Asia. Instead, India has been a haven for many peoples and faiths that have found refuge on its shores.

Language makes community, for communication builds and binds people together. Words convey not merely sounds but collective images and ideas etched in memory. Script and writing provide wider locomotion to words and language over space and time and represent the historical signature of a people. No surprise then that language has preceded nation and is a prized marker of identity and being that arouses deep emotion.

States and empires have long existed as expressions of territorial power rather than as exclusive preserves of distinct communities and peoples. The nation state was late in coming and Europe witnessed a reorganization of states after the Treaty of Westphalia in 1648 that saw an end to wars of religion. The process of new state formation thereafter by and large followed a pattern of linguistic singularity, barring exceptions like Switzerland and Belgium, though fringe populations remained along borders. It took time for the Balkans to be reorganized, most recently after the break up of Yugoslavia. Most states were virtually inhabited by members of a single faith, though even here denominational rivalries contained seeds of conflict as between Catholic and Protestant in Ireland or Flemish and Walloon in Belgium and, more recently, French Catholic Quebecois and English-speaking Protestants in Canada.

Linguistic pluralism

In India, four great speech-families, the Indo-Aryan, Dravidian, Austric-Mon Khmer and Sino-Tibetan, have interacted over 3000 years. Panini and Tolkapiyam wrote their famous grammars in 6 BC and between 2 BC and AD 2 in Sanskrit and Tamil respectively, and Sanskrit emerged as a pan-Indian medium of communication. In Nehru's view, it was 'not only the vehicle of the highest thought and some of the finest literature, but it became the uniting bond for India, even though there were political divisions'. Pali, used for Buddhist canonical literature, and the more popular Prakrits gave way to regional tongues that were influenced by Sanskrit and local dialects and grew into major languages with a rich literature of their own. Though each of these dozen languages developed their own scripts, some closely related or influenced by Devnagari, they uniquely had a common phonetic alphabet. In addition, there flourished innumerable dialects and tribal and other lesser languages. That there should be so many major languages need occasion little surprise for Europe west of Russia, a territory of somewhat similar size and population, is home to some twenty nations with as many languages.

Many observers over the centuries have testified to India's linguistic pluralism. It was, however, left to the seventeenth century Orientalists to discover, explore and codify the true range and nature of this Babel. The missionary William Carey perhaps undertook the first linguistic survey of India in 1816. Interestingly, he noted 'Hindee' as one among many Hindi dialects such as Dogri, Bikaneri, Jaipuri, Udaipuri, Marwari, Haruti, Malwa, Braj, Bundelkhandi, Awadhi, Magadhi and Maithili, to which others would add Chhattisgarhi, Bhojpuri and so on. Islamic rule had brought in Persian, Arabic and Turkish and the interaction with the local 'Hindi' dialects produced a less Persianized Dakkhani in the South and, gradually, Urdu, a camp language, born from the intermingling of Persian and Hindi, and Hindustani, with a further admixture of Khari Boli, a literary high Hindi. The Mughals made Persian the court language; but Hindustani, written in both Devnagari and Persian scripts, became the lingua franca.

Terrain and history

George Abraham Grierson was officially commissioned to do a more thoroughgoing Linguistic Survey of India, which he completed in twenty-nine years and published in 1927. Though this excluded Madras Presidency and the states of Hyderabad and Mysore, it identified 179 languages and 544 dialects, 723 in all. The 1961 Census was the next landmark. This listed 1,652 languages spoken at home and among kinship groups, including 103 foreign and 530 unclassified languages. This number may be compared with the latest linguistic survey done by the Anthropological Survey of India, under the People of India project (Volume IX, 1993), which enumerates 325 home and kin-group languages. Presumably some dialects are dying or are being absorbed into more dynamic and empowering languages. More will be known with the next major linguistic survey of India that is now being undertaken as a ten-year project under the auspices of the Central Institute of Indian Languages in Mysore.

Suniti Kumar Chatterji, the noted linguist, has it that the Indo-Aryan languages of North India started taking shape after AD 1000 and the Hindi we know today scarcely existed prior to 1850 by when the Dravidian languages of the South were well formed, Tamil first, then Telugu and Kannada and, finally, Malayalam. Incidentally, it is all too often forgotten that Hindi is a Persian word that was used to describe the people of Hind or Hindustan, from which the British coined the further derivative, Hindu, to describe followers of the large residual non-Christian, Islamic and Buddhist faiths with which they lacked familiarity.

Macaulay's famous Minute of 1835 was to change the course of India's linguistic fortunes. He wished Indians to be educated and given an appropriate medium or vehicle for their educational advancement. He told protagonists of Sanskrit and Arabic/Persian that there could be no alternative to English. He said he had read translations of the most celebrated Sanskrit and Arabic works and conversed with men distinguished by their proficiency in Eastern tongues. And then, perhaps more exuberantly than accurately,

> I am quite ready to take Oriental learning at the valuation of the Orientalists themselves. I have never found one among them who would deny that a single shelf of a good European library was worth the whole native literature of India and Arabia.

Max Mueller and Romain Rolland were later to speak with reverence and awe of India's contribution to the world of literature and thought.

However, Hindustani (in two scripts) replaced Persian in 1837 as the official language of British administration in India, with the appearance that same year of the Delhi Gazette, the city's first English-language newspaper. The English branch of the Delhi College found its enrolment soar with the new-found opportunities for those with knowledge of English. (Pernau, 2006) It was not long before English took over from Hindustani with the founding of the three Presidency Colleges and the spread of English education. Incidentally, the dalit problem also surfaced during the same period with the drive for education as upper-caste teachers excluded dalit children from schools, compelling a policy of separate dalit schools in various parts of the country. (Prasad, 2006)

The 1857 uprising had awakened a sense of nationalism in the country but this insidiously sowed the seeds of what was to deepen into a communal rift. A Hindu reform and Hindi movement in the latter part of the century saw the founding of the Arya Samaj, a cow protection agitation in eastern Uttar Pradesh, and the revival of Hindu festivals by Tilak. The Nagari Pracharini Sabha was established in 1893 to propagate Hindi in the Devnagari script and seven years later the United Provinces administration sanctioned its use alongside Urdu in all provincial offices and courts. However, Hindustani remained a bridge as three influential north Indian Hindu communities, the

Kayasthas, Khatris and Kashmiri Pandits, were steadfast in their loyalty to Persian and Urdu. As late as the Census of 1931, both Hindi and Urdu were classified as Hindustani. On the other hand, Sir Syed Ahmad Khan established the Mohammadan Anglo-Oriental College, the precursor to the Aligarh Muslim University, to encourage Muslim youth to take to modern education in English and be able to compete with the best.

The Indian National Congress was founded in 1885 and conducted its proceedings in English. Having converted the Congress into a mass movement, Gandhi lamented, 'Our love for the English language in preference to even our own mother tongue has caused a deep chasm between the politically minded classes and the masses'. The Congress in 1920 mooted the goal of linguistic states and reorganized its provincial units on this basis. The Mahatma favoured Hindustani written in both scripts and had launched the Dakshina Bharat Hindi Prachar Sabha in Wardha with branches in Madras in 1918, Trivandrum in 1922 and Hyderabad in 1936.

The framing of the Constitution witnessed a great deal of heartburning over language. The tussle was between Hindi and a two-script Hindustani but the Congress Parliamentary Party finally adopted the former by a single vote. That sealed the issue. The matter of Devnagari versus international numerals, which are of Indian origin, was, however, settled in favour of the latter. The next issue to be confronted related to the official language. Hindi/Hindustani, the mother tongue of a little under 40 per cent of the population, was admittedly the most widely understood language in the country. But an increasingly Sanskritized Hindi in the Devnagari script had displaced Hindustani. The question now was whether it should displace English for official purposes, and when. Hindi zealots did not help the cause by urging undue haste and casting aspersions on those pleading against forced measures. South Indian members and those from Bengal feared that too sudden a transition could place non-Hindi speakers at a disadvantage and would breed resentment. Two factors rankled, especially in the South. Hindi 'imperialism' or 'chauvinism' was associated with fears of both north Indian (Aryan) as well as Hindu upper-caste dominance. Any brute majoritarianism was unacceptable. Fortunately, saner counsels prevailed and the compromise finally reached was that English would continue as an associate official language for fifteen years until 1965, and that the regional languages would enjoy a similar status in the states. Further, English would remain the language of the superior courts and legislative transactions would also be in English.

Two further assurances provided for primary schooling in the mother tongue and the appointment of a Commissioner for Linguistic Minorities to ensure implementation of requisite safeguards. Further, Article 351 enjoined that Hindi should serve 'as a medium of expression for all the elements of the composite culture of India', and that this be accomplished by its enrichment by assimilating the forms, styles and expressions of Hindustani and other Indian languages, particularly Sanskrit.

Linguistic Reorganization of States

With the promulgation of the Constitution, there were demands for immediate implementation of the long-standing Congress commitment to linguistic states. However, even by the 1940s Nehru had begun to worry about linguistic rivalries that could tear the country apart and spoke of other considerations such as economic viability, administrative efficiency and, above all, national unity that must be kept in mind. The trauma of Partition, the divisive tendencies it fostered and the rise of communal tendencies weighed heavily with him and he began to see merit in composite states and cosmopolitan cities like Bombay and Madras.

Three months into the Constituent Assembly, Nehru spoke his mind (King, 1997):

> There are numerous urgent demands in the economic and other spheres . . . First things must come first and the first thing is the security and stability of India. Before we can undertake any major schemes we must have a strong state and smoothly running governmental machinery . . . If India is enfeebled, all the component elements grow weak . . . It is necessary to have a reconstitution of the provinces, or some of them. But if we tackle this problem in a large way at

> present, there is grave danger of our energies being diverted from some of the more urgent tasks . . .

In other words, Nehru did not see linguistic reorganization as urgent or unifying but as debilitating and divisive. He conceded justification for Andhra but baulked at the creation of Maharashtra and Karnataka 'as any marked change will powerfully affect the structure and economy of the provinces concerned'. The official Dar Commission (1948) and JVP (Jawaharlal Nehru, Vallabhbhai Patel, Pattabhi Sitaramiah) Committee of the Congress Party (1949) also counselled caution. However, events did not wait. Potti Sriramulu died in December 1952, fasting for Andhra, forcing the government's hand. Andhra was conceded and a States Reorganization Commission (SRC) was announced in December 1953.

Prior to Independence the British had carved out administrative units on the basis of conquest with little consideration for language, community or culture. The only exception occurred in 1936 when Orissa was carved out of Bihar and Sind from Bombay Presidency. The nearly 600 princely states were a mixed lot, many unilingual but some, like Hyderabad and J&K, polyglot. Their integration and merger after Independence altered the map of India. Many were absorbed in neighbouring (linguistic) provinces; others were grouped together. The SRC transformed the political geography of India, consolidating a welter of territories into somewhat homogeneous units. Nehru lamented the vivisection of the composite state of Hyderabad, which he held as a model of composite India. Two exceptions stood out as sore thumbs and were to cause bloodshed: Bombay, which included Maharashtra and Gujarat, and Punjab, where a Punjabi Suba was not conceded.

These were errors of judgement. The arguments were unconvincing. Bombay city, a cosmopolitan metropolis and financial capital of India, was claimed by both sides while in Punjab there was a linguistic–communal divide, with a raging battle between Gurmukhi and Devnagari for writing Punjabi fought out through the medium of Urdu!

In the event, both demands had to be conceded within a few years. Gujarat and Maharashtra were separated after avoidable strife. In Punjab, the Akalis were demanding not a Sikh-majority state but a linguistic Punjabi Suba that would have included what is now Haryana and part of Rajasthan (Ganganagar) where Punjabi was and is popularly spoken. In the result, Hindu resistance to Punjabi Suba on the issue of script ultimately resulted in the formation of a Sikh-majority Punjab state (Dhillon, 2006).

The background to this denouement goes back many years and is enshrined in Sikh history. The founding of the faith by Guru Nanak in the fifteenth century broke away from the ritualism and clash of Brahmanical Hinduism and Islam to find salvation in a monotheism influenced by both Bhakti and Sufism, preaching universal brotherhood. Persecution led to revolutionary change and the formation of the Khalsa in 1699 under the tenth Guru, Govind Singh. The tangled history of Punjab need not detain us here but in 1920 the Shiromani Akali Dal was formed to regain control over the Sikh gurudwaras from Hindu mahants. Thereafter, with every step towards Independence Sikh anxieties mounted as they pondered their place in the emerging situation amid sharpening Hindu–Muslim rivalries that spilled over into the issues of language and script. The Akalis mooted a separate Sikh state should India be divided but this proved a non-starter. As Partition approached, Nehru said in 1946 that he could envisage arrangements in northwest India where the Sikhs too might enjoy 'the glow of freedom'.

The wave of migrations in the wake of Partition resulted in enhancing Sikh numbers in East Punjab and the consolidation of the five Sikh principalities of Patiala, Kapurthala, Jind, Faridkot and Malerkotla in the Patiala and East Punjab States Union (PEPSU). With a linguistic reorganization of states in the offing, it seemed the time for Punjabi Suba had come. Therefore its denial by the SRC was a bitter blow, a seeming betrayal. (SRC Report, 1955) While Hindus spoke Punjabi, their women in particular used Devnagari to read the scriptures. The SRC found the Hindi spoken very akin to Punjabi and concluded that 'the problem of language in the Punjab is, therefore, primarily one of scripts; and in this battle of scripts, sentiment is arrayed against sentiment.' In sum

> The creation of a Punjabi speaking state would offer no solution to the language problem; the present arrangements

> for the recognition of both Punjabi and Hindi could not be done away with, and the controversies would not in all probability come to an end, and while no major problem would be solved, both languages might suffer.

The Commission's recommendation favouring a Maha Punjab, including Himachal, as a compromise formula, was galling.

> From the point of view of the Sikhs themselves, the solution which we have proposed offers the advantage that the precarious or uncertain political majority which they seek will be exchanged for the real and substantial rights which a sizeable and vigorous minority, with a population ratio nearly one-third, is bound to have in the united Punjab in the whole of which they have a share.

Nobody was pleased. The Himachalis were not particularly happy while the Haryanvis began to speak of economic discrimination and neglect of their region. The Sikhs saw no glow of freedom in an arrangement that they believed was designed to put them down. Trouble was in store.

It was Indira Gandhi who finally decided to concede Punjabi Suba, but not without a bitter pill. Chandigarh was carved out as a joint capital of the successor states of Punjab and Haryana within a Union Territory and would only be given to Punjab in exchange for Abohar and Fazilka, which would go to Haryana (with a corridor to provide access). The Bhakra-Beas Management Board was also placed under Central control. The entire issue was poorly handled and politicized on all sides in a manner that was to lead to the sponsored rise of Bhindranwale, Operation Blue Star and Indira Gandhi's assassination.

Thereafter no linguistic states as such have been created. The reorganization of the Northeast established ethnically oriented states with a dominant language, such as Nagaland and Mizoram, and Meghalaya to a lesser extent. Within the region, autonomous and regional councils have been formed, some with a linguistic resonance, and a Bodo homeland and Darjeeling Gorkha Hills Council area has been established. The struggle for linguistic identity has permeated downwards, with apex councils formed in non-territorial jurisdictions for the Rabhas, Tiwas, Mishings and some others in Assam, and for the people of Leh (Ladakhis) and Kargil (Baltis) in Jammu and Kashmir. Most significant of all, of course, has been Assam's movement against cultural and political marginalization by an influx of Bangla migrants.

Anti-Hindi agitation

Meanwhile, even as these events were unfolding, the South was slowly coming to a boil over the approaching fifteen-year deadline before Hindi replaced English as the sole official language. The Official Language Act of 1963 provided that English 'may' continue to be used indefinitely with Hindi as an official language beyond 1965. The importance of English had been realized and Nehru emphasized its importance for mastery of science and technology and for keeping abreast of modern thought. English was by volition largely included in the three-language formula laid out for schools. This mandated instruction in the mother tongue, Hindi (or any other vernacular in non-Hindi areas) and a third language, which could be a foreign language. This meant that Hindi was mandatory in the South but in non-Hindi areas students could offer Sanskrit or some other language and not necessarily a South Indian vernacular. Southerners saw the Sanskrit option for the third language in northern schools as a deviant response.

The protagonists of Hindi began to worry. Ram Manohar Lohia, the fiery socialist, launched his *Angrezi hatao* (scrap English) movement for fear that English, once entrenched, would never allow Hindi to take its due place. The South and Bengal felt threatened by what they saw as Hindi illiberalism and feared a competitive disadvantage as well as Hindi dominance if English was relegated. There was also apprehension that Hindu revivalism lurked within the Hindi Trojan horse. The strident cow-protection movement lent grist to these mills. The constitutionality of the total ban on cow slaughter imposed by Uttar Pradesh, Bihar and Madhya Pradesh was challenged. The Supreme Court ruled that only milch and draught animals merited protection and noted that protection of useless animals would cost the country Rs 18–19 per head of cattle per annum as against the total national per capita expenditure on education by all public authorities in 1955–6 of just Rs 4.9. (Ram, 1968)

The DMK took a lead in the anti-Hindi movement. The party registered gains in 1962 on a social development and anti-Hindi platform with a further pitch for an independent Dravida Nadu. This set off alarm bells and the Centre hurriedly enacted the Sixteenth Amendment to the Constitution on 3 October requiring candidates to any legislature to take an oath of allegiance to the sovereignty and integrity of India. The DMK responded a month later by amending its party constitution to delete the reference to Dravida Nadu. This cooled the hardliners but the anti-Hindi agitation mounted and anti-Hindi riots broke out in Tamil Nadu on 26 January 1965 when Hindi was to replace English as the official language of the Union. This was sparked by the self-immolation of a DMK protestor. C. Subramaniam resigned from the Union Cabinet. Indira Gandhi rushed to Madras to pacify the protestors and the prime minister, Lal Bahadur Shastri announced that English would remain an associate official language for as long as necessary, the states would be free to determine their own official languages and English would continue to be used for Union Public Service examinations. This defused the crisis. But, leaving nothing to chance, the DMK's landslide electoral victory in 1967 saw the putting in place of a Central Unlawful Activities (Prevention) Act against any kind of secessionist activity. This let C.N. Annadurai, the DMK leader, off the hook as he had been uncomfortable with the secessionist plank.

Foreign observers had long wondered how a polyglot India would survive as it was never a real state ever before, having been largely glued together by the Raj. Selig Harrison, an American journalist very well disposed towards India, wrote warningly after his tenure in this country of India's approaching 'dangerous decades'. Another correspondent, Bernard Nossiter, was even more sceptical. But then many, including Churchill, had written off the very idea of India only to be proved completely wrong.

Robert King, the Canadian scholar cited earlier, gives credit to Nehru for his policy of 'benign neglect' of the Hindi question. Certainly India did not splinter like Pakistan, which discovered that Bangla nationalism trumped Islamic nationalism in the creation of Bangladesh. Nor did the government display the kind of linguistic chauvinism witnessed in Sri Lanka where the Tamils were driven to the wall. Canada has had less of a problem than India by far but has handled French Quebecois concerns with maturity and aplomb.

Language policy

India's policy of encouraging primary schooling in the vernacular and softening strident Hindi voices must be commended as also its attempt to nurture lesser linguistic traditions and tribal dialects as important cultural expressions that should not be lost even while promoting language as a vehicle of commerce. How well these policies have been implemented may be questioned but the effort was made. All India Radio too has been used to promote local languages and cultures with some stations in the Northeast uniquely broadcasting cultural programmes in five, ten or more languages, something that would be hard to match anywhere in the world. The Sahitya Akademi and its state counterparts and translation bureaux and the assistance given to folk and regional theatre have played a part in assuaging linguistic and cultural pride. Sahitya sabhas (literary associations) abound in the Northeast and have been focal points for assertion of linguistic and cultural identity. Each has provided a safety valve.

Notwithstanding all this, the government's language policy, or lack of it, can be strongly critiqued. The policy of inscribing languages in the Eighth Schedule has been needlessly restrictive. The only constitutional requirement or benefit from such scheduling is that 'official' Hindi is encouraged to borrow from scheduled languages—as if these things happen by anybody's leave—and that official language committees should draw membership from speakers of scheduled languages. The real importance is psychological, that of vesting a scheduled language with the 'status' to look Hindi or any of the other 'major' languages in the eye. In the play of identity politics, a huge and continuing issue in India, as dormant diversities 'emerge' with empowerment and seek a place in the sun, grant of such 'status' is an effective way of lowering tensions. Once accommodated, the 'cause' tends to lose intensity even if it does not vanish. Yet it took up to

1967 to include Sindhi in the Schedule and it was not until 1992, and some intervening trauma, that Manipuri, Nepali and Konkani were scheduled. Bodo, Dogri, Santhali and Maithili were added still later, to bring the total number of scheduled languages up to twenty-two.

More important of course is the fact that nation building requires a lingua franca. Here was India, an ancient civilization, being born anew as a nation. In what language should it speak to itself? English was adopted as the 'link language' but amazingly two of the most powerful nation builders of the earlier post-Independence period were handicapped by language. Maulana Azad could not speak to audiences that did not know Hindustani while Kamaraj, the kingmaker so-called, needed an interpreter to address anybody who did not know Tamil. Parliament and state legislatures and other major auditoria and conference halls even today lack the human resources and technical facilities to provide simultaneous interpretation so that all Indians can converse together. Conferences are organized on the basis of who understands what language. Participation is necessarily selective. There are inadequate facilities or employment avenues for translators.

The approach to propagating the 'official language' has been discouraging in the extreme. There was (and is) little effort to produce bilingual lexicons, especially for Hindi, or a basic Hindi vocabulary to promote 'learn Hindi in 10 days'. There has been no attempt to standardize scripts in order to be able to use the coincidence of a common alphabet to promote inter-lingual cross fertilization, and only a limited effort to produce attractive books for the young in Hindi (this task having been taken up in the 1960s and 1970s by the Soviet and Chinese governments, both of whom produced some wonderfully illustrated books at throwaway prices and distributed them through footpath sellers in Delhi to be picked up by enthralled children).

Worse, it was left to All India Radio, the country's most powerful language disseminator, under the then Information and Broadcasting Minister B.V. Keskar, to promote a stilted, Sanskritized Hindi that few could comprehend. Instead of making the language inclusive (as Article 351 and commonsense enjoined), it was made highly exclusive. Even as late as during 1966–8, Indira Gandhi's monthly national broadcasts were prepared in Hindustani, then 'translated' into Hindi to be spoken by a bewildered Prime Minister who had to negotiate small linguistic bargains with Hindi Pooh-Bahs to make sure she understood what she was saying. In the name of 'socialism', only a single manufacturer, the public sector Hindustan Teleprinters Limited (HTL), was licensed to produce these machines for national print transmission and communication. HTL commenced production with English keyboards and only later went on to manufacture Devnagari teleprinters. The result was that newspapers, government offices, business houses and others had to transliterate their Hindi/ Marathi, Bengali, Kannada, and other vernacular copy into English for inter-office transmission cross-country, there to be unscrambled into the relevant language again. The moral: three or four carefully devised standard keyboards (with a few additional keys for special sounds and symbols) and lexicons made available at subsidized prices, translation bureaux and language learning and interpretation facilities would probably have done more for India's linguistic integration after Macaulay's Minute than all the bombast, fussy notings and wasteful expenditure that the country has had to bear in the name of official language. If India taught simple Hindi in the manner French is taught by Alliance Francais or German by the Max Mueller Bhavan there would be many takers for learning Hindi across the country. Sadly, there is nothing as well done for convenient Hindi-learning even sixty years after Independence even though the Central Hindi Directorate has been running correspondence courses for non-Hindi learners since 1968.

The clever answer could be, 'So What? India managed'. It did. But it might and should have managed better. Indonesia, with multiple languages and dialects and 6,000 islands, put together Bhasha Indonesia thanks to Sukarno who smartly decided to promote the national language through the bazaar in preference to the secretariat. Bollywood has done more to bind India together linguistically through its movies and lyrics than the Indian government and Parliament combined. Its formula has been reliance on an inclusive and expressive pan-Indian Hindustani. Madras, the heart of Tamilness, 'produces' a number of Hindi movies as there are state-of-the-art processing laboratories in that city that attract Bombay producers there for post-production finishing. Money speaks and neatly distinguishes commerce from culture. Not for nothing is the denominational value of all Indian currency notes printed in fifteen Indian languages. Old barriers are gradually falling. Jayalalithaa, the AIADMK leader, went campaigning during the May 2007 Uttar Pradesh elections and spoke in Hindi.

Turning away from Urdu was a tragedy for a language born to and in India of 'Hindi' and Persian parentage. It is in every sense an Indian tongue, spoken by Hindus, Muslims, Sikhs, Jains and others alike, and not a 'Muslim' language per se as it was perceived to be through communally-tinted lenses. The language has declined. Osmania University in Hyderabad gave it up as a medium of instruction but a by-product of the Urdu Committee the government set up under Inder Kumar Gujral was the establishment of the Maulana Azad University that uses Urdu as a medium. Urdu is recognized as a second official language in Uttar Pradesh and Delhi and a number of Urdu newspapers are still published in various parts of the country and especially in Jammu and Kashmir, where Urdu is an official language. (Urdu Committee Report, 1975)

English has grown over the years and opposition to it has diminished with its growing utility as an international language and a medium for education, science and business. English (or Hinglish) is widely spoken and more and more ordinary people wish to give their children an education in that language so as to enhance their future prospects.

With increasing literacy, knowledge of all Indian languages is fast growing as evidenced by school enrolments and by rising newspaper circulations. Union Public Service Commission statistics too show that while a majority of short-listed candidates for the all-India services write their papers and take the interview in English, the number of those opting for the vernacular is steadily rising—from 151 candidates in 1998 to 280 (out of 1,162 interviewed) in 2004. In the 2006 civil service examinations, of the top twenty candidates selected, two wrote their papers in Hindi. A trend analysis of the results indicate that those writing the all-India service examinations, and more especially those being selected, are increasingly coming from smaller towns rather than the metros, and from lowlier backgrounds and not just from elite homes.

The well-known historian, Ramachandra Guha believes that the country has been successful in handling the prickly language question, which has more or less been laid to rest. Many will concur. Certainly, language issues continue to crop up from time to time, but India will not break on the language question. Indeed, it is the linguistically homogeneous societies of the West that are facing language problems with the growth of multiculturalism. The United States has left the states to grapple with language policies. Spanish is now taught in some states while various Asian tongues are increasingly spoken elsewhere in the country. The response to this trend has been a movement to enforce 'English only' or 'Official English' policies in certain other states. (Chandhoke, 2007)

Religious diversities

Language, however, is only one aspect of India's diversity. There is a defining characteristic of the plurality of India that is little understood though it lies at the very heart of the nation-building project. It is not a melting pot like America in which different minerals emerge from the cauldron as one metal. Although predominantly of one kind, India is a garden in which even the dominant species consists of many distinctive varieties, interspersed with little tinges and broader splashes of colour; many subtle, others brilliant. The garden had in some ways a formal design, with everything in its own particular place. But no longer; it remains with all its hues, but the design has begun to show bewildering change.

Christianity was brought to the Malabar Coast in AD 52 by St Thomas, the Apostle of Christ who founded what remains one of the very oldest living churches anywhere in the world. Islam also came early, in the lifetime of the Prophet, along with Arab traders who plied the west coast, and was well established well before the Islamic conquest or the rise of Islamic political power in India. Jews and Parsees likewise found hospitality on these shores centuries ago and became respected and responsible members of society, rising to positions of great honour and trust.

Although conquerors came and empires rose and fell, the intruders stayed and became part of the people, adding something to the country or community. Life at the bottom continued much as before with people of all faiths sharing the same joys and sorrows. That is, until the British, who came from afar not to settle but to rule and exploit a vast market and its resources. The rise of nationalism and struggle for independence saw the beginnings of linguistic and communal discords, which the British did not a little to encourage, in order to divide and rule. But until 1857, the communities lived together despite occasional strains and tensions. Indeed, at the Great Uprising in 1857, Hindus and Muslims alike turned to Bahadur Shah Zafar, the last Mughal, as their sovereign among moving scenes of communal amity. (Dalrymple, 2007)

The suppression of the Great Rebellion was followed by repression, the brunt of which fell on the Muslims. Emperor Bahadur Shah, a man of literary pursuits and without any real power, was led away in chains to Rangoon. The Union Jack was hoisted over the Red Fort and other hallmarks of courtly Delhi were levelled. The court language, Persian, had already given way to Hidustani in 1837. Muslims suffered a loss of prestige, patronage and self-esteem, accentuated by the new education policy that gave primacy to English and modern learning. The Hindus quickly adapted to these changes and the opportunities they presented while the Muslims sullenly turned inward until the advent of Sir Syed Ahmad Khan.

Lord Mayo, the Viceroy, asked whether Indian Musalmans were bound by faith 'to rebel against the Queen'. The query evoked a response by a Bengal civil servant, William Hunter, who in his book of 1871, *The Indian Mussalman*, analyzed the Muslim condition taking as its starting point the role of the puritanical Wahabi sect that had grown from the 1820s under the inspiration of Sayyid Ahmad, a soldier turned preacher, a messianic figure whose influence was soon to be felt. His followers hailed him as an imam and he spoke of a crusade against the infidels who now ruled India that had become *dar-ul-harb* (Abode of War). Traditional sources of wealth and employment such as military commands, revenue collection and judicial and political positions were now largely barred to them. Muslim higher education was undermined by the new educational and language policy and Friday ceased to be an official holiday. The insularity caused by Muslim withdrawal symptoms made the community non-competitive even as Hindus marched ahead.

Growing communal divide

Resentments grew, waiting to be fanned. With modern education, the periodization of history mistakenly portrayed different epochs under communal labels. Thus, Ancient, Medieval and Modern India were designated as Hindu, Muslim and British periods respectively. The focus on dynastic history and the achievements, foibles or tyranny of rulers rather than on social history and the lives of the common people compounded the distortion. This sowed the seeds of pride and prejudice as between rulers and subject peoples. Real or assumed wrongs were thereby subconsciously laid at the door of communities rather than individual despots.

The Congress was born in 1885 and with talk of representative government in the air the demand for separate Muslim electorates was conceded in 1909. The earlier partition of Bengal in 1905 was seen as a communal separation and led to protests culminating in its annulment some years later. Certain Hindu reform movements were not without a revivalist slant, setting in motion a chain of interactive anxieties and responses that were exploited by the Government to entrench its own power. (Kanpur Riots Committee, 1933). Lord Elphinstone, the Governor of Bombay, advocated the Roman policy of 'divide et impera', divide and rule, in a minute dated 14 May 1858. This was not the first or last time such advice was offered. The Directors of the East India Company were until 1793 reluctant to permit Christian evangelization in India lest it unite the native communities and recoil on the Raj. The same view was heard in 1813 in evidence before the House of Commons. Following the Afghan War of 1843, Lord Ellenborough, the Governor-General, informed the Queen that the sandalwood gates of the famous Somnath Temple, allegedly carried away centuries earlier by Mahmud Ghazni, had been brought back to India and it was his intention to carry it in triumphal procession to Somnath for reinstallation. Writing separately to the Duke of Wellington, he opined, 'it seems to me most unwise, when we are sure of the hostility of one-tenth, not to secure the enthusiastic support of the nine-tenths which are faithful.' India historians regard the entire story as a concoction as the gates brought back by the British were left unnoticed in the Agra Fort.

However, the two major communities appeared to be on collision course. The 1916 Lucknow Pact brought about short-lived unity with the Congress conceding separate electorates. The rift soon widened and there were communal riots in Arrah and Saharanpur districts in 1917 and 1918, followed by the Moplah rebellion in Malabar in 1921, which assumed communal overtones with the forcible conversion of some Hindus. This was the signal for an intensification of the *shuddhi* and *tanzim* movements under Swami Shraddhanand and the Tablighis. The cow-protection movement initiated in Punjab led to extensive riots in Bihar and the United Provinces in 1893. Subsequently, demands for cow protection would be matched by protests against the playing of music before mosques. The decade 1921–31 witnessed a rash of riots all over North and East India.

The great Kanpur riots in March 1931 sent alarm bells ringing. The Congress set up an inquiry committee but the government banned its report. It had focussed on the underlying factors rather than just the killings and tore aside the veil behind which communal influences had been at work. The chairperson of the committee observed, that the Kanpur riots were the result of 'germs fostered in the body politic of India for some generations'after 1857. The report exposed the perverted view of Indian history as told by colonial authors in the nineteenth and early twentieth centuries and subsequently given currency by partisan Indian historians.

Communalism is of more recent, post-1857 origin and not an age-old and persistent malaise. On the contrary there is much historical evidence to show that Hindus and Muslims lived together for centuries as good neighbours and evolved a rich common culture despite wars and the clash of kings. Indeed, the commonly perceived notion that Islam spread in India by the sword after the Muslim invasion in AD 1000 is very misleading. Islam was well established in large parts of the Deccan and East India well before any Muslim invasion of those regions in the thirteenth century and later. Indeed, it is noteworthy that the largest concentration of Muslim communities in India is to be found in states like Kerala and Assam that were never brought under Muslim dominion and not in northern India which faced Muslim invasions from the eleventh century on. According to the Kanpur Riots Committee, by AD 1000 Buddhism in India was struggling to retain its supremacy as a reformist movement against the tide of an orthodox Brahmanical revival that excluded a vast section of the Hindu underclass.

> The Kshatriyas and other higher castes also cooperated (in stamping out Buddhism) because the upheaval in the lower castes, which Buddhism had greatly helped, was antagonistic to their interests and undermined their social monopoly and influence. This combination of the most organised and resourceful sections of society wiped Buddhism out of India and, side by side, gradually crushed the rebellion against the established order which Buddhism had inaugurated.
>
> . . . This mostly accounts for the success which Islam seems to have met on its arrival in India. It was not spread by the sword of the invader but by indigenous caste tyranny.
>
> The tragic immobility of the Hindu system and its failure to respond to the call of its own reformers continued to increase the numbers of converts to Islam. Islam satisfied a crying need of the social system which Hinduism continued to neglect and whose satisfaction was essential in the wider interests of nationalism and humanity.

Conversion, the Committee concluded, was a deliverance for leather workers, weavers and other socially-discriminated elements in society. The Report of the Kanpur Riots Enquiry Committee is a remarkable document and its recommendations, alas, continue to have a contemporary ring.

The communal problem came to a boil over Partition. The savage riots and mass migrations were a monumental tragedy that solved little. Having won Pakistan on the basis of the two-nation theory, that country lost its eastern wing to Bangla nationalism, proving once again that religion by itself is no guarantor of nationhood, sovereignty or security. The crowning irony is that the battle for a separate Islamic homeland in the northwest of the subcontinent was fought by the Muslim League in the provinces that now territorially constitute India where the League feared Hindu majoritarian dominance. Thereafter, several of its elite cadres moved to what is now Pakistan, where Muslims were already in a majority and had never felt threatened and had therefore been politically lukewarm about Pakistan until the very last stages. In so doing, the makers of Pakistan left behind an orphaned, traumatized and bewildered Muslim Indian community, loyal to India but suspect in the eyes of many among the majority and, more particularly, communal elements within it.

Largely bereft of an elite leadership outside the circle of so-called Nationalist Muslims, Muslim Indians clung emotionally to symbols such as Urdu, personal law and Aligarh. The residual Muslim leadership now consisted of a few princes, zamindars and other feudal interests who soon disappeared from the scene with the integration of princely India and zamindari abolition. What remained was the clergy and orthodoxy, and it is to this element that the Government of India largely turned as the guide and arbiter of Muslim opinion and interests. Liberal and modern Muslim elements, such as the so-called Muslim Progressive group in Maharashtra were officially subordinated to Islamic conservatism in the name of secularism in the 1950s and 1960s as the result of a profoundly mistaken even if unintended policy.

Muddled thinking is again evident in continuing 'nationalist' objections from time to time to the very correct use of the term 'Muslim Indian' rather than the more commonly used but less appropriate expression, 'Indian Muslim'. A moment's reflection will show that the former refers to Indians who happen to profess Islam whereas the latter speaks to Muslims who happen to be Indian, a subtle but important distinction as 'Indian Muslim' connotes pan-Islamism or faith rather than Indianness or nationality.

India is a deeply religious society that has found space for every kind of religious and cultural manifestation. Yet, in the background of post-1857 history and the events leading up to Partition, the Congress had all along stood for a secular society in which all sections would be free to profess and practise their faiths, with the State as a neutral guarantor of this right. Everything in the Constitution stresses the secular ideal though the word 'secular' did not occur until a Constitution amendment introduced it into the Preamble as late as in 1976. The constitutional expression employed was Fraternity, a term broader than 'secular' and richer in content. Ambedkar employed that word repeatedly and with feeling. Extraordinarily, no other leader or manifesto has ever done so.

The secular society is a Western concept going back to the Renaissance and Age of Reason. It entailed separation of State from Church and Church from School and heralded the process of modernization and scientific inquiry untrammelled by dictates of scriptural heresy. The Indian adaptation adopted the first part but ignored the second. Secularism came to be understood as a policy of state-equidistance from all faiths, but the meaning of secularisation as a process was lost. Equal respect for all faiths soon came to mean pandering to everybody's orthodoxy or religious bigotry in the name of keeping faith with 'secularism'. Thus social and religious reform has in some ways become an unintended victim of a misplaced Indian secularism, which, like every ism, has acquired a certain degree of rigidity. In practice, equal respect for all faiths has sometimes come to mean equal respect for everybody's communalism. Hence the bizarre spectacle of 'respect' for or tolerance of religious land grab, loudspeakers blaring forth to deaf gods, the invasion of public space in the name of faith, excommunication, provocative routing of processions in celebration of religious festivals, the forcible undoing of inter-religious and inter-caste marriages, competitive religiosity, state subsidies for going on *haj* or pilgrimage to Kailash and Mansarovar and, worse, to creation of communal vote banks.

Mandal and Masjid

Reservations are a useful and legitimate means of affirmative action. But these have been operated in a manner that has created new vested interests (in the absence of an exit policy) and become a means to burke the universalization of primary education, the enforcement of social rights and meaningful social reform. Untouchability shamefully continues and the lynching of dalits in Jhajjar in Haryana in 2002 could still be passed over with the brazen remark that a cow's life was more valuable. The constitutionally ordained National Commissions for Scheduled Castes and for Scheduled Tribes are hollow bodies for which neither Parliament nor successive governments have had much time. Nevertheless, the dalits and the underclass are on the march. Nothing can halt them, though opposition and obstruction may delay their progress. The May 2007 Uttar Pradesh assembly election result gives hope that a dalit-led rainbow coalition of all castes and minorities under Mayawati's Bahujan Samaj Party may just have defeated the use of caste as a political pawn for collateral partisan gain.

The bid to expand the listing of 'other backward classes' and empower them through reservations in accordance with the recommendations of the Mandal Commission (1989) was interpreted by the religious Right as a sinister bid to fragment and politically weaken Hindu society. This was countered by Hindu mobilization through *rath yatras*, the demolition of the Babri Masjid, the denunciation of 'pseudo-secularism' and 'minority appeasement' and the rise of the Vishwa Hindu Parishad and Bajrang Dal as the militant face of the Sangh Parivar.

Hindutva has been defined to mean all things to all men. The 'cultural nationalism' of Hindu Rashtra is built around the idea of one nation, one flag and one people whose place of origin, motherland and holy land is Bharat. This casts Christians, Muslims, Parsees and Jews as 'foreigners' or Indians on probation who somehow need to prove themselves. This has been and will be indignantly denied. But one has only to read Savarkar's 'Who is a Hindu' and Golwalkar's 'We or Our Nationhood Defined' (which Savarkar wrote but to which Golwalkar incredibly lent his name as author) and the tenth standard Social Studies school textbooks officially brought out and used in Narendra Modi's Gujarat to see that this is so. More recently, L.K. Advani, as home minister in the NDA Government, patronized a volume entitled *Religious Demography in India* with a Foreword and a formal seminar launch. This classified Hindus, Buddhists, Jains and Sikhs as 'Indian religionists' suggesting, conversely, that Christians, Muslims, Parsees and Jews must be non-Indian religionists, not 'we' but 'them'. He spoke of the 'strategic pressures' of internal and external demography and alluded to the pressure being put on Indian religionists by Christians and, more particularly, Muslims. (Joshi, et al., 2003) The thesis was mischievous and misconceived. Among the more absurd arguments advanced in its support is the allegedly high growth rate of India's Muslim population. Hence the bizarre advocacy by none other than the RSS chief that Hindu women should each bear sixteen children, or at least nine by reference to Krishna's order of birth!

Meanwhile, the findings of Professor Roop Rehka Verma's recently published '*Study of Textbooks in Non-Governmental Schools in Uttar Pradesh*' are disquieting. Her survey of books used in RSS schools, including the large chain of Saraswati Vidya Mandirs, reveals an uncritical glorification of Brahmanism and associated notions of hierarchy. More generally, the appropriation and rewriting of history and the politicized striving to seek present-day revenge for real or assumed historical wrongs and an 'imagined Hindu victimhood' have bred violence and communal discord and are deeply divisive, breathing new life into a discredited and discarded two-nation theory which, incidentally, Savarkar was the first to propound. Hindutva, as a narrowly exclusivist, authoritarian doctrine, is a rejection of the idea of India.

The Gujarat holocaust of 2002 was only possible with the crass complicity of the State and was hailed by ideologues as witness to a 'successful experiment' in Hindu consolidation. The Tehelka tapes released in October 2007 merely confirmed on hidden cameras the chilling self-confessions of some of the principal BJP, VHP and Bajrang Dal actors in that carnage. Even five years later, a visit to Ahmedabad is a saddening experience. Outwardly, there is all the evidence of a bustling city, with a new skyline, an international airport, malls and other symbols of a consumerist, upwardly mobile society; that is until one sees the wall along what is called 'the border', a wall of fear and hate. This separates Vejalpur, a well-lit middle-class Hindu colony with three- and four-storey buildings, from Juhapura, a crowded, poorly-lit quarter with pot-holed streets and minimal services, home to some 350,000 Muslims herded together in a ghetto. Vejalpur residents built the wall and later further raised its height and topped it with barbed wire. They have left no exit to the street that once connected them with Juhapura, involuntarily consigning themselves to a self-made ghetto of another kind.

The 'border' marks a line where safety and camaraderie end and fear and hate begin on either side. Muslims suffer an economic and social boycott. Juhapura reportedly does not have a single bank or public office. A well-known Baroda professor, Juzar Bandukwala, who would be an ornament in any society, recounts the not uncommon experience of wanting to live in a cosmopolitan locality only to be rejected time and again as soon as his Muslim identity was revealed. Housing agents plead that real estate values would fall and they would be out of business should they breach this unwritten code.

There are fundamentalists and mafia goons on both sides of the 'border', some cloaked in religiosity. There are very many more decent, civilized people but they have been unable to confront the hate-mongers, who control state and civic power, and their ideological mentors. Unfortunately, the Gujarat Opposition, trade unions, academia, Gandhians, religious leaders, the corporate world, even the media and civil society have momentarily collapsed, barring some notable exceptions.

The Nanavati–Shah Commission of Inquiry into the Godhra-Gujarat killings plods on its weary way. Many known and named perpetrators of violence roam free while witnesses are afraid to come forward. Encounter killings of Muslims continue. Those assisting with legal aid have been threatened. The filing of first information reports has been resisted and compensation given has been ridiculously small or remains to be paid. Livelihoods have not been restored. The recent demolition of one more roadside dargah in Baroda has sent out another chilling message, adding more bricks to the walls of hate and fear.

However, the formula of Hindu consolidation will not work as Hindus represent a differentiated mass of which only a fringe is sympathetic to the Hindu right. Yet periodic riots, for which very few have been punished, have kept tensions alive, though it would be unfair to suggest that the provocation has always come from only one side. The Centre has introduced a Communal Violence (Prevention, Control and Rehabilitation of Victims) Bill. This has some good points and could be improved; but legislation cannot help if political will is lacking.

Recent run-ups to elections have seen strenuous efforts to stir sectarian passions whether on Ayodhya and other 'disputed' temples or on issues relating to cow protection, religious conversions, minority appeasement and personal law. There have been various crude acts of vandalism, censorship and violence in the name of moral policing, and a strident campaign to stop the supposed destruction of Ram Setu or Adam's Bridge by the excavation of the proposed Sethusamudram

Navigation Canal across the Palk Straits, which Hanuman's legions are said to have built to enable Rama's army to cross over to Lanka in order to win back Sita from the clutches of Ravana. This agenda has been variously furthered by unrestrained hate speech, the distribution of *trishul*s (tridents), jingoism and inflammatory rhetoric. There have been limited gains for the Hindu Right but much revulsion too.

Contrapuntally, there have been manifestations of Islamic fundamentalism as well and resort to terrorism, some, or much of this, with cross-border support and sustenance. Sikh militancy disappeared after the Khalistan upsurge despite a passing contretemps more recently over a blasphemy charge against a Dera or sect leader. The siege mentality lingers among Muslims. The Muslim Personal Law Board avoidably inveighed against a Supreme Court order to the Centre and states to frame rules for compulsory registration of marriages in order to secure gender justice to deserted wives and to curb child marriage. Until now, only Maharashtra, Gujarat, Karnataka and Himachal have legislated in favour of compulsory marriage registration. The Court's ruling evoked an inference of a lurch towards a uniform code. Likewise, clerical opposition to another more recent court ruling, that a triple talaq uttered by an inebriated husband shall be deemed invalid on voluntary retraction, is difficult to understand. Fatwas are still issued by impassioned clerics. Fortunately, the new amir or chief of the Jamaat-e-Islami-e-Hind, Maulana Syed Jalaluddin Umri has called for change 'which is not possible through the *ulema* (clergy) who, despite being born in the 21st century, are mentally and intellectually living in the 6th and 7th centuries'. (*Indian Express*, 23 May 2007)

Sachar Committee

Increasingly self-assured and competitive Muslim Indians are emerging out of their shell despite more recent traumas. Significantly, no Muslim Indians were found among the Taliban in Afghanistan. However, the sense of helplessness and despair sweeping the Islamic world over the past few decades has bred extremist violence and fundamentalism. Some of these negative jehadi influences have spread to India, giving a further fillip to Hindu fundamentalism and setting in motion a vicious cycle detrimental to tranquillity, social development and modernization.

The secular Muslim leadership in India has to play a more active role in leading the community out of the ghetto and conservatism within which some elements would try and confine it. Equally, the State has a duty to assist through targetted education and other opportunities. It is time also for the community to practise *ijtehad* or reinterpretation of the Shariah so that Muslim Indians are better able to assume their rightful place in a fast changing world. Change has to come from within. Fortunately, the government has woken up to its responsibility. We now have the thoughtful yet sombre report of a Committee appointed under former Justice Rajindar Sachar to look at the Muslim condition sixty years after Independence. (Sachar Report, 2006) Making nonsense of the charge of Muslim 'appeasement', the report card represents a national indictment of gross discrimination and benign neglect. The Muslim condition is not uniform. By and large the southern states are better off while the situation in Uttar Pradesh, Bihar, West Bengal and Assam give cause for concern. Overall, Muslims stand a cut above the Scheduled Castes and Tribes but rank below the OBCs. The Report debunks some myths: that Muslims shun modern education and flock to madrasas (only 4 per cent do so); that they are averse to family planning (fertility rates are in decline); and that demographically they will before long swamp the rest.

Two factors lie at the root of the Muslim problem—educational backwardness and socio-administrative mindsets. Of these, the first is the more fundamental. Education opens the door to equality of opportunity, with schooling as the foundation having due regard to access, retention, the quality of teaching, textbooks and infrastructure, and instruction in the mother tongue, Urdu. Given this, vocational and higher and professional education will follow. But to accomplish the first step satisfactorily and soon, the Sachar Committee recommends, as for other matters, that the fifty-eight districts of Muslim concentration be targetted for social development. Simultaneously, madrasas should be enabled to modernize and issue recognized certificates so that their alumni can be mainstreamed into higher education. Girls' education merits particular emphasis, with provision for more female teachers, scholarships and hostels as a necessary adjunct.

Livelihoods follow. The comparative statistics of employment are dismal, whether in government, public sector units or the corporate and private sectors. Muslim job ratios are a quarter or less of their population. This cannot be happenstance or solely attributable to lower educational attainments. Because of their lower visibility in public spaces—in the administrative, police and security services, in the judiciary, corporate world, professions and public life, especially at local body levels of democratic participation and decision making—Muslims are diffident to compete and do not come forward in sufficient numbers. The Committee, however, points out that several constituencies of Muslim concentration are reserved for Scheduled Castes when other constituencies would better qualify. Such aberrant delimitation must be corrected.

The community has a perception of being discriminated against. Though exaggerated in some cases, discrimination is certainly evident in access to social infrastructure (health, water supply and sanitation, transport and communications) and bank finance. Muslims are also unable to rent accommodation in cosmopolitan areas/buildings, leading to involuntary ghettoization. Some handicaps are general rather than community-specific and stem from poverty. Extant poverty alleviation and basic needs programmes and achievement of the Millennium Development Goals can cure many. But targetting of such programmes is also necessary.

Muslims fall into three broad caste categories, the *ashraf*s or upper castes, the *ajlaf*s, who are OBCs, and *arzal*s, equivalent to the Most Backward Castes who perform menial tasks. Muslim OBCs account for 40 per cent of the community and 15 per cent of the overall OBC cohort and are particularly disadvantaged. The Committee recommends affirmative action as a means of ameliorating the condition of the ashrafs but would lump the ajlafs with the OBCs and the arzals with SCs for reservation. The Committee is of the view that the process of promoting inclusive development and mainstreaming would be greatly assisted by a constantly updated national data bank and the establishment of appropriate fast-track mechanisms to ensure equal opportunities. Affirmative action could be furthered by reference to a suitably constructed diversity index. Entities earning high diversity ratings could also be eligible for various incentives on a sliding scale.

The suggestion that Muslim participation in all spheres of political life be buttressed through 'a carefully conceived "nomination" procedure' is more problematic. Nomination could become a dangerous crutch and lead to charges of partisanship to win political support. There is much the community can do on its own. One instrumentality would be better-managed and suitably reformed Wakf Boards whose properties could yield an annual revenue of Rs 12,000 crore for a variety of projects that benefit the community.

Uniform Civil Code

The failure to confront issues of social reform and effect necessary 'structural adjustments' that could prise people out of polarized and parochial grooves is disturbing. Illustratively, an issue that periodically generates great excitement but has yet to be liberated from wilful obfuscation and rank prejudice is the enactment of a uniform civil code as enjoined by Article 44 of the Constitution. The Muslim Personal Law Board has, however, formally taken the position that Muslims be excluded from any such civil code. Apart from being an obscurantist view, this is tantamount to asserting that any and every religious community should have the right to veto India's social progress in the secular domain. This is the mirror image of the BJP/RSS's equally perverse view that a political majority has the constitutional right to override 'freedom of conscience and the right freely to profess, practise and propagate religion' guaranteed under Article 25. Both positions are products of the huge confusion that successive governments, political parties, academics and the media have ingrained into public thinking by proclaiming that adoption of a uniform civil code must entail the abrogation of personal law. The Constitution and laws of India say no such thing. On the contrary, Goa has a uniform civil code while elements of a uniform civil code are to be found in the existing, though not altogether satisfactory, Special Marriage Act. Neither is ultra vires.

There are many personal laws relating to every faith in India and the gamut of Hindu Code Acts are only one among several Hindu personal laws that are extant. Their codification is a most desirable objective but is not to be confused with enacting a uniform civil code. The latter, currently limited to the Special Marriage Act, is optional and available to couples that choose cross-cultural alliances and marry outside their faith, caste, regional or ethno-cultural categories. Indeed, in some cases, no such cross-cultural marriages can be legally solemnized under personal laws unless one or other spouse converts. In such cases, recourse can fortunately be had to the Special Marriage Act.

India's enormous diversity is manifesting itself as cohort after cohort of the underclass gets empowered. With the country's innate multiculturalism thereby increasingly coming into its own, there is desperate need for a modern, liberal uniform civil code or national family law even as each community takes steps to codify its own personal laws in keeping with the times. This applies equally to customary tribal laws, many of which, contrary to popular belief, discriminate against women. A uniform code would also go a long way towards overcoming gender discrimination on secular issues in keeping with the values of the Constitution.

The absence of a uniform civil code was not so keenly felt earlier when most Indians lived out their lives in little compartments or boxes in their 'native place' among people of their own kind. Thus, even 'modern', 'foreign returned' Indians would invariably marry into their own kind, whether defined by community, gotra region or language. Even if they lived and worked outside their 'native place', they would often retire to their 'ancestral home'. This is changing. There is today increasing social and regional mobility and cross-cultural integration. Home is anywhere and everywhere and the concept of 'native place' is fast becoming a conundrum.

In this new and rapidly evolving context, Indian pluralism is increasingly coming into its own, and the idea of Fraternity is acquiring a new dimension. Those opposing a uniform civil code are no longer quaint, old-fashioned conservatives but, in fact, socially menacing forces inimical to the Idea of India. For as soon as a couple decide that they want or need to get out of the confines of traditional group identity boxes or 'ghettoes', they come up against a united front of 'secular' and 'fundamentalist' zealots fanatically blocking their path towards assuming a larger Indian identity. An uninformed people have made Fraternity hostage to clerics and revivalists and a pawn in vote-bank politics. The Hindu Right has not helped by making a uniform civil code an anti-Muslim bogey. Such a code can legally be enacted by any state and does not necessaily have to be centrally legislated. Yet no BJP government, Central or state, has ever attempted to legislate such a code. Why?

Religious extremism of any kind is neither politically nor socially sustainable and the idea of India will ultimately triumph. For this to happen, sooner rather than later, there is need to redefine the meaning and practice of secularism and return to that richer, nobler and more meaningful concept of Fraternity and togetherness. The language of discourse must change.

Religion and culture

The failure to distinguish between religion and culture has only added to confusion. The two are by no means synonymous as sometimes mistakenly assumed. Culture represents a wider range of living experience than faith. Indonesia is the largest Islamic nation in the world but boasts a proud Hindu culture. Thailand and Cambodia are similarly devoutly Buddhist by faith but exhibit a strong Hindu cultural underlay in terms of language, art, architecture and so much else. Indian culture is eclectic and traditions have blended seamlessly to create rare new styles and textures of shared cultural spaces that have brought enjoyment and acclaim. This can be seen in food, dress, art, music, dance, language and literature, architecture, arts and crafts, fairs and festivals, and in the inter-faith congregations that visit so many shrines and dargahs. This is truly a celebration of diversity and should not be cause for exclusivist concerns. Urdu was a major casualty of narrow thinking and now some would question M.F. Husain's 'right' to paint Hindu deities or frown on ceremonies like *bhoomi puja* or lighting a lamp for Vishwakarma or recitations from the scriptures to invoke divine blessings on any secular venture. Some secularists objected to the Mahabharata and Ramayana being serialized over the State-owned Doordarshan. Not surprisingly, the serials were hugely popular across communities and regions. They were broadcast not as religious programmes but as much loved epics deeply ingrained in Indian culture and with a universal message. It has been argued by some that the television serial helped mobilize Hindutva opinion in support of the Ramjanambhoomi issue. This seems an appealing theory but is of doubtful validity.

Equally worrisome is the tendency to view religious minorities, to whom the Constitution offers special protection, in exclusively numerical terms. This immediately translates into political demography, impacting on elections and power equations. That this should be so is understandable in view of the colonial history of separate electorates and representation indexed to numbers, leading to Partition. Yet, with the constitutional guarantee of equal citizenship without discrimination on grounds of race, religion, caste, gender or region, this should no longer be a primary consideration. To describe 140 million Indian Muslims, possibly the second largest concentration of Islamic followers anywhere in the world, as a minority, is to strain meaning. (Canada now refers to the Inuit people or Eskimos as its second majority). Moreover, Muslims, just as much as Hindus, Sikhs or Christians, have multiple identities of which faith may not necessarily be the most important for most or for most of the time. Witness Bangladesh. At home, Sikhs are a minority in India, but constitute a majority in Punjab but are again a minority in the city of Amritsar. Maybe a more sophisticated definition is necessary regarding who or what constitutes a minority. There was consternation when a UP High Court judge suddenly declared that the 18 per cent Muslims in the state did not constitute a minority. A division bench quickly overturned this runaway ruling. However, stung by this or otherwise, the Government of India now contemplates legislation leaving it to the states to determine who are minorities and, presumably, to lay down the criteria, which could conceivably be a percentage of the state population. In other words, there will be national minorities and state minorities. By this token, Hindus could be declared a minority in Mizoram or Kashmir and enabled to enjoy minority rights.

The politicization of community and caste in relation to numbers has led to vote-bank politics and the competitive exploitation of communal sentiments. This has tended to entrench sectarian tendencies and stoke tensions and negative memories. 'Minority', more truly, represents an attitude towards self and nation. Those weak, uncertain and rejected feel threatened, irrespective of numbers. Parsees and Sikhs, by and large (1984 notwithstanding), do not behave as 'minorities'. They are self-assured and competitive. However, many Sinhala politicians and the Sangha speak of majority oppression by the minorities, a striking manifestation of their own insecurities and minority complex with the nightmare image of Tamils surrounding them on every side. Hindutvavadis reflect the same minority or insecurity–inferiority complex.

Hinduism, a richly eclectic way of life made up of multiple strands, is not a monolithic faith of the Book and cannot be cast in a single mould. It too is in need of reform to end outworn and ritualistic practice and caste oppression. Sanskritization is a slow process and limited by the caste hierarchy. Hindutva, on the other hand, is power-driven and talks of Hindu consolidation and cultural nationalism in political terms. It is not sufficient merely to co-opt dalits, tribal peoples and even OBCs into the Hindutva fold. They have to be enabled to become full citizens with all the rights and privileges that it entails. The answer lies in the social and economic empowerment of the disadvantaged and underprivileged.

Conversion

Dalits continue to seek a way out of the stranglehold of caste by resort to conversion and the hope it brings of a new beginning within a framework of equality and dignity. Recall the conversion to Islam in Meenakshipuram in the deep Tamil South in 1981.

More dramatically, a reported 100,000 nomadic Scheduled Castes and Scheduled Tribes people embraced Buddhism en masse at a ceremony in Mumbai on 27 May 2007 under the auspices of the Republican Party on the fiftieth anniversary of Ambedkar's renunciation of Hinduism for Buddhism.

Regrettably, the Church has been unable to shake off caste and has in some ways been instrumental in upholding it by petitioning for continuing reservations for SC Christians, a contradiction in terms. Christianity has grown in India since Independence, especially among dalits and tribals, particularly in backward and neglected regions. They have been attracted by Christian service and caring and, in the case of certain tribal groups, as a means of differentiation or modernization. Conversion 'by force and fraud' is probably rare, and is certainly against tenets of the faith and punishable under the law, which must take its course. One must also deplore the brash conduct of certain so-called revivalist or charismatic foreign churches and missions that exude attitudes of cultural arrogance and fundamentalism that are offensive and unacceptable in a plural society. This is a menace that the Indian Church must address.

The Sangh Parivar has in recent years made considerable efforts at working among tribal communities and spreading education. This is to be welcomed, but will cause concern if the effort is directed towards building political constituencies in a new form of vote-bank politics. It has been strident in advocating anti-conversion laws (to prevent conversion by force and fraud, which is already an offence under other laws) and has repeatedly used violent and coercive means to uphold this norm on the basis of rumour and allegation outside the law and to practise re-conversion (*grih vapasi* or religious homecoming). Arunachal, Madhya Pradesh, Gujarat, Tamil Nadu, Orissa and Himachal have legislated anti-conversion laws, some even requiring that advance notice of conversion be given to the district magistrate who must establish the facts and give his prior consent before the act of conversion. Despite such legislation, nobody seems to know clearly just how many cases of conversion by 'force and fraud' have been detected, and where. The allegations are loud, the evidence slender. Meanwhile, to make a district magistrate the arbiter of faith is surely an assault on the very notion of secularism.

Social reform, textbooks, parochialism

India needs social reform across the board. A coalition of enlightened citizens, religious leaders and the State is required to further such a movement. The Preamble promises Liberty, Equality and Fraternity. Though progress may be halting and disappointing, some efforts have been made to promote political and economic reform. But the debate on social reform and building Fraternity has yet to be truly joined as Indian 'secularism' actually discourages forays into what it regards as forbidden ground. A committee of the resurrected but sadly dormant National Integration Council would perhaps be an appropriate forum to thrash out delicate and complex social issues and come to broad conclusions regarding what might be done by governments, political parties and civil society respectively. This would be a problem-solving approach that provides opportunity for constructive debate and collective thinking rather than to lock horns in the streets.

The controversy over the writing and rewriting of history and social studies textbooks, whether with a Saffron or Marxist slant, has raged off and on over the years. One community's heroes are sometimes tyrants and oppressors to others. Everybody wants his heroes to look good, minus any warts, but falsification of history is wrong and pandering to populist sentiments to create a historically misleading feel-good factor can be dangerous. It is here that regional identities and chauvinism also come into play, in the clash of local folklore and championship of regional heroes who have become the stuff of ballads and legend. Local pride is understandable and is part of the heritage of any society, but things can get out of hand when the past is treated as part of a continuing present where affronts and triumphs have to be relived from day to day. Here again, angularities can be smoothened in the manner in which history is written and presented, especially to children.

Nevertheless, regionalism is a lurking danger and continues to vent local linguistic particularisms from time to time. The Kannadigas, progressive and well up in the IT sector where Bangalore reigns, are sometimes prone to be obsessed by localism. They recently decided on a change in brand image by renaming Bangalore, Bengalooru. This indeed is what Kannadigas call it; but has the makeover made any great difference to anybody? Are Mumbai and Kolkata too any the better for their renaming? Karnataka has also de-recognized private institutions for changing their registered medium from Kannada to English, whereas the schools presumably made the change in response to parental and public demand and employment trends. Tamil Nadu has been chafing for the High Court to transact business in Tamil in addition to English, though the Bar and the Bench have warned about making any changes without a sufficiency of translators and other preparation.

Migration and sons of the soil

A matter of more serious import has been the repercussions of inter-state migration on issues of identity and employment. The ULFA in Assam has been targetting Hindi-speakers around Tinsukia while a Shiv Sena mob stormed a Railway Recruitment Board examination hall in Pune and drove away all non-Maharashtrians in a familiar replay of the sons-of-the-soil syndrome of territorial versus ethnic identity. Regional and international mobility is responsive to push and pull factors and has been responsible for the domestic and international Indian diaspora. It is not merely the availability of jobs, land or of opportunity that people seek but a better quality of life. Hence the direction of migration is always from deprived to more affluent areas. Demand and supply equations are at work but social and political factors cannot be disregarded either. The swamping of Tripura by Bengali speakers and of Sikkim by Nepalese has given rise to extreme anxieties in Assam, the Northeast generally and West Bengal with regard to the continuing illicit influx of Bangladeshis into the country. The change wrought in the demographic complexion of Assam caused a political upheaval through the 1980s and to this day, resulting in much agitation and violence and fencing of the Bangladesh border.

The problem of migration will not go away and has been closely analysed at many levels. (See Myron Weiner, 1978) While its positive effects in providing necessary manpower and skills will be welcomed, reducing inter-regional and trans-border disparities can mitigate its negative impacts. An urbanizing India will, however, necessarily invite migration as new, rising cities grow more by the talent they attract than by natural increase. They tend to be more cosmopolitan and less prone to pander to regional and ethnic identities. As prosperity increases people are less paranoid about identity. Malaysia is a good example. At the time they won their independence four decades ago, the Malays felt disadvantaged in relation to the Chinese and Indians who were ahead of them in trade and the professions. Hence, a Bhoomiputra policy that put sons of the soil first. Forty years on, with its economy thriving, Malaysia is beginning to place merit above ethnicity.

Democratic decentralization and participative governance through greater federal and local body devolution to the states and panchayati raj institutions could reassure regional and local communities that their cherished identities are in safe hands. At the end of the day, education and young people hold the key. Campus diversity programmes that bring students together and teach them of their shared common heritage could instil pride and ownership in a larger Indianness. There is much to unlearn too. As the country's diversity continues to unfold in the years ahead, it is respect for and accommodation of that diversity that will maintain the bonds of national and regional unity and community harmony. For that has been the genius of India.

{8}

From the 'Other' to Just Another

Along the journey, quaintly written by the roadside, the sign reads, 'Caution: Men at Work'. Sixty years after Independence, and contrary to doomsday forecasts, the Idea of India has translated into a vibrant and going concern as a state-nation but yet remains work in progress. The state-nation is a recent concept developed to differentiate multi-cultural and plural entities from the familiar nation states that emerged out of Europe in the nineteenth century, each essentially dominated by a single nation enjoying a largely homogeneous culture. (Linz et al., 2007). Even as it lurches along, India is on its way cunningly melding an astonishing multitude of diverse threads into new cloth.

There is much to regret about what has not been accomplished or left undone thus far. There is also cause for legitimate anxiety over the manifold tasks that lie ahead as latent diversities transmute into jostling, impatient, raucous demands for instant satisfaction. Many less privileged have waited a hundred or maybe a thousand years and rightly claim justice here and now. But patience comes with assurance of inclusive and equitable progress for the remaining journey and the knowledge that, direction set, it is necessary to travel in order to arrive.

The present, being known, is familiar while change essays a journey into the unknown with attendant risks. Yet there is a yearning for change while clinging to *a present rooted in the past*. The perils of transition cannot be avoided but safety nets can insure against danger and provide assurance in moving ahead. This entails risk-taking together with hand-holding for vulnerable sections and communities. It would be reckless, even criminal, to shout 'fire, fire' in a crowded hall and cause a panic stampede. Yet that is what some critics are prone to do when confronting change.

Two theorems to remember

Diversity entails difference not sameness and a layering or spread of otherness. This need not be threatening, though it is often made out to be so because of ignorance, prejudice or self-interest. By defining oneself as the chosen people, one invites or demands preference, especially in situations of shortage, whether of land, shelter, employment or opportunity, or at times of conflict, danger, crisis or uncertainty. Hence, the attachment to or insistence on or perception of a singular identity in the 'other'. This can be misleading, for humankind exhibits and projects manifold identities to claim access and participation in myriad different situations.

It has almost become a reflex in India to proclaim unity in diversity as a magic mantra. The slogan is used as a shield against differences or divisiveness and, hence, instability, and to invoke stability and order. Unconsciously perhaps, this has sometimes bred resistance to change. However, a moment's examination will show that the problems apprehended may stem not from too little stability, but from too much of it, which serves to buttress an unchanging permanence of the long-established social and economic order with its many cruel inequities fashioned in times past and kept in place through congealed violence. And all too often, when the cry goes up for maintenance of law and order, the subconscious appeal is not necessarily to the rule of law as much as to the executive facility to employ the law to maintain or reclaim the established order.

Facile projections of proclaimed national unity for long ignored latent diversities whose expression was muted for lack of voice or fear of reprisals. This has now changed with empowerment and has yielded to a boisterous clamour for equality and entitlements. This churning can be loud and sometimes exaggerated but represents democratic energy that can be diverted to constructive purpose. If persistently thwarted, it can turn into or be used to instigate mob violence. Two broad theorems therefore underlie India's quest for unity in diversity.

Stability comes from ordered change and unity is best assured by respect for diversity.

India's human diversities are both hierarchical and spatial. The Constitution vests sovereignty in the People. This is a differentiated mass, with tribals and dalits at the bottom of the heap. The poverty and inequities they suffer have been aggravated by the exponential growth in population that is just beginning to slow down. Even so, the net addition of some twelve million to the labour force each year constitutes a crushing number that compels mounting competition for common natural resources and man-made opportunities. The de jure WE, the sovereign people is in reality a fragmented 'we', divided by yawning gaps that remain to be bridged.

Imperative of inclusive growth

India's record in this department is disappointing despite impressive achievements under other counts. As many as 270 million people or 26 per cent of the population live below a poverty line drawn so improbably low, essentially to leave almost double that number living at not much above subsistence levels. Such deprivation is not commensurate with the dignity of the individual. With rapidly rising political and social consciousness and international comparisons at hand, excessive disparities are untenable. The stupor of ignorance or sullen acceptance has yielded to more insistent and organized protest. Dual societies, Bharat and India, cannot coexist. There must be inclusive development and India must shine for all, else 9 or 10 per cent growth iniquitously distributed will not endure. That is obvious enough. The question is how to ameliorate that condition.

The focus too long has been very largely though not exclusively on political management and the manipulation of vote banks and 'growth' as a statistical number more than a shared value through distributive justice. The social sector, education, health, housing, employment and other basic needs that give quality to life, has been relatively neglected alongside social reform to rid society of encrustations of dead habit. Between them they have constituted a powerful social depressor.

India's very diverse eighty-five million tribal people, the world's largest, may not be 'indigenous' in every sense but represent elements of a primordial society that remains marginalized. They are by definition backward, even primitive, remote, and isolated, and shy of contact with the outside world. Occupying the heartland of the Middle India plateau and highlands, they have been systematically alienated from their lands and forest habitat with which they shared a symbiotic relationship as guardians and beneficiaries. Though children of the forest, they have found the woods 'reserved', 'protected' and otherwise closed to them, step by step, and diverted for 'public purposes' and the greater common good in which they have been denied any stake or benefit. This tragic story has been made sorrier by deliberate defiance and default of law against land alienation and the constitutional promise of consultation through the gram sabhas and their informed consent in case of changes in land use and mineral development and industrialization that entail displacement or threaten the sustainability of local livelihoods.

The Fifth and Sixth Schedules and the Panchayats (Extension to Scheduled Areas) Act, 1996, have been described as a constitution within the Constitution for India's tribal people. But they have not been implemented in good faith. On the contrary, they have been ignored and violated with impunity not just by functionaries of the State, but by moneylenders, contractors, the forest mafia and a small, co-opted tribal elite. Governors enjoy wide powers for 'the peace and good governance' of Scheduled Areas and the Centre may issue administrative directions to the states in this regard. Few governors have cared to exercise these powers purposefully and Raj Bhavans are not well equipped to discharge this onerous responsibility. Indeed the appointment of governors, especially to states with large tribal populations, should be made with care so that only those with the requisite capacity and bent of mind are selected. They should be given instruments of instruction for guidance and provided with a sufficiently senior tribal affairs officer on their staff for independent investigation and advice. State legislatures and Parliament too must show more serious interest in debating and monitoring tribal affairs. Hopefully, the revamping of panchayati raj institutions and the implementation of the provisions of the Scheduled Tribes and Other Traditional Forest Dwellers Act will spur appropriate action from below.

The dalit condition is perhaps a shade better but essentially little different. Here too there has been a failure to heed Ambedkar's warning about the contradictions flowing from the huge social deficit inherent in a harshly restrictive and hierarchical caste system. The upper intermediate castes have made gains since Independence, especially with the first round of somewhat disappointing land reforms and the green revolution, but have thereafter tended to sit on the lid to prevent competition from below.

Land has become a class–caste issue and class struggle even among Leftist groups is barely indistinguishable from caste struggle. Agricultural decline has only aggravated matters, with growing landlessness and fragmentation of holdings below viable levels. Unemployment has mounted. Coupled with this has been rising anger among awakening dalits. They are no longer willing to suffer in silence the indignities and atrocities practised against them. They are now politically organized and the BSP victory in Uttar Pradesh in May 2007 is possibly a portent of things to come, with dalits grasping hands across the social spectrum to fight for common rights alongside higher caste groups and minorities.

The cynical use of caste for electoral mobilization by all sides must be deplored. Realization is, however, dawning that at the end of the day all may be losers by debasing the political coinage and promoting divisiveness on sectarian lines that devalues fair competition and merit. The monopolization of reservations by the upper crust is also perverting an otherwise laudable exercise in affirmative action. The failure of the clergy and community leaders to attack caste discrimination, an irreligious excrescence on true faith, has also impeded social reform. This cannot, however, extenuate the State from doing its duty in accordance with the secular mandate of the Constitution. Laws have been passed and institutions established but all too often only to be sidestepped for lack of political will. The effete nature of the Commission for Scheduled Castes and the total absence of any 'endeavour' to adopt a constitutionally mandated optional uniform civil code tell their own tale.

Ideologically, the former Naxalites and present-day Maoists have stepped into the breach to exploit historical grievances and injustices within a wider agenda of wresting state power to establish an altogether new revolutionary social order through violent means, not excluding class annihilation. There is today something of a 'Red Corridor' that runs down the spine of Middle India under a united CPI (Maoist) party. Various other Left-wing Extremist (LWE) splinter groups are struggling to maintain a presence and relevance in pockets elsewhere, while some have come to terms with electoral politics in parallel with building up mass organizations and sponsoring mass struggles. Every agitation is seen as an opportunity to forge, participate in and, if possible, take over 'people's movements', whether in opposition to SEZs, the Tata plant at Singur, mineral-based projects in Orissa and Jharkhand, or dams and ports elsewhere and most recently in Nandigram.

Extremists fill void

The Maoists have built up a base and boast a liberated zone in Dantewada in Chhattisgarh and along the Jharkhand–Orissa border from where they have made forays into the greater Dandakaranya area and beyond, attacking police posts, consolidating their strongholds and impeding connectivity and development which threaten their support base. The problem is basically socio-economic but is overlaid with issues of rights and dignity. These are not without substance, but the methods employed are unacceptable. Equally, the State's response has been overly law and order oriented. Andhra Pradesh has been relatively successful in curbing LWE activities through a combination of firm, mobile security responses and development initiatives. It also engaged in prolonged peace negotiations through the good offices of a Concerned Citizen's Group though these came to naught.

The Chhattisgarh approach of building up tribal resistance through the Salwa Judum, a supposedly popular movement, has gone seriously awry both conceptually and in practice. It has become part of the problem, with innocent people becoming cannon fodder in the crossfire. Unfortunately, this is not as yet realized by the state government or the Centre, which continues to back this misadventure.

Any socio-economic programme also requires a good delivery mechanism. This is lacking. The administration in LWE-areas is generally weak and poorly motivated and the infrastructure poor. This has resulted in a seeming vicious circle that cannot be broken merely by licensing mega-projects, as some would believe. The latter are necessary but have to be part of an overall programme of development and good governance in which governors can play a pivotal role as guardians of tribal interest and public good under the Fifth Schedule. But this implies that these dignitaries are well selected, well motivated and properly assisted to discharge their constitutional responsibilities.

Mechanism for conflict resolution

Meanwhile, there is no reason to baulk at dialogue with the Maoists and other LWE groups. The door should certainly be kept open. The Centre has said that it is prepared to talk with any group abjuring violence. In the interim, credible NGOs and citizens groups can play a role in establishing contact, ascertaining priorities for action on minimal demands and issues that can be met or resolved to create a climate for further negotiations on more substantial issues. The idea of schools as safe zones has been mooted and is something that could be tried experimentally.

It is a great pity that India lacks a neutral body that could intervene in matters of conflict avoidance, conflict management and conflict resolution. The Gandhians once played that role, as in mediating with the Chambal dacoits, but were decimated during and after the Emergency by a vindictive State. Religious leaders have filled the breach occasionally—Swami Agnivesh and a group of Good Samaritans during the Akali–Dera Saccha Sahib crisis in Punjab in May 2007, and, earlier, the Baptist Church in Nagaland. Some professionals did endeavour to get together farmers from Tamil Nadu, Karnataka and Kerala to discuss the Cauvery issue at the height of that water dispute and were able to build some bridges. There have been many cross-border Track-II initiatives by bodies like WISCOMP (Women in Security, Conflict Management and Peace) to build constituencies of stakeholders in dialogue. The National Human Rights Commission has been able to intervene in areas within its remit. All these have been valuable initiatives. But there is no standing all-India institutional mechanism that can intervene in all situations to parallel in the area of peacekeeping what is being built up under the national disaster management programme.

The one agency that could conceivably intervene constructively is the Indian Red Cross, but only if cast in a new mould. The International Committee of the Red Cross, ICRC, has played a quiet, behind-the-scenes role and has been a valuable mediator and overseer of international humanitarian law as a result of the high credibility and trust that it enjoys. Could a wing of the Indian Red Cross Society be similarly structured in the internal context, free of political or partisan agendas? The Society is presently headed by the President of India, with governors and deputy commissioners chairing the state and district units. This is perhaps well suited for its present mandate of disaster management and medical relief, providing ambulance and health services and blood banks, assisting in pulse polio and HIV/AIDS programmes and running several health-related awareness campaigns. But a conflict avoidance/management mechanism would require an altogether different charter and structure. The idea merits exploration.

The National Integration Council and its committees can also be useful instrumentalities if reconstituted. The NIC has had a fitful existence but is overwhelmingly governmental and political in composition and bureaucratic in operation. This has been a major weakness. Should it be recast as a largely non-governmental body with high-level political and governmental backing it could be a useful deliberative and consultative mechanism in many ways. But it would still not exclude the need for an alternative non-state and non-political mechanism. At both Nandigram in West Bengal and Kalinganagar in Orissa, protestors embattled themselves behind barricades and severed roads to exclude the State and its functionaries as well as other 'opponents' from the area for weeks and months on end. Such a situation is quite bizarre and no State can long accept such exclusion or abdication of its sovereign responsibilities. Yet there has been no body that could intervene here or in J&K and the Northeast where abductions, detentions and disappearances give rise to rumours and aggravate tensions. Who is there to intervene?

Not backwardness but merit

India must be the only country in the world where people struggle and kill to be declared backward and revel in social regression in reversal of the whole story of civilization. Sadly, official policy and partisan politics tout and cultivate such nonsense. This monstrous aberration, that stigmatizes and deforms Indian society, is a product of warped thinking and ad hoc action that legitimizes and rewards crude behaviour and social contradictions against which Ambedkar had so presciently warned.

The Gujjar–Meena 'caste war' witnessed in Rajasthan in the summer of 2007 was a fallout of the vote-bank politics and policies practised over the years by all parties across the board to score petty points, stoke fires and win cheap kudos at the cost of the national interest. Gujjars in Rajasthan, an OBC, do not face wilful discrimination in writing exams and entering the civil or other superior services. However, living beside them, the Meenas have made considerable advances through reservation, having long back been declared a tribal community. The Jats in Rajasthan, by no means a particularly disadvantaged people, were some time back also listed as an OBC, enabling them to appropriate a slice of the reserved quota. So when Rajasthan's Gujjars argue that it is now their turn to get a golden key, with what logic can they be denied? After all, Gujjars in J&K, Himachal and Uttarakhand have been scheduled as tribes and derive certain entitlements from that status. But the criteria of being backward, remote, isolated and shy of contact, by state determination for Central and, ultimately, presidential consideration, provide little justification for such selection. In J&K, some years ago, all those living in Leh tehsil were declared tribes on a territorial rather than any sociological basis. So, by straining logic and reason, political expediency has come to dictate far-reaching decisions that have a bearing on the national interest. The story has been repeated in the eastern region where Rajbongshis are SCs, STs or OBCs depending on the state where they are domiciled. A process of de-Sanskritization and re-tribalization has been unleashed, the price for which, as in all too many situations around the country, varies from burning X number of public buses and killing Y number of people, or the other way about, depending on the prevalent 'ideology' in vogue.

There is reasonable ground for reservation for Scheduled Castes and Scheduled Tribes and maybe other disadvantaged groups (who may not necessarily be traditional OBCs), accompanied by a well-defined exit policy subject to periodic review, so that the benefits seep down to the least privileged. Thereby the entire quota can be steadily depleted and extinguished within a finite period as originally constitutionally conceived, and not perpetuated and open-endedly enlarged as at present. Yet the very idea of a 'creamy layer' is derided by those who have fattened on the cream to the detriment of others more deserving.

A further major flaw lies in not adequately expanding education and vocational and professional training at all levels and in all regions to build competence, merit and equal opportunity, backed by scholarships. Distance learning, correspondence courses, workers' education and extra-mural studies are all well-known methodologies. Certainly something has been done in this direction but too little and too late.

Private education has been needlessly thwarted or sought to be over-regulated, a contemporary example being the Karnataka government's move to de-recognize Kannada-medium schools for switching to English, which, presumably, is what parents and the job market, would prefer. It is nobody's case that Kannada or the mother tongue should not be taught; but why impose what parents believe to be a handicap on their children? The object of all right-thinking people should be to enlarge the cake, so that there is more for more, and not to reduce the size of the pie and then dole out starvation rations to burgeoning numbers of job-seekers looking for better opportunities and a richer life. There is nothing like a crisis to crystallize the mind. Hopefully, both governments and people will jointly fashion a better response to the huge challenge of inclusive development and social change.

If casteism remains a threat, the monster of communalism is yet to be slain. Here again, the mischief lies in political and ideological mobilization of the 'chosen people' to win numbers, domination and preference. One of the most pernicious aspects of this process is revivalism, the ideological glorification of the past, often by distorting history, the selective rewriting of texts and seeking redress or even revenge for historical wrongs, whether real or imagined. Such conditioning of the mind—and wars and riots begin in the minds of men—breeds chauvinism, fear, hate and mistrust, and scarcely encourages reconciliation. In this case too, State inaction if not partisanship has bred impunity. In sixty years since Independence very few have been punished for acts of communal violence. The Gujarat holocaust of 2002 represents the acme of bestiality, of acts perpetrated not in moments of mob frenzy but as a result of cold calculation accompanied by an official campaign deliberately to prevent the succour of law and deny justice.

Closing old divides

The UPA government's resolve to implement a series of measures in keeping with the recommendations of the Sachar Committee report on the Muslim Indian condition, hopefully, marks a new beginning of inclusiveness and justice for a beleaguered community and, indeed, all minorities. While the government must surely take a lead, the Muslim Indian community too must assert itself and come out of its shell. Wherever the latter have done so, they have fared wonderfully well, equal to the best.

The cause will, however, be greatly furthered if the ghosts of 1947 are laid to rest. The road map spelt out by Dr Manmohan Singh and President Musharraf for the Indo-Pakistan peace process that has been under way holds out promise of a long-awaited settlement that may take time but could also come sooner than many anticipate. An honourable resolution of the J&K imbroglio without altering existing boundaries but rather making them irrelevant, possibly with semi-confederal characteristics, could help give quietus to ancient Indo-Pakistani animosities over the Kashmir question on which right-wing religious fundamentalists on both sides have traded. It would, as Jinnah had hoped, enable Pakistan to become a modern, liberal, plural and democratic society without need for Kashmir or the Indian 'other' to define itself. Fraternity and reconciliation are mutually reinforcing and the route to communal fraternity in India may to some extent possibly run through Srinagar and Islamabad. A dynamic South Asian community could enable its members to find regional solutions to national problems. This would enhance prosperity and all-round security within the region and enable SAARC to take its place as a major and mature global player.

Amid the welter of castes and communities and myriad diversities that abound in India, one man's aspirations can become another's apprehension in a competitive environment. The most basic and efficacious solvent for this problem is education and provision for equal opportunity. Universalization of elementary education was a constitutional priority that awaits fulfilment. While that goal will be reached soon, the country's sights have to be set on making available quality education and higher, vocational and professional education to all on demand. Skilled manpower is in any case imperative if higher growth rates are to be sustained; and stipends and loan scholarships should ensure that none is shut out. This will lay the basis for equality of opportunity. In addition, it is necessary that children and young people reflecting the country's plurality be brought together in campus diversity programmes so that they may not only work, play and live and eat together but also learn about one another and discover the truth that the 'other' is just another, whatever their names, faiths, festivals, dress, food habits, language, customs or domicile. The promotion of common schooling, alas spurned when first proposed by the Education Commission in the mid-1960s, would also help bridge the class divide. Stipends, the ensuring of good facilities and excellence, and a marginal credit point preference for entry into institutions of higher learning or certain levels of job entry could provide an incentive for enrolment in these institutions.

Cultures need not divide for they are not necessarily rivals or competitors but can co-exist and enrich one another through interaction and fusion. The kind of cultural or moral policing, including various forms of censorship, witnessed in recent times is reprehensible and a product of small minds. Caste panchayats have sometimes played a vicious role in honour killings and excommunications to protect not merely castes but gotras, to keep alive ancient social fault lines. Matters of taste and standards should by and large be left to the artistic and literary community and to public opinion. There is no place in an open society for self-serving regulation by cultural zealots acting on behalf of the State or of private or sectarian interest groups.

Gender discrimination is another ill that has to be overcome. In some ways Indian women are very advanced, having entered the portals of universities, politics and power ahead of most of their sisters around the world. Gandhi brought women into the forefront of national life by making them equal partners in the freedom struggle. Indira Gandhi's very presence in office as prime minister fired the imagination of Indian womanhood and invested them with a sense of empowerment. But Indira Gandhi would also say that Indians deified women by calling them 'devi' (goddess), and then went on to exploit them cruelly. The adverse sex ratio, female foeticide, the treatment of widows, purdah and triple talaq, the continuing practice of *sati* and the *devadasi* system (of dedicating virgins to temples) in certain places, and the annual observance of child-bride marriage festivals are testimony to the fact. Tribal women, too, do not enjoy full rights even though some like the Khasis follow a matrilineal tradition. Women must have equal rights and opportunities if India is to progress.

Insurgency remains a worrying manifestation in parts of the Northeast. Here too the Naga and Mizo insurrections represent the only genuine insurgencies, with a significantly large section of people rising against the State. The latter has been happily resolved. Unrest among a section of the Nagas continues. Some groups have come to terms with the government. Others are negotiating terms of possible settlement, hopefully short of secession but with a greater degree of autonomy, embroidered with appropriate symbolism representing a unique identity, and even going to the extent of a separate associate constitution within the Constitution to underline a special status. Negotiations are in progress with the IM (Isak Swu–Muivah group) and the seemingly one major stumbling block, the demand for the integration of all Naga-inhabited areas across four states, can perhaps be overcome by suitably conceptualizing a non-territorial pattern of integration that may lack the form but satisfies the core substance of the demand.

There is no reason to fear a domino effect, with similar demands from other quarters. The Naga issue, like the J&K question, is sui generis. Demands may be made but will not be sustainable. Some observers would write off other Northeastern 'insurgencies' as lawlessness by criminal gangs or adventurers or as terrorism in pursuit of money or self-aggrandizement clothed in the garb of identity, ideology and imagined grievances. Typical of this would be the ULFA in Assam, which has lost public support. In the Imphal Valley, seventeen groups of extortionists at war with the State and with one another hardly qualify singly or collectively to be identified with 'insurgency'. In Tripura and elsewhere, local grievances have triggered armed violence.

Better and firmer governance, multi-layered development, connectivity and market access that provide jobs and opportunities to a modernizing youth are what is needed. Peace and development go hand in hand and without the latter the former must remain elusive. A genuine opening out of the Northeast to its international neighbours, who share 98 per cent of its external perimeter, could also promote both peace and development and legitimize much underground and clandestine activity and traffic. Instead of merely 'looking' East, India needs to 'act' East and not merely gaze across fenced or seemingly uncertain boundaries. Simultaneously, it must develop a border policy, presently lacking, to strategize the kind of border development and trans-boundary relationships it wishes to develop with its immediate neighbours.

Physical secession is nowhere on the cards as the Indian State will not be further vivisected. It is instead the little acts of emotional secession that are cause for worry, for these are unseen and can fester. The causative factors might vary from a sense of neglect to alienation, deprivation or injustice. Good governance, social action and the creation of rising opportunities for all through creative development based on informed consent constitute the tripod on which policy must rest. A single-window administration manned by something like the former Indian Frontier Administrative Service (sadly abolished in 1968) is what is needed for the Northeast, the Himalayan marches and the tribal heartland in Middle India to deliver governance and development at the grass-roots rather than from distant secretariats.

Federal safeguards

One important safeguard in empowering plurality is India's federal polity. This has been further enhanced by constitutionally entrenching democratic devolution or three-tier panchayati raj as an institution of local government. The Seventy-third and Seventy-fourth Constitutional Amendments enacted in 1992 made mandatory and explicit what had until then been voluntary and largely implicit. Despite that it took much pressure and cajoling to get all states on board. The importance of this massive reform for the management of diversity is the access and participation it gives to vast numbers at the grass-roots to become decision-makers and governors rather than mere pawns on a vast political chessboard. Consider the numbers. Some 240,000 rural and urban grass-roots institutions in the country have elected 3.6 million representatives, the largest democratically-elected assembly in the world. Of these, 22 per cent represent Scheduled Castes and Tribes and a third are women whose election constitutes the largest single act of female empowerment anywhere in the world at any time. Some twenty-nine subjects have been devolved on the panchayats and governance is conducted through the principle of subsidiarity and on the basis of district-level planning or planning from below. A similar pattern exists for urban bodies.

In practice, governance nearer the point of delivery entails greater participation, transparency and accountability. With the right to information, people know what has been decided, what matching disbursements have been made, who is to execute any given contract within a stipulated timeline and so forth and can therefore monitor progress and ask questions. District planning allows local aspirations or wish lists to be translated into programmes of choice whether it is a school and its location and staffing or a road and its alignment. Such processes make for inclusiveness and can accommodate diversities, minority views and aspirations and plural representation. Admittedly, there have been teething troubles and imperfections in execution. Nevertheless, a participatory system is in place and is steadily beginning to operate more effectively and responsively. Likewise, various grass-roots schemes of employment such as the National Rural Employment Guarantee programme and safety nets are being put in place to smooth the transition and enable people to withstand the shocks of change.

There are obviously gaps to be filled and more efficient outcomes must be ensured. But a beginning has been made and as in all things, as stated earlier, one must travel in order to arrive.

Gandhi's injunction in 1947 was that the purpose of Independence must be to wipe the tear from every eye. That objective remains a distant goal. Nehru started the process of planned development in 1952, but on the eve of the Eleventh Five-Year Plan the country still has to lift roughly 26 per cent of the population above the poverty line (a dollar a day per capita) and perhaps 500 million to a level of life with dignity (two dollars a day per capita). Not everything can be blamed on population growth, though this has obviously imposed an enormous burden of numbers. There have been failures of policy and performance as well. India was ahead of most Third World countries at the commencement of post-war decolonization but has fallen behind many in terms of social, economic and corruption indices. Many good things have happened too—the development of some fine institutions of professional learning, strong industrial capability and a sound technological base among them. But parts of the foundation are weak: education and health, agriculture, the infrastructure and the capacity for large non-farm employment generation. Climate change too is upon us.

Broadly stated, this is the challenge the country now faces. Fashioning new strategies to meet that challenge has generated new uncertainties and fresh controversies, some ideological, some ecological, others social. Challenging old verities breeds new uncertainties and rapid change, aggravated by regional and social disparities, has spawned new anxieties. Parts of India and certain elements within them are certainly shining. But, as a wag might put it, an average annual growth rate of 9 or 10 per cent for India maybe translates into *a mere* 1 or 2 per cent growth for many in Bharat but 15 per cent or more for others. Some might counter that the rising tide will lift all boats but others will retort that in the long run a lot of people in Bharat could be dead and that this is already happening as witnessed by farmer suicides.

The new departures planned entail change and taking the road less travelled. At whose cost and for whose benefit, comes the cry? New insecurities surface or perhaps these are merely old insecurities in another garb that redefine 'the other', imparting sinister meaning to even familiar diversities.

Beware 'Landism'

Adding grist to the mill, ideology makes enemies of otherness too. The ideologues of the religious Right have their communal, social and cultural turf to exploit while the ideologues of the Left continue to battle 'Imperialism' and have an old-fashioned economic agenda to which they cling, paying obeisance to China when it suits them but unmindful of the very pragmatic twists and turns of market socialism and reform that the Chinese diligently practise. Buddhadeb Bhattacharjee has been a market socialist and pragmatist in West Bengal but has come up against opposition from within the Leftist fold and sundry Left intellectuals. He has been bold enough to make marginal mid-course corrections while staying the reformist course he has set for West Bengal and India, promoting industrialization, frowning on mindless general strikes or coercive hartals and bandhs that do little to encourage investment and innovation, setting a new trajectory for agricultural revival and regeneration and working out new land use patterns in a crowded countryside that will enhance factor productivity and maximize employment. (In 2004, West Bengal accounted for 75 per cent of days lost countryside in work stoppages, mostly from lockouts, while Communist unions opposed a scheme for workers' stakeholding in a reconstituted tea plantation company in the state).

In West Bengal, Left intellectuals and other critics of the Singur small car project (occupying 997 acres all told) have spoken eloquently of the loss of fertile areas, the displacement of farm workers and a consequent threat to India's food security from increasing diversion of farms lands to industry and urbanization. Simultaneously, Left critics in Kerala have slammed the Left Front government and communist trade unions for killing paddy farming in the state by preventing use of any farm machinery for years. In the result, Kerala's paddy acreage fell from 753,000 ha in 1961–2 to 276,000 ha in 2005–6 with a corresponding loss of paddy production by more than 50 per cent since 1981. Paddy lands are being diverted to cash crops or for infrastructure and construction and people are migrating to the Gulf for jobs in a globalized economy that profits the state through large remittances though this is ideologically anathema. The contradictions are gaping and show how nimble-footed ideologues can be.

The good earth and farming constitute both livelihood and a way of life. But when population explodes, as it certainly has in south Bengal, farmers with fragmented, unviable holdings must move off the land and jobs must be created in the non-farm and urban sector. Clinging to land in a situation of unviable farms and low factor productivity is much like hanging on to a chronically sick industry that 'earns' losses that ultimately other poor must bear so that some not-so poor idle workers may continue to idle. Such 'landism' (clinging to the past) is akin to Ludditism, the anti-machine movement in Britain at the start of the Industrial Revolution.

Displacement by land acquisition has been an understandable concern as peasants, tribals and other inhabitants of simple societies in particular have a deep attachment to the land, forests and natural heritage. Yet land uses will change with changing circumstances as they have throughout history. The Land Acquisition Act is merely a mechanism and not the problem. While the State's right of eminent domain remains in reserve, negotiated settlements are obviously to be preferred. Those taken off the land must be well compensated and trained to avail of unfolding opportunities that call for new and different skills. However, the transition must be made as smooth and painless as possible so that the trauma of insecurity and uncertainty is obviated even as the assurance of a better future is realized. R&R packages are constantly being upgraded with project-affected families being offered a shareholding or stake in proportion to their loss and the community a share in the future stream of project benefits or profits. Industry is also being urged to assume corporate social responsibilities in excess of and beyond the tax benefits that may be available. The response has been cautiously encouraging and will become increasingly positive as industry and other land users realize that a happy community means time and, therefore, money saved and the creation of an environment that is conducive to productivity, creativity and goodwill, all of these invaluable social and economic assets.

Ecological damage is often pleaded and must necessarily be mitigated and compensated to the extent possible even if it cannot be altogether avoided. The notion that all human interventions despoil nature is untrue. Some improve nature by reclaiming swamps and deserts. Yet none should be so technologically arrogant as to believe that he can play god and, like King Canute, order nature to do his bidding. Ecological damage can also be compensated over time and space and restorative works after, say, minerals have been won from a mine, can rejuvenate derelict areas. The grime and soot, surface subsidence and underground mine fires, eroded gullies, bare hills and waterlogged swamps one sees are admittedly no advertisement for certain kinds of 'development'. But sensible people can and do learn from experience though greed often comes in the way. It is here that good governance and community sanctions can play a role.

A certain class of touch-me-not environmentalists has condemned large dams and inter-basin water transfers as satanic disasters. Dam building and water transfer is as old as mankind. The critic may cite bad examples that should serve as a warning, but tend to ignore many good examples that prove that such projects, designed and executed with care, are not without merit. Yes, dams do silt and must ultimately be retired. But the time bought often enables humankind to find other and better solutions. There is a cost for doing nothing and, sometimes, a high opportunity cost of delay. Ultimately, it is the critical balance that matters. The addiction to land as an absolute value in the demand for R&R on the basis of land for land represents a status quoist approach. With rapidly rising population densities and a growing demand for land for non-farm uses, there is no 'surplus' land. An interesting distinction can be made between the dominant environmental philosophy of India, agrarianism, and that of the United States, which is based on preservation of the wilderness. (Guha, 2006)

'Land' in traditional societies essentially denotes security, employment and status. Modernization, a catchword for industrialization, urbanization and emerging milieus, offers other routes for the assurance and enjoyment of all three in different ways. 'Modern' and modernizing Indians, for example, are not going back to the land or to their 'native place', which was the centre of their universe a generation or two ago. Different ages espouse different values and, unless one is caught up in a time warp, nostalgia lingers but life moves on.

Fashioning new paths

Some would question industrialization and urbanization, as does Medha Patkar, though she would qualify her objection with the adjective 'indiscriminate'. But what is 'indiscriminate industrialization'? Is anything short of full employment or persisting low wages, abject poverty and the country's inability to pay its way an acceptable alternative to 'indiscriminate' industrialization? Some would romanticize tribal life and eulogize an existence that has sometimes barely risen above subsistence and dire want. Who dare choose for others what one considers unacceptable for oneself and one's own kind? It is perverse to condemn others to a lifestyle that is 'nasty, brutish and short'. This is not to suggest that tribal societies and cultures should be overrun or overwhelmed in the name of 'development' and the common good. Once again, the right balance must be found and change wrought with due care and informed consent.

The licensing of SEZs has sparked much controversy. Criticism regarding the objectives and operational details must be met on their own merits and adjustments and improvements made where necessary and possible. However, what must be questioned is the blunt attack on industrialization and urbanization per se as antithetical to farming and Arcadian bliss. Gandhi saw violence in Western civilization, which he condemned as 'the creation of Satan'. His views were elaborated in *Hind Swaraj*, a tract written in 1908, reiterated in 1921 and once again in correspondence with Jawaharlal Nehru as late as in 1945. Ambedkar critiqued these views in unambiguous terms.

Gandhi wrote in 1921, 'I feel that if India would discard "modern civilisation" she can only gain by doing so'. *Hind Swaraj* made out the case against railways and lawyers, the first symbolizing machinery (other than the Singer sewing machine) and the other litigation, a by-product of competition in acquisitive societies fuelled by greed more than need. He advocated a slow unhurried life of voluntary poverty. He would eliminate class war and class struggle and strife between capital and labour, landlords and tenants. He reconciled the contradictions inherent in prevailing industrial and agrarian relations by advocating the principle of trusteeship which Ambedkar dismissed as no more than a 'spiritual obligation' especially as the Mahatma simultaneously embargoed strikes and tenant agitation against zamindars. Gandhi also wrote in 1925 explaining varna or caste as an antidote to competition, class struggle and class war. 'I believe in the *varna* system as it fixes the duties and occupations of persons'. (Rodrigues, 2002) Like his advice to Jews in Germany to confront the Nazis with non-violence, did Gandhi's idealism sometimes disdain realism?

The village India of Gandhi's dream was just that—a utopian ideal. Nehru rejected the *Hind Swaraj* thesis as 'completely unreal'. He saw no reason to believe that the village necessarily embodied truth, non-violence, progress, culture or national security. The present arguments against industrialization and urbanization would seem to echo earlier Gandhian and philosophic refrains. Nostalgia is a worthy emotion provided one does not live in the past or remains fearful of the future. The unfamiliar poses uncertainties; but societies must and do find ways and means to insure themselves against undue risk. There is a dark side to industrialization and urbanization too. However, there are many examples of how these ills have been overcome in the workplace, in working relations and in the larger living and cultural environment. The choice is not between agriculture and industry, town and country, big and small but an appropriate blend of all of these as circumstances demand and opportunity dictates, with improvements at every stage and level.

There is, however, yet another criticism. The direction the economy and society are taking is not self-willed. The forces of globalization that have taken over with market reforms are involuntarily propelling the country. This too is an exaggeration. India was always globalized from the earliest times and there was an ebb and flow of commerce, culture, faith and ideas along the Silk Road and spice routes that linked India to the world by land and sea. Greece, Rome, the Levant, West Asia, Russia, Africa, Southeast and Central Asia, the Arab world, Iran and China were all well known to India and Indians. Indeed, Mohammad bin Tughlak thought nothing of asking the medieval Arab traveller, Ibn Batuta, who visited Delhi, to be his ambassador to China, whither he was bound. This open-door policy only lapsed with

Western colonial dominance until the Asian Relations Conference in Delhi in 1947 sought to renew old contacts. Nehru said:

> Vivekananda was an internationalist. I am, he said, thoroughly convinced that no individual or nation can live by holding itself apart from the community of others, and wherever such an attempt has been made under false ideas of greatness, policy or holiness—the result has always been disastrous to the secluding one. (Nehru, 1947)

The communications revolution has annihilated space and time to make One World a reality. There is little choice to opt out and a high cost for doing so. India was a late convert to market reform but opened up its economy on its own volition and at its own pace. The growing Indian diaspora is forging new cultural and commercial links and India is steadily emerging as a major regional player or even global power with a growth rate touching 9 per cent. However, huge internal challenges remain to get rid of poverty and hunger, discrimination, violence, disparities, et al. and make this a country of equal opportunity. There is much to be gained from thinking globally but acting locally so that balance is maintained.

Lifestyle choices

Growth has to be not merely combined with social justice but must be sustainable, nationally, regionally and globally. The Club of Rome may have been premature in its thesis forecasting very early limits to growth. Decades later the clock would seem to read a bare minute to midnight. The world's scientists have set a deadline. The Inter-Governmental Panel on Climate Change declared in 2007 with a 90 per cent level of confidence a measurable acceleration in global warming. The IPCC's global alert is simple. Anything beyond a two degree Celsius rise in global warming could prove catastrophic if unchecked. With business as usual, this threshold will be reached eight years from now. But meaningful and concerted global action with immediate effect can contain temperature rise to within that critical two-degree margin at a cost of no more than 0.12 per cent of the world's annual GDP. This is a small burden to bear to save the planet and its ecologically vulnerable population who are located in the tropical latitudes that are scientifically more susceptible to climate change. However, none anywhere will be altogether spared.

It would be immoral for richer or less vulnerable nations or sections within them to plead the triage doctrine of superior survivability. That can scarcely be a prescription for preserving civilization, especially as the wealthier of the species have historically contributed most to global warming, maybe only because they progressed earlier and more rapidly than the rest, irrespective of the means employed. Nor can those with a lesser responsibility for global warming refuse to do whatever little they can. For as John Donne said long ago, 'Send not to ask for whom the bell tolls; it tolls for thee'.

So as India prepares to launch on its Eleventh Five-Year Plan and target 10 per cent growth it must ask whether it is doing enough to combat global warming. The imperative of escaping from poverty cannot justify ostentatious consumption or a higher count of billionaires. Thus far the argument has been that poor nations like India must produce more in order to be able to distribute more. It is time to consider both production and distribution in tandem in order to build a just and contented society rather than one with an unbalanced load of riches while the other half decays. We have to be concerned with sustainable lifestyles and trajectories and, beyond a threshold, social consumption more than self-indulgence.

What then should be India's growth trajectory? If it escapes poverty and ensures sustainability, should it stop trying to keep up with the Joneses and move notionally some way towards the Bhutanese goal of maximizing Gross National Happiness, howsoever defined? This would not sacrifice national security or scientific advance or good living but, in keeping with Gandhian principles, would place social consumption above ostentatious personal consumption. Thus the emphasis would be on public transport and mass transit rather than on more personal transport, on more public housing than fancy private real estate development, on preventive and community health and public health facilities than on private super-speciality clinics, on recycling and renewable energy, all this within a framework of inclusive growth. Beyond a point, Indians can choose to *Be* more rather than go on yearning to *Have* more. This is where civilizational values might weigh in.

Will the centre hold?

The rest of the world too is grappling with problems of diversity. Europe is struggling to become a unified entity and is trying to come to terms with multiculturalism, learning from India. It has yet to decide whether to accept Turkey, 'Muslim' but secular and with an 'Asian' civilization, into the fold. The Irish question has at last been settled, but the Basques are once again calling for independence from Spain and France. Belgium is being pulled apart by the Flemish and the Walloons. Chechnya battles on. Turkey, Iraq, Syria and Iran are wary of Kurdish nationalism. The LTTE is fighting for Tamil Eelam. Pathans in Pakistan seek Pakhtunistan or Pakhtunwa. One can add to the list. Scotland? Corsica? In a symbolic move of reconciliation, the French-speaking people of Quebec have been recognized as a nation within a united Canada, but not before a minister resigned on the ground that he could not accept ethnic as opposed to civic nationalism.

At home, some linguistic boundaries are still in dispute: Belgaum between Maharashtra and Karnataka, Kasargod between Kerala and Karnataka and Chandigarh and Abohar–Fazilka between Punjab and Haryana. There are purely territorial border disputes over forest lands between Assam and Arunachal, Meghalaya, Mizoram and Nagaland. Statehood is being demanded for Vidarbha and Telengana, and many similar demands will no doubt follow. These will be resolved. There have been sporadic outbursts of regionally driven cultural chauvinism in the Northeast, Karnataka, Tamil Nadu, Maharashtra and Jammu and Kashmir based on language, ethnicity and caste. Caste and tribal conflicts continue, with caste mobilization for electoral gain as a major driver. Alienation has driven some into the arms of Left-wing Extremism. All these are cause for concern.

There were seventy-seven political parties in the fray at the time of the first general elections in 1952 but a single dominant party countrywide, the Congress. Single-party dominance cracked in 1967 and disappeared in 1977 when two dominant formations emerged. The Janata Party gave way to the National Front and then the BJP-led National Democratic Alliance to oppose the rival Congress-led formation, the United Progressive Alliance, each a coalition of a dozen and more parties. Similar coalitions have emerged in a number of states.

Some observers see in this a cause for worry. With strong regional parties steadily becoming virtually co-equals of the core party (the Congress or BJP) at the Union level, will the Centre hold? Will ideological, sectarian and regional warlords manipulate the Centre for their own aggrandisement? If that were to happen, would national unity be subject to unbearable strain as local agendas will be less prone to look at regional and ethnic balance? Already India's South and West have had occasion to chafe over in-migration from what they regard as demographically and economically improvident northern and eastern states. Delimitation of electoral constituencies in favour of states with more rapidly growing populations could tilt the political balance against others while the redrawing of reserved seats could upset delicate ethnic balances in the regions. For example, Kokrajhar, the Bodo Autonomous Territory capital, is in some danger of being de-reserved as a tribal seat. Chhattisgarh, a so-called tribal state, is similarly threatened with the loss of tribal seats in favour of some additional general constituencies. All these pose delicate issues of principle and practical adjustment, special exceptions and so forth. It will take much wisdom in addition to just the juggler's skill to keep these several balls in the air.

Such fears are not entirely unfounded but can be exaggerated. The problems looming ahead are in some ways puny compared to the enormous challenges that India has overcome. And the India of today is far more united, democratically cohesive and stable than the India of 1947, 1952, 1964, 1975, 1984 or 1990. Regional parties may well grow in strength. That would strengthen the federal character of the polity but need not stultify the Centre. Regional and local parties do have local and regional agendas. But they also have a vision of India and know that they must think nationally while acting locally if local and regional agendas are going to find fulfilment. They know, as the people do, that India is more than the sum of its parts. India must shine for them; and if that happens, the million mutinies of which Naipaul spoke will be resolved and will not add up to a great, unsettling uprising.

Where the mind is without fear

There is no ground for complacency but every reason for hope. Identity matters and always will. But most people have multiple identities and exhibit or prioritize one or another as circumstances demand. The projection of a singular identity, generally privileging ethnicity, faith or language, stems from insecurity, which may itself be rooted in a sense of discrimination or injustice. The market cannot build a nation; good governance can. What ordinary people think about and aspire to is often based on what they hear and read. The media has an enormously significant role in setting agendas, communicating facts and ensuring transparency and accountability. More the pity, therefore, that the Indian State has been callous and careless in virtually jettisoning public service broadcasting and in constraining the growth of community radio. Prasar Bharati is not to be viewed as an instrument of state propaganda, but as a vehicle of information and empowerment that targets the citizen rather than the consumer. Almost half of India's citizens live outside or beyond the market from which the commercial media earns its keep.

We need instrumentalities of communication, education, institutions and policies to help negotiate the country's myriad diversities in the years ahead. Centuries ago, the Rig Veda proclaimed the ideal of *vasudhaiva kutumbakam,* the world is my family. That spoke of a universal brotherhood that the Indian Constitution enshrines in the call to Fraternity. Tagore lighted the path towards that goal in Gitanjali when he prayed that India become a land where the mind is without fear or insecurity; where the head is held high, with a sense of dignity and incorruptibility; where the world is not broken up by narrow domestic walls of caste, community and ethnicity; where the clear stream of reason is not lost in the dreary desert sands of dead habit, entrapped in superstition, bigotry and hate; and where tireless striving would stretch its hand towards perfection, implying constant negotiation to do what is right and for the common good.

To enter that 'heaven of freedom' Tagore envisaged we need to move from the primacy of minority–majority vote mobilizing calculations and complexes and of group identities, which are not unimportant in their limited sphere, to the idea and ideal of a common citizenship. The Indian Constitution is a very liberal document that has been very liberally interpreted. All the rights and entitlements anybody might claim are subsumed in the grand charter and social contract laid out in the chapter on Fundamental Rights. We are moving in that direction, step by step, not without occasional stress and tribulation. Sixty years from Independence is not a long time in the life of a nation. Given half as much time again we could truly make that tryst with destiny.

Unchanging and timeless, India is changing and is being born anew, its diversities adding new harmonies, colour and riches to the landscape and mindscape. Negotiating diversity calls for both navigating the way forward, a directional challenge, as much as a consultative process that builds consensus and discovers unity in diversity through Fraternity. India is on the move. But, as Debray put it in *Revolution in the Revolution?*, 'History advances in disguise . . . . We see the past superimposed on the present, even when the present is a revolution.'

Maybe thirty years from now, Indians going about their occasions and meeting together might suddenly discover, perhaps to their own great surprise, that the stranger they just passed or encountered is not the 'other' but just another. For a stranger is but a friend you had somehow not met before.

References

Agragramee,Vidhya and Achyut Das. 2004. 'Tribal Women: Rights over Natural Resources', Kashipur.

Alagh, Y.K. 2006. *Community Organisations and Rural Development in the 11th Plan*. S.K. Dey Memorial Lecture, Hyderabad: National Institute of Rural Development. September.

Ambedkar, B.R. 1945. *What Congress and Gandhi Have Done to the Untouchables*. Bombay: Thacker and Co.

_____. 'Who Were the Sudras?' 1946.

Anwar, Ali. *Masavat Ki Jung*. 2005. Delhi: Indian Social Institute.

BALCO Employees Union vs Union of India & Others. 2001. Supreme Court, 10 December, from *Report of the Expert Group on Prevention of Alienation of Tribal Land and its Restoration*. Delhi: Ministry of Rural Development. October 2004.

Banerjee, Abhijit Vinayak et al. 2007. 'Beyond Nandigram: Industrialisation in West Bengal'. *Economic and Political Weekly*, 28 April.

Bandhopadhyay, Debabrata. 1978. 'Indra Lohar and the due process of Law', *National Labour Institute Journal*.

Barpujari, H.K. 1992 and 1994. *The Comprehensive History of Assam*. vol. 2 and vol. 3. Guwahati: Publication Board, Assam.

Biswas. Prasenjit and C.J. Thomas. 2006. *Peace in India's Northeast, Meaning, Metaphor and Method. Essays of Concern and Commitment*. ICSSR-NER, Shillong. Delhi: Regency Publications.

Bhuria, Dileep Singh. 2007. Personal conversation. New Delhi. March.

Chandhoke, Neera. 2007. 'Negotiating Linguistic Diversity: A Comparative Study of India and the United States', in Shankar Bajpai (ed.), *Democracy and Diversity, India and the American Experience*. Delhi: Oxford.

Committee of Concerned Citizens. 2002. First and Second Reports, 1997–2002, Hyderabad. December.

Dalrymple, William. 2007. *The Last Mughal: The Fall of a Dynasty*. New Delhi: Penguin Books India.

Das, Arvind. N. 1992. *The Republic of Bihar*. Delhi: Penguin Books.

Dasgupta, Manas. 1998. *Tea Garden Labour*. Delhi: Gyan Chand, Delhi.

De Bary, T. (ed.) 1958. *Sources of Indian Tradition*. New York: Columbia University Press.

Debray, Regis. 1967. *Revolution in the Revolution? Armed Struggle and Political Struggle in Latin America*. New York: Grove Press, Inc.

Desai, A.R. 1979. *Peasant Struggles in India*. Delhi: Oxford University Press.

Dhagamwar, Vasudha. 2006. 'The Paradip Project: Harbinger of Light or Darkness?', *Social Change*. Council for Social Development Special Resettlement Issue, Vol. 36, No. 1. March.

Dhillon, Kirpal. 2006. *Identity and Survival: Sikh Militancy in India, 1978–1995*. Delhi: Penguin Books India.

Dubois, Abbe, J.A. 1906. *Hindu Manners, Customs and Ceremonies*. Third edition, Oxford: Clarendon Press.

Durgadas (ed.) 1972. *Sardar Patel's Correspondence, 1945–50*. Ahmedabad: Navjivan Publishing House.

Dutta, Anuradha and Ratna Bhuyan (eds.) 2007. *Genesis of Conflict and Peace: Understanding Northeast India Studies*. Vols 1 and 2. Guwahati: Omeo Kumar Das Institute and New Delhi: Akansha Publishing House.

Economic and Political Weekly. 2006. Special Issue. Maoist Movement in India. 22 July.

Economic and Political Weekly. 2006. A Rejoinder by 'Azad', official spokesman of the CPI (Maoist), 14 October.

Elwin, Verrier. 1957. *A Philosophy for NEFA*. Reprinted 1958, 1964. Shillong: Government Press.

Expert Group on Prevention of Alienation of Tribal Land and its Restoration. 2004. Report of Ministry of Rural Development, Delhi: Government of India. October.

Ghurye, G.S. 1957. *Caste and Class in India*. Bombay: Popular Book Depot.

Guha, Ramachandra. 2006. *How Much Should A Person Consume? Thinking Through the Environment*. Delhi: Permanent Black.

Guha, Ramachandra, Harivansh, Farah Naqvi, E.A.S. Sarma, Nandini Sundar and B.G. Verghese. 2006. *War in the Heart of India: An Enquiry into the Ground Situation in Dantewara District, Chhatisgarh*. Delhi: Independent Citizens' Initiative, July 20.

Heimsath, Charles. 1964. *Indian Nationalism and Hindu Social Reform*. Princeton: Princeton University Press.

High Level Committee on Food and Public Distribution. Report. 2001. Delhi: Department of Food, Government of India.

Hunter, William W. 1871. *The Indian Musalmans*. Reprint 2002. Delhi: Rupa and Co.

Hutton, J.H. 1946. *Caste in India: Its Nature, Functions and Origins*. Delhi: Oxford University Press.

Joshi, A.P., M.D. Srinivas and J.K. Bajaj. 2003. *Religious Demography in India*. Chennai: Centre for Policy Studies.

Kanpur Riots Inquiry Committee Report: The Communal Problem. 1933. Reprint 2005, Delhi: National Book Trust.

King, Robert D. 1997. *Nehru and the Language Politics of India*. Delhi: Oxford University Press.

Linz, Juan J., Alfred Stepan and Yogendra Yadav. 2007. '"Nation State" or "State Nation"? India in Comparative Perspective', in Shankar Bajpai (ed.), *Democracy and Diversity: India and the American Experience*. Delhi: Oxford University Press.

Mason, Philip (ed.) 1967. *India and Ceylon: Unity and Diversity*. Delhi: Oxford University Press.

Mehor, Rajkishor. 2006. *Globalisation, Industrialisation and the State: A Sociological Study of Tribals' Reaction to Industrial Development in Orissa*. Bhubaneshwar: Nabakrushna Chaudhury Centre for Development Studies. February.

Mishra, Vinod. 1999. *Selected Works*. Delhi: CPI (ML).

Misra, Udayon. 2001. *The Transformation of Assamese Identity: A Historical Survey*. Shillong: The North East History Association.

Mitra, Meera. 2007. *It's Only Business: India's Corporate Social Responsiveness in a Globalised World*. Delhi: Oxford University Press.

Mullick, B.N. 1972. *My Years With Nehru, 1948–64*. New Delhi: Allied Publishers.

Mumford, Lewis. 1961. *The City in History, Its Origins, Its Transformations and Its Prospects*. London: Secker and Warburg.

Murugkar, Lata.1991. *Dalit Panthers Movement in Maharashtra*. Bombay: Popular Prakashan.

Nadkarni, M.V. 2003. 'Is Caste System Intrinsic to Hinduism? Demolishing a Myth.' *Economic and Political Weekly*, 8 November.

Nagaland Bapist Church Council. 2006. Dialogue on Healing and Reconciliation of the Naga People. Kohima. 12 August.

Nanda, B.R. 2004.*Three Statesmen: Gokhale, Gandhi and Nehru*. Delhi: Oxford University Press.

National Commission on Agriculture. Reports. Part IX, Forestry. 1976. New Delhi: Ministry of Agriculture and Irrigation, Government of India.

National Commission on Farmers. Reports. 2007. New Delhi: Ministry of Agriculture, Government of India.

National Institute of Rural Development: Rural Development Report. 2005. Hyderabad. August.

Nayak, Nihar. 2006. 'Maoists in Orissa: Growing Tentacles and a Dormant State.' *Faultlines*, Delhi. 15 February.

Nehru, Jawaharlal. 1946. *The Discovery of India*. Reprint 1947. Bombay: Asia Publishing House.

Nuh, V.K. 2002. *The Naga Chronicle*. ICSSR—Northeastern Regional Centre. Delhi: Regency Publications.

PACS Programme at www.empowerpoor.org. 2007. Delhi: Development Alternatives.

Pandey, Sachidanand. 1985. *Naxal Violence: A Socio-Political Study*. Delhi: Chanakya Publications.

Patel, Aakar, Dileep Padgaonkar and B.G. Verghese. 2002. Editors Guild of India Fact-Finding Mission Report. *Rights and Wrongs: Ordeal by Fire in the Killing Fields of Gujarat*. New Delhi. 3 May.

Pernau, Margrit. 2006. *The Delhi College; Traditional Elites, the Colonial State, and Education before 1857*. Delhi: Permanent Black.

Planning Commission. 2006. 'Towards Faster and More Inclusive Growth: An Approach to the 11th Five Year Plan.'Government of India, Delhi. December.

Prabhu, Pradeep. 2003. In 'Endangered Symbiosis: Evictions and India's Forest Communities.' Report of the Jan Sunwai (Public Hearing), 19–21 July. Dahanu, Thane District, Maharashtra: Campaign for Survival and Dignity.

Prasad, Chandra Bhan. 2006. *Dalit Phobia, Why Do They Hate Us?* Delhi: Vitasha Publishers.

Radhakrishnan, S. 1927. *Indian Philosophy*, Vol. 1. London: George Allen and Unwin.

Raghavaiah, V.R. 1979. Background of Tribal Struggles in India in A.R. Desai (ed.), *Peasant Struggles in India*. Delhi: Oxford University Press.

Ramunny, Murkot. 1988. *The World of Nagas*. New Delhi: Northern Book Centre.

Ram Mohan. 1968. *Hindi Against India, The Meaning of DMK*. Delhi: Rachna Prakashan.

Risley, H.H. 1891. *Tribes and Castes of Bengal*. 2 Vols. Calcutta: Bengal Secretariat Press.

Rodrigues, Valerian (ed.) 2002. *The Essential Writings of B.R. Ambedkar*. Delhi: Oxford University Press.

Sachar Committee. 2006. Social, Economic and Educational Status of the Muslim Community of India. Chairman, Rajindar Sachar. Cabinet Secretariat, Delhi. November.

Saikia, Yasmin. 2005. *Assam and India: Fragmented Memories, Cultural Identity, and the Tai-Ahom Struggle*. Delhi: Permanent Black, Delhi.

Samatha vs State of AP and others. Supreme Court Cases 191, Civil Appeal Nos. 4601–02, 1997. 2001. In *Tribal Affairs in India, The Crucial Transition*, B.D. Sharma. Delhi: Sahyog Pustak Kuteer (Trust).

Sanyal, Kanu. 'More About Naxalism', in Prakash Singh, *The Naxalite Movement in India*.

Sattanathan, A.N. 2007. *Plain Speaking: A Sudra Story*. Delhi: Permanent Black.

Sharma, B.D. 2000. *Dalits Betrayed*. Delhi: Sahyog Pustak Kuteer.

Shiva Rao, B. 1967. *The Framing of India's Constitution*, Vol. 5. Delhi: Indian Institute of Public Administration.

Singh, K. Suresh. 1992. *People of India. An Introduction*. Vol. 1. Anthropological Survey of India, Calcutta: Seagull Press.

Singh, K. Suresh. 1994. *People of India*, Vol. 3. The Scheduled Tribes. Delhi: Oxford University Press.

Singh, Prakash. 1995. *The Naxalite Movement in India*. Revised edition 2006. Delhi: Rupa and Co.

Simeon, Dilip. 2006. 'Rebellion to Reconciliation', In B.G. Verghese (ed.) *Tomorrow's India: Another Tryst With Destiny*. Delhi: Penguin Books India.

Smita. 2006. *Locked Homes, Empty Schools: The Impact of Rural Migration on the Rural Poor*. Delhi: Zubaan.

Standing Committee on Inter-Sectoral Issues Relating to Tribal Development. 2005. Chair, Dr B. Mungekar, Member, Planning Commission, serviced by the Union Ministry of Tribal Affairs, Government of India, Delhi.

States Reorganisation Commission Report. 1955. Government of India, Delhi.

Status on Land. 2006. Kolkata: West Bengal Department of Land and Land Reforms.

Srikanth, H. and C.J. Thomas. 2006. 'Challenges & Predicament of Naga Nationalism'. *Eastern Quarterly*, Vol. III, Issue IV, Jan–March. Manipur, Delhi: Manipur Research Forum.

The State of the Panchayats: Mid-Term Review and Appraisal. 2006. Panchayati Raj Ministry, Government of India, Delhi.

Thorner, Daniel. 1965. *The Agrarian Prospect in India*. Second edition, 1973. Delhi: Allied Publishers.

Tiger Task Force. Report. 'Joining the Dots'. 2005. Delhi: Union Ministry of Environment and Forests, Government of India.

Tyler, Mary. 1997. *My Years in an Indian Prison*. London: Gollancz.

Urdu, Committee for the Promotion of, Report. 1975. Chairman, I.K. Gujral, Delhi: Ministry of Human Resources, Government of India.

Verghese, B.G. 1996, 2004. *India's Northeast Resurgent: Ethnicity, Insurgency, Governance, Development*. New Delhi: Konark Publishers.

Verma, Roop Rekha. 2008. A Study of Textbooks in the Non-Government Schools in Uttar Pradesh. Report in http://www.aiccindia.org/news/school_textbooks_in_uttar_pradesh_promote_hindu_bias. In *Through the Gender Lens: Looking and Nation and Identity in School Texts*. Delhi: Nirantar.

Visaria, Leela. 2007. 'Demographic Trends in South India.' Paper presented at a Workshop organized by the Population Foundation of India, Hyderabad. 12 February.

Weiner, Myron. 1978. *Sons of the Soil*. Delhi: Oxford University Press.

Weiner, Myron. 1991. *The Child and the State in India*. Delhi: Oxford University Press.

Witsoe, Jeffrey. 2006. *India in Transition: India's Second Green Revolution?* Philadelphia: Centre for the Advanced Study of India, University of Pennsylvania.

Index